ANTHROPOLOGICAL PAPERS OF
THE UNIVERSITY OF ARIZONA
NUMBER 30

THE HODGES RUIN
a Hohokam Community in the Tucson Basin

ISABEL T. KELLY
with the collaboration of
James E. Officer & Emil W. Haury

edited by Gayle Harrison Hartmann

THE UNIVERSITY OF ARIZONA PRESS
TUCSON, ARIZONA
1978

About the Author . . .

ISABEL T. KELLY has headed field expeditions in the southwestern United States, Mexico, Bolivia, and Pakistan during her nearly fifty-year career in archaeology and anthropology. After receiving a doctorate from the University of California at Berkeley in 1932, she began ethnographic research among the Southern Paiute and Coast Miwok Indians of California. Other fieldwork during the 1930s included the Hodges Ruin excavation in Tucson, and applied anthropology projects in West Mexico. In 1940 Dr. Kelly moved to Mexico, where she has been involved in independent research since 1960.

THE UNIVERSITY OF ARIZONA PRESS

Manufactured in the U.S.A.

I.S.B.N. 0-8165-0619-1
L. C. No. 78-4029

Library of Congress Cataloging in Publication Data

Kelly, Isabel Truesdell, 1906–.
The Hodges Ruin.

(Anthropoligical papers of the University of Arizona; no. 30)
Bibliography: p.
Includes index.
1. Hodges Ruin, Ariz. I. Officer, James E., joint author. II. Haury, Emil Walter, 1904– joint author. III. Hartmann, Gayle Harrison. IV. Title. V. Series: Arizona. University. Anthropological papers; no. 30.
E99.H68K44 979.1'77 78-4029
ISBN 0-8165-0619-1

CONTENTS

TABLES

FIGURES

PREFACE AND ACKNOWLEDGMENTS

Manuscripts, unlike wine, do not improve with age. Some unidentifiable process causes a general deterioration and the older a manuscript becomes (no matter what its original condition), the more difficult is the task of preparing it for publication.

Isabel Kelly, the author of this report, is a thorough and meticulous investigator and writer. Since her work in Tucson she has pursued an archaeological career in Mexico; she currently resides in Mexico City. Her Hodges work has survived relatively well its forty-year dormancy at Gila Pueblo and in the archives of the Arizona State Museum library. However, certain problems have resulted from this long period of neglect. A primary difficulty has been the location of specimens. Some of the artifacts from the Hodges site have never been fully catalogued. As a result, they could not be located and therefore could not be photographed. In the text, the discussion of certain specimens is not accompanied by figures because, in almost all such cases, the artifacts in question could not be found. In addition, it has not been possible to use all the ceramic developmental charts that accompanied the original manuscript, because some of the material could not be located.

Another, perhaps more pervasive difficulty (at least from an editorial point of view), results from the fact that archaeology as it was done in the 1930s is not quite like archaeology in the 1970s. There are differences in methods of analyses, in terminology, and in emphasis. The Hodges excavations represent a pioneering effort of enormous importance to an understanding of the archaeology of the Tucson Basin. In fact, all subsequent publications dealing with Tucson Basin archaeology are based on the typologies created by Isabel Kelly. Therefore, because of this report's value as a historic document, no major effort has been made here to amplify the analyses, or to change terminology or emphasis. The only changes of any consequence have been in the first three chapters which in the original draft were entitled Introduction, Summary of Excavations, and Relationship to the Gila Basin. These are presented here in slightly condensed form as Chapter 1: Introduction. Other changes in the text have been made only if a usage was clearly outdated and would confuse the reader, such as the use of "ware" instead of "type." Some artifact descriptions have been added, and a few that were clearly outdated have been modified. In a few cases, conclusions reached by Kelly have since been modified by other researchers. In such instances, her statements in the text have not been changed but are followed by an editor's note mentioning the more recent information. Occasionally more recent references are inserted with no additional note. Readers should note that Officer's 1956 work has been listed by some authors as a reference separate from Kelly's. To avoid possible confusion, it should be re-emphasized that Officer's material is included in this report and is not listed as an independent reference in the bibliography.

In an effort to clarify the extent and location of the source material on which this publication is based, I have prepared a guide to the Hodges documents and artifacts. This guide is on file at the Arizona State Museum library; it describes the various drafts, correspondence, and field notes in the library archives and also lists maps, sketches used in illustrations, and artifacts in the Museum collection.

Archaeologists work with long spans of time, and perhaps as a result, sometimes seem to feel no urgency about publishing their results. The forty-year "prepublication period" in this case, though resulting from various circumstances over which the author had no control, is a demonstration of this lack of urgency. During that time the Hodges site has become something of a legend in Hohokam archaeology. Isabel Kelly's unfinished manuscript has been widely quoted in other works on the archaeology of the Southwest. The site itself has undergone frequent inspection by professionals and received considerable attention of the "pot hunting" sort by amateurs.

Carl Miller began excavations at the Hodges site in 1936. Assisting him and providing financial support were Mr. and Mrs. Wetmore Hodges who, during the year, purchased some of the land on which the ruin is located. At this time the site was known generally as the "Gravel Pit Ruin."

Digging continued through 1937 and 1938 still supported by the Hodges, but now under the auspices of the Gila Pueblo Archaeological Foundation in Globe, Arizona. Isabel Kelly was in charge of excavations during these two years. The late winter and early spring were devoted to fieldwork, the other months being taken up with laboratory analysis and preparation of the manuscript. Dr. Kelly's appointment with Gila Pueblo expired before she could complete her report and late in 1938 she turned to other research. The only major work on Hohokam archaeology published at that time was the Snaketown report, "Excavations at Snaketown, Material Culture'' by Harold S. Gladwin, Emil W. Haury, E. B. Sayles, and Nora Gladwin. The plan of Kelly's manuscript is strictly in accordance with that of the Snaketown report.

Kelly's notes, the uncompleted manuscript (including information from Miller's review of the 1936 season), and collections from the site remained in the possession of Gila Pueblo until 1944, when, at the Hodges' request, Emil Haury transferred all material relating to the site to the Arizona State Museum in Tucson where it has remained.

Early in 1955, Haury asked James Officer, then a graduate student in the Department of Anthropology, to undertake the completion of Kelly's manuscript. Officer's work included analyzing the shell, bone, and certain stone materials, writing the sections dealing with those objects, and writing the chapter on disposal of the dead. Many of the specimens were photographed at this time and some illustrations were drafted by his wife, Roberta M. Officer. But much illustrative material (particularly in the chapter on ceramics) was not prepared for publication; the manuscript had no conclusion and had never been edited.

Pressures of urban land development in the 1960s and 1970s have literally obliterated the Hodges site. Most of it is under residential subdivisions; the ball court and adjacent portions were bulldozed in 1972 during construction of a trailer park south of Ruthrauff Road and west of La Cholla Boulevard. A survey in early 1977 showed continuing rapid buildup of the area, although vacant lots still exist adjacent to the excavated portions of the Hodges site. Sherds presumed to be associated with Hodges have been found in these areas. To the north, they thin out about a block east of Kain Avenue. To the south, sherds were found in open areas west and north of Flowing Wells Junior High School, north of Wetmore and west of La Cholla.

The Hodges site was by no means the only prehistoric community in this area. Thirty additional prehistoric sites are listed in the site file of the Arizona State Museum within a few miles of Hodges. Most of these are just above the floodplain of Rillito Creek or the Santa Cruz River and all have been heavily damaged or completely destroyed either by erosion or by urban development.

The earliest site identified in this area is the so-called Jaynes Ruin (Arizona AA:12:13?) discussed by Huntington (1914: 52) and by Kelly in Chapter 1 of this publication. Twenty-three of the recorded thirty sites were surveyed in 1937 and 1938 by Frank Mitalsky, then a student at the University of Arizona; he describes eleven of the sites as villages or parts of villages and twelve as campsites or sherd scatters. One of the villages, Arizona AA:12:31, was apparently nearly the size of the Hodges site. It contained Gila Polychrome as well as earlier ceramic types, suggesting that it was inhabited after Hodges had been abandoned.

That the Hodges report is finally being published is largely due to the encouragement and boundless enthusiasm of Stephen M. Larson, president of the Arizona Archaeological and Historical Society from 1973 to 1975. Discovering that he had purchased a home near the Hodges Ruin and on top of Arizona AA:12:31, he made it a project during his term of office to encourage publication of a complete manuscript. At his urging, I began the task of readying the manuscript for publication. I received assistance from numerous persons, all of whom deserve thanks. Bruce Huckell and Steven Fuller examined and re-identified some of the lithic artifacts. Walter B. Miller and Carl Christensen in Biological Sciences at the University of Arizona re-identified some of the shell specimens. Alice Holmes provided invaluable aid by locating specimens which, in the interval between 1944 and 1975, had been housed in a variety of locations in the Arizona State Museum. Stephen Larson photographed artifacts and printed old negatives—a task that had been only partially completed. Charles Sternberg, Sharon Urban, and Joyce Rehm finished the numerous drafting chores. The manuscript was typed by Melinda Curry, Faye Larson, and Suzy Horning. William K. Hartmann suggested numerous editorial changes, and David E. Doyel and Sharon Urban read parts of the manuscript. William J. Robinson provided drafting service, storage space, and encouragement. Emil W. Haury read the entire manuscript and wrote the long-missing conclusion; I am especially grateful to him for his advice and for his interest in forty-year-old problems.

Through the auspices of Edward Ronstadt, president of the Arizona Archaeological and Historical Society from 1976 to 1977, Carl Miller kindly sent to the Museum numerous photographs and draft materials dating from the early excavations at Hodges. These arrived during final preparation of this publication and are being catalogued into the Museum archives.

A number of persons were acknowledged both by Isabel Kelly and James Officer in their manuscripts. Rather than publish their acknowledgments verbatim, I have chosen to list the individuals and their contributions.

Harold S. Gladwin and E. B. Sayles gave advice on many problems. Emil W. Haury excavated the ball court and provided information about the University Ruin then being excavated by Julian Hayden. Norman Gabel, then of the University of Arizona, measured the few intact burials. A.T. Erwin of Iowa State College identified vegetable remains, D.D. Davis of the Field Museum of Natural History in Chicago identified animal bones, and George Kanakoff and Howard Hill of the Los Angeles County Museum identified shell. Virginia Ross, a student at Yale University, provided laboratory assistance. The original maps were by J.R. Strickland and T. Blanton of Tucson.

GAYLE HARRISON HARTMANN

In response to a plea by the Arizona Archaeological and Historical Society the following people contributed financial support toward the publication of this work. Their help is gratefully acknowledged.

Alice Carpenter
R.D. Cunningham
E. Douglass
Wendell Eckholm
Paul H. Ezell
Gloria J. Fenner
Alan Ferg
Prof. and Mrs. C. W. Ferguson
Emilie Friedenthal
Dr. Theodore R. Frisbie
Frances Gillmor
Reed J. Hallock
Robert S. Hardy
Mr. and Mrs. H. F. Harrison
Mr. and Mrs. E. C. Hartmann
Emil W. Haury
Alden C. Hayes
Marion Anne Hennessy
William B. Hubbard, Jr.
Wm. S. Hurley
Wilma Kaemlein
Dr. and Mrs. Ronald J. Knudson
Albert J. Levine
Karl Reinhard
Mr. and Mrs. T.A. Riehl
William J. Robinson
Mr. and Mrs. Edward Ronstadt
Gerd Schloss
Susan Small
Landon D. Smith
Watson Smith
C.P. and V.L. Sonett
Clara Lee Tanner
Mr. and Mrs. R.F. Torrance
Sharon F. Urban
R. Gwinn Vivian

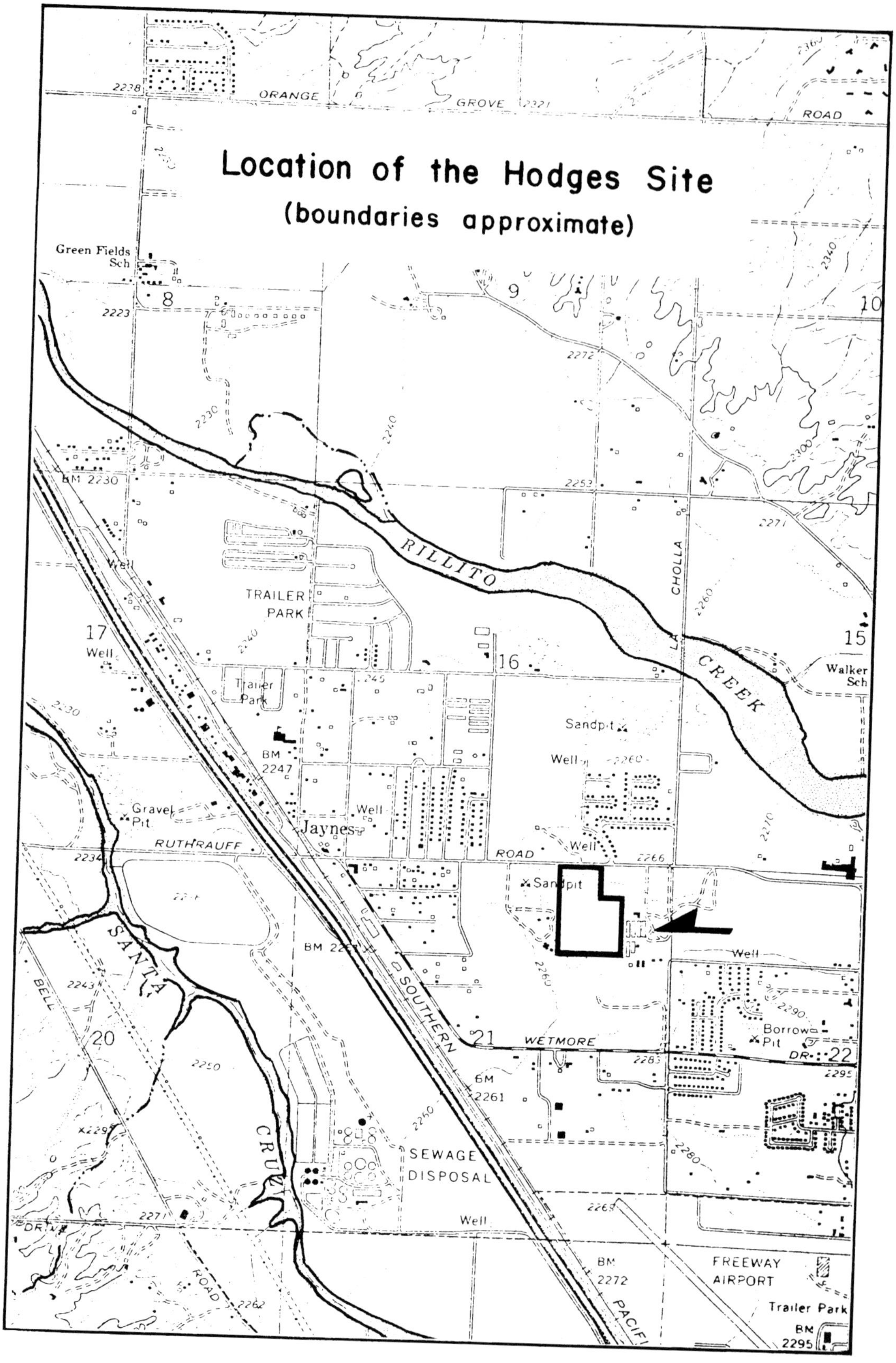

Fig. 1.1 Location of the Hodges site. This map is part of the 1968 U.S.G.S. Jaynes, Arizona, 7.5 minute quadrangle. Considerable construction has taken place since this map was drawn; most of the Hodges site now is covered by a trailer park.

1. INTRODUCTION

SITE LOCATION

The Hodges Ruin (Arizona AA:12:18) is located approximately one-half mile east of the intersection of Ruthrauff Road and the Southern Pacific railroad tracks, just to the northwest of the 1975 Tucson city limits. It lies in the triangular point of land formed by the junction of Rillito Wash with the Santa Cruz River (Fig. 1.1). It is east of the Santa Cruz on the edge of the second terrace above the alluvial floodplain.

The surface features of this site were described by Ellsworth Huntington (1914), who regarded it as an annex of his "Jaynes Ruin." The main Jaynes village (AA:12:13?), however, lay at a lower level "upon a gravelly tract which now rises perhaps 10 feet above the main alluvial plain" (1914:52). This area, between the railroad tracks and the river, is now under cultivation. Sherds are plentiful and indicate an extensive occupation.

On the higher terrace where the Hodges Ruin is located, the zone of concentrated occupation—marked by surface sherds and later determined through testing—covers approximately 30 acres (0.12 sq. km). However, to the west a considerable portion has been cut away by gravel pit operations, and scattered sherds both north and southeast indicate former extensions of the village. Artificial relief on the site is provided by the ball court. Beneath the surface, accumulations of cultural soil and debris vary in depth from 0.5 to 2.0 m. The underlying material is sterile, consisting for the most part of red desert soil, with localized gravel and caliche deposits.

At the time of excavation, the surface of the site (Fig. 1.2) was gently rolling, with a gradual slope off to the west and northwest. The dominant vegetation was creosote bush and its associates, intermixed with barrel and various cholla cacti. Clumps of mesquite and catclaw occur where the subsoil moisture is sufficient to support them. [*Ed. note:* As noted by Officer in his 1956 draft portions of this manuscript, "The area of excavation is now bounded on the south by farm land and a dairy cow feed lot; on the west by the gravel pit and several homes; on the east by a chicken farm; and, just to the north, by Ruthrauff Road."]

This location must have been unusually favorable for early occupation, provided defense was not a vital factor. Although agricultural modifications within the last 100 years have made the Santa Cruz River a more deeply cut channel, in prehistoric time the river meandered across the floodplain. The site is well above flood level but is immediately accessible to the ample bottom lands of the Santa Cruz and Rillito rivers, which were available for cultivation. Flood farming evidently was practiced; at least no prehistoric irrigation canals have been found. [*Ed. note*: Excavations in 1974, just east of the Santa Cruz River within a mile of the Hodges site, located a segment of at least one and possibly two prehistoric canals (Kinkade and Fritz 1975).]

Because of the presence of arable land and an assured water supply from the Santa Cruz River, occupation was long and continuous. On the basis of Snaketown parallels, the lifespan of the village may be placed at about a thousand years, from A.D. 300 to about 1300. Huntington (1914: 52) emphasized the depth of debris, writing

> In this village and in the adjacent main area of the Jaynes ruins the pottery is so thick and extends to such a depth in the ground that we can scarcely doubt that the villages were densely populated for a long time.

Assuming the same frequency of houses as in the Sabino Canyon site where he counted foundations, Huntington estimated the Hodges occupation at 500 houses and 2000 individuals. This estimate is too high for the area excavated, but since we cannot now determine the extent of the remaining occupied area, no substitute hypothesis with respect to population can be suggested.

The long time span and the relatively limited area of concentrated occupation meant incessant rebuilding in a given spot. Later houses were dug into or built over earlier ones; early rubbish and cremations were churned by excavation for later houses. Unfortunately for archaeologists, continued occupation of this nature destroys its own stratigraphic evidence.

Sheet, rather than mound, rubbish was common and characteristic. As previously mentioned, the accumulation of surface soil and trash varied from 0.5 to 2.0 m, with the latter rare. Pits of pure trash were infrequent and consequently less significant than at Snaketown. Several low rises gave promise of stratified refuse; although numerous tests were made, invariably the results were unsatisfactory.

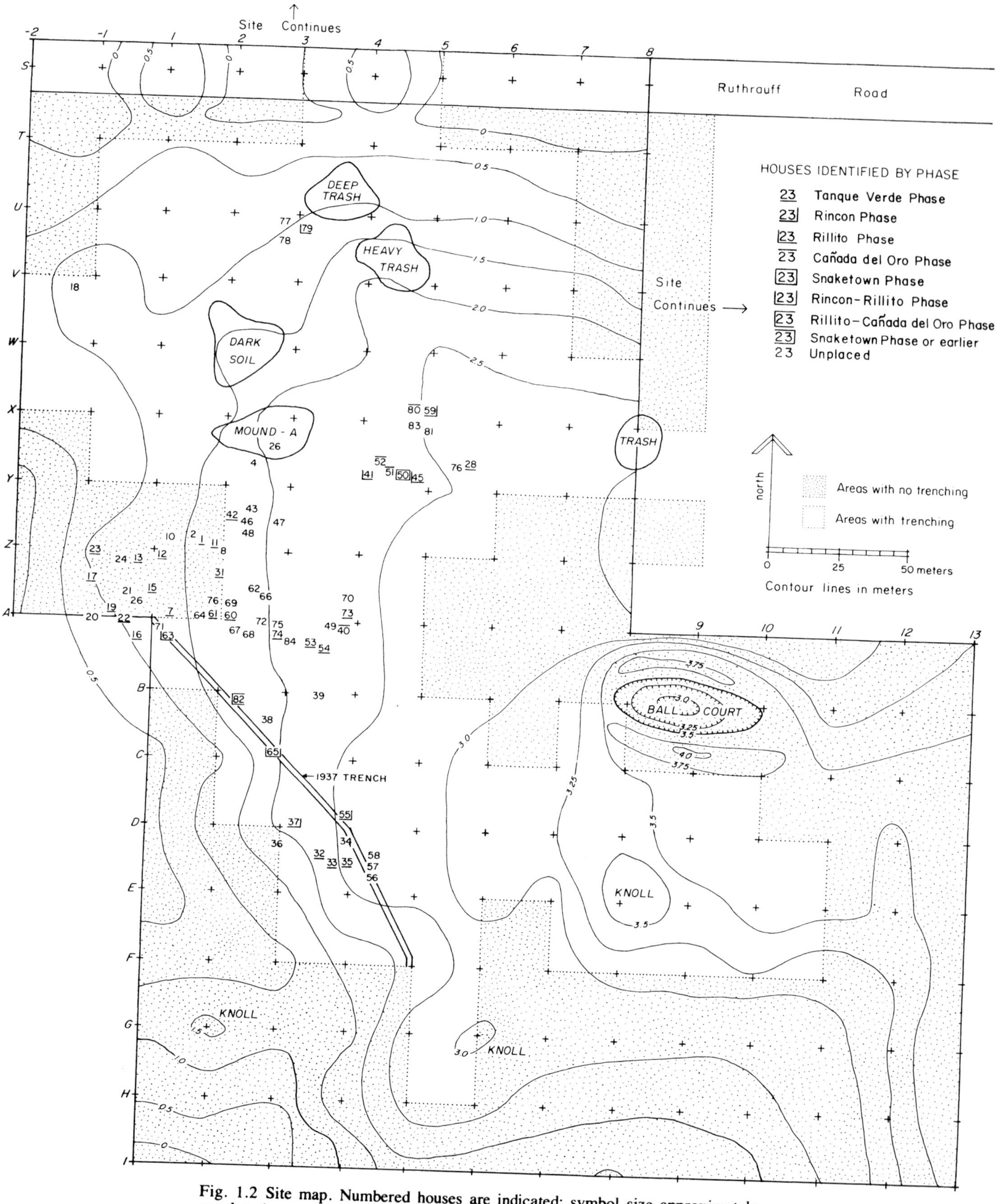

Fig. 1.2 Site map. Numbered houses are indicated; symbol size approximately equal to house size. Original records indicate that some houses were recorded too poorly to be located on the site map. Therefore, all houses are not shown.

SUMMARY OF EXCAVATIONS

At the start of the 1937 season the site was laid off in 25-m blocks, lettered from north to south and numbered from west to east. The original block designations ran from A to I and 1 to 13; later, extensions north and west were accommodated by a reverse order of the alphabet, extending northward from A, and by a series of minus numbers extending westward from 1 (Fig. 1.2).

The 1936 work was largely confined to a fan-shaped area west, north, and east of 1A, with concentration in 1Y, 2Y, -1Z, and 1Z. In addition, two isolated houses were cleared, one each in 2X and 5X. Thirty-one houses were excavated; the only identifiable ones belonged to the latest phase, which we have called Tanque Verde. Houses were chiefly of the standing-wall variety, but certain other fundamental and presumably earlier styles were represented. These were not datable, and, as no house floors were cut through, the sequential order was uncertain.

In pottery, too, there was ample evidence of material earlier than the Tanque Verde phase, particularly in the sherds from a low mound to the northeast, in 2X-3X. From testing of this rise came pottery primarily of the type later distinguished as the local equivalent of Gila Butte Red-on-buff.

A relatively good cross section of the Tanque Verde phase resulted from the 1936 excavations. Several houses provided a generous amount of decorated ceramics, and a number of cremations amplified the picture. Consequently, at the start of 1937, we set out to locate, if possible, earlier material, both architectural and ceramic.

Test pits 1.5 × 0.5m were cut in each 25-m block, so spaced that one fell every 25-m north and south, and east and west, and every 12.5-m on the diagonal. House remains proved to be scattered over the entire site, except in the southeastern blocks, which were almost sterile.

The area of densest occupation appeared just south and east of the 1936 excavations, on a diagonal axis from 1A to 4D. There the sherd yield indicated concentrated occupation and a considerable time span, and the chances for stratigraphic data seemed excellent. To the west of this diagonal line the ground slopes away to the alluvial plain and test pits showed less promise.

Stratigraphic tests were uniformly disappointing and were eventually abandoned. During the 1937 season, 29 houses were cleared, more or less in the order they presented themselves. There was ample superposition of houses, and we ended the season with a knowledge of the range of major types and a fair idea of their sequential order. With a few exceptions only the late Tanque Verde phase houses produced restorable decorated vessels, however, and we were unable satisfactorily to equate the remaining houses with ceramic material. Unfortunately this, in part, is still the case. During 1938, we concentrated upon filling this gap and on establishing the phase affiliation of the nonpottery industries. Sections of the site not already excavated were tested intensively.

Testing took the form of rows of pits 0.5 x 0.2 m, alternating every 2 m, with the rows 4 m apart and the pits of adjacent rows staggered. This season we were more eclectic with regard to house clearing and confined our excavations to those which gave promise of being datable, to houses occurring in conjunction therewith, or to those which were of particular interest for other reasons.

As a result of the wholesale testing during the 1937 season, several cremation areas were revealed. Cremations were of particular importance at the Hodges site, giving us our largest and most secure association of plainware and minor artifacts with decorated pottery.

RELATIONSHIP TO THE GILA BASIN

Tucson pottery appears to be intermediate between Hohokam red-on-buff and Mogollon red-on-brown, an ambivalence entirely expectable from its intermediate location. On the one hand, it has pronounced Mogollon affinities in its close-grained paste, its polish, its relative absence of slip, its utilization of smudging, and, in certain vessel forms, a preference for geometric ornament. The Gila Basin rose-colored paste with its excessive porosity, its chalky slip, its fugitive pigment, and its matte surface seems generally foreign to the Hodges site.

On the other hand, shape and ornamentation adhere closely to Gila Basin patterns. The relationship between the two areas must have been intimate, for in some of our excavations intrusive Gila Basin sherds run as high as 40 percent of the decorated types. Moreover, Gila Basin importations occur with frequency in cremations. Recognizable Gila Basin intrusives are from the Gila Butte through Sacaton phases, with Santa Cruz and Sacaton the strongest. The sole exception to this range is a Casa Grande Red-on-buff jar from a cremation.

Our local series begins with the Snaketown phase. We were not able to isolate equivalents of the Vahki and Estrella phases; even the Sweetwater phase is sparsely represented. Sherds of the Sweetwater and Snaketown phases are indistinguishable from comparable types of the Gila Basin; hence, the same phase names have been retained. Beginning with the Colonial period, however, there is divergence, and the term Cañada del Oro distinguishes the Tucson version from that of the Gila Basin.

Despite this divergence in the Cañada del Oro (Gila Butte in the Gila River area) phase, the relationship between the Hodges red-on-brown ceramics and the Gila Basin red-on-buff remains very close. Cañada del Oro sherds show the same preference for the serrated scroll and for exterior scoring as do those of the Gila Butte phase. Similarly, in the Rillito phase as in the Santa Cruz phase, jars with flaring rims, flare-rim bowls, fringing, small elements, and exterior trailing lines are favored. There are similar parallels between the Rincon and Sacaton phases, and between the Tanque Verde and Soho phases, although in the latter case comparison is hampered by our scanty knowledge of Soho.

In any case, it is possible to establish a series of painted types exceedingly close typologically to those of the Gila Basin. It follows almost necessarily that in both cases, the styles succeeded one another in the same relative order. Upon this inference we base, in part, the suggested ceramic sequence in the Tucson area (Table 1.1).

The Hodges site, characterized by sheet rubbish (with deeper rubbish almost invariably mixed) gave little good stratigraphic evidence. Houses occur in clear-cut superposition, but many lack correlatively superimposed pottery. Together with associated ceramics, house superposition gives definite evidence (although not strong quantitatively) of the following sequence: Tanque Verde, Rillito, Cañada del Oro, and Snaketown. Also from house stratigraphy we know that Rincon is later than Cañada del Oro, but we cannot place it with regard to either Tanque Verde or Rillito. Although our stratigraphic data from trash are weak, we do have several indications of a Tanque Verde–Rincon–Rillito sequence. Typologically, this is precisely parallel to the well-known and well-established Soho–Sacaton–Santa Cruz series in the Gila Basin and makes the postulated order almost certain.

In the last analysis, therefore, our dating rests upon the establishment of local phases stylistically, and presumably temporally, equivalent to those of the Gila Basin. What local data we have are definitely confirmatory, with nothing seriously contradictory. The few examples of multiple, restorable vessels from house floors are almost invariably of a single phase. Each of two houses, whose types were predominantly from the Tanque Verde phase, has a Rincon-type jar. This overlap is more understandable than it would be if the phases were remote from each other in time—such as Tanque Verde and Snaketown. Even stronger quantitatively is the evidence from cremations, where the association likewise is pure. This means almost necessarily that in both cases, the styles succeeded one another in the same relative order. This would seem adequately strong evidence for the validity of the suggested chronological sequence at the Hodges site.

TABLE 1.1

Ceramic Sequences for the Hodges Site and the Gila Basin

Ed. note: These 1937 dates have since been slightly revised. See Haury (1976) for more recent dates.

Period	Estimated Dating Gila Basin	Gila Basin Phase	Hodges Site Phase
Classic	A.D. 1300–1400	Civano	Tucson[a]
	A.D. 1200–1300	Soho	Tanque Verde
Sedentary	A.D. 1100–1200	Santan[b]	——
	A.D. 900–1100	Sacaton	Rincon
Colonial	A.D. 700–900	Santa Cruz	Rillito
	A.D. 500–700	Gila Butte	Cañada del Oro
Pioneer	A.D. 300–500	Snaketown	Snaketown
	A.D. 100–300	Sweetwater	Sweetwater[c]
	100 B.C.–A.D. 100	Estrella	——
	300–100 B.C.	Vahki	——

[a] The Hodges site terminated with the Tanque Verde phase, but the Tucson phase is well represented in the same general area. Prominent late ruins include the University Indian Ruin, the Martinez Hill Ruin, and the large, unexcavated ruin in the Sabino Canyon area. In general, the Tucson phase was characterized by two-storied houses, polychrome pottery (both Gila Basin and Tucson types) San Carlos Red and San Carlos Red-on-brown. Tanque Verde Red-on-brown also continues into the Tucson phase. The latter, however, tends to become more micaceous in the late period, and Hayden (1957) calls this pottery Pantano Red-on-brown. The abundance of mica in the Pantano paste is the only difference between it and Tanque Verde Red-on-brown.

[b] The Santan phase is a local specialization confined to the eastern part of the Gila Basin. Gladwin and others (1937: 264) regarded it as the forerunner of the Salado movement. It is distinguished chiefly by architectural innovations and by the presence of a distinctive redware, Santan Red. Sacaton Red-on-buff continues into this phase (Gladwin and others 1937: 170). All told, the absence of a Tucson phase equivalent to Santan is not a major deficiency, despite the fact that we are hard-pressed to account for the abrupt change from curvilinear to rectilinear pottery designs which occurred between the Rincon and Tanque Verde phases.

[c] Represented only by random sherds and four restorable or near-restorable vessels.

2. BALL COURT

Available data on ball courts in southern Arizona have been summarized by Gladwin and others (1937). As a result, two major types have been established. One, uniformly larger than the other and consistently oriented east and west, has been designated as the Snaketown type and is Colonial period in age. The other, the Casa Grande type, is smaller, with a north-south orientation. It has been dated to the Sedentary and Classic periods. [*Ed. note:* See Wasley and Johnson (1965:81–86) for a more recent, detailed discussion of ball courts.]

The ball court at the Hodges site is of the Snaketown variety. It lies roughly east and west. The side embankments reach a somewhat higher elevation than do the ends, although the latter are by no means open, as in the Casa Grande type. The ends are flanked on the outside by an apron-like embankment.

Emil Haury amiably agreed to excavate portions of the ball court during the Easter season of 1937. He dug two axial trenches, designed to determine the profile and to locate the central and end markers. A cross section of the north-south trench is shown in Figure 2.1.

The court, as will be seen from the illustration, is dish-shaped, with low walls that merge into the floor. This contrasts with the comparable Colonial period court at Snaketown (Gladwin and others 1937: Fig. 12), which is characterized by a relatively high wall and a sharp wall-floor angle. The difference is significant, not only because it establishes a local variation in court form but because it implies that here the game may have been played somewhat differently than was the corresponding Mexican game.

The court appears to have been made by sinking the floor approximately a meter into the sterile red soil and caliche that underlie the site. The core of the north wall is virgin red soil; in the section tested, it contained no sherds. However, the core of the south wall may have been built up artificially. It contained several sherds, none decorated.

Once the major excavation for the court was accomplished, pockets in caliche presumably were filled, the red soil leveled, and a relatively even floor produced. The inner surface of the wall (number 4 in Figure 2.1), and perhaps also the floor, was plastered. Along the south wall some plaster remained, but the floor was badly weathered and was difficult to trace. The strata numbered 2 and 3 in Figure 2.1 may represent additions to increase the height of the wall. Stratum 1 in Figure 2.1 is trash, probably also a deliberate rather than natural accumulation.

No central goal or marker of any sort was found, and the end markers were identified somewhat dubiously. At the east end was a slightly oval break in otherwise continuous caliche. This depression, 35 by 40 cm and 30 cm deep, contained only red soil. At the west end of the court, caliche gives way to red soil; embedded in this soil (20 cm below the supposed floor level) was a small, much worn hammerstone, its long axis upright. Identification as goals or markers is dubious, but both the cavity in the caliche and the hammerstone occurred in the expected locations, with no other depressions or objects in the immediate vicinity.

A number of tests were made to ascertain the pottery styles associated with the ball court. Although the resulting decorated sherds proved to be few, they, nevertheless, confirm the assignment of this court to the Colonial period. The fill from test areas at the northern and southern ends of the lateral trench was screened but produced no sherds later than the Rillito phase. However, at the south end of this trench, a three-level stratigraphic test was made in the trash banked against the outer wall. The two upper levels produced several Rincon Red-on-brown sherds. These may be chance sherds, but, if they were in trash deliberately banked against the south wall, we may have evidence that the use of the court continued into Sedentary times. The general fill, from the two axial trenches, contained sherds of all phases, Snaketown through Tanque Verde.

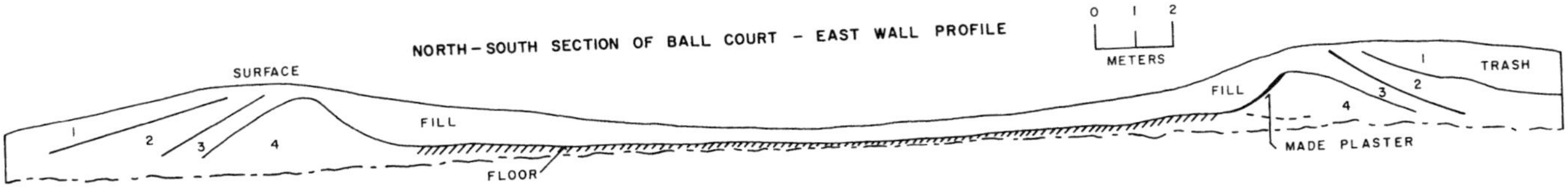

Fig. 2.1 Profile of ball court

3. HOUSES

Eighty-four houses and house fragments were excavated. The structures described here present certain general aspects that may be summarized at the start. First and foremost, they were essentially domestic, without special features that would suggest ceremonial function. Occasional, isolated firepits, surrounded by a poorly defined circle of floor, may have been out-of-door kitchens. Presumably, much domestic activity took place in the open, and some houses are so small that they would have served better for storage than for living quarters.

Second, houses were consistently semi-subterranean. Presumably, the actual depth below the surface was of little significance—it must have varied directly with the depth at which suitable foundation soil was found. There was, however, no aversion to house building in rubbish, and Tanque Verde phase houses, in particular, rested more often than

[*Ed. Note:* Houses 1–31 were excavated and drawn by Carl Miller.]

Fig. 3.1 House with burned posts still in place

not upon trash and, incidentally, upon the remains of earlier houses. In rare instances (three only) the walls of the excavation functioned as the lower walls of the house. Generally, the pit itself was not incorporated so intimately into house construction.

A highly characteristic feature was the covered entry or vestibule. The vestibule usually entered the long side of the house, but end entries occur. Opposite the entry was the firepit, a shallow, heavily-plastered depression in the floor. In contrast to Mogollon practice, graded vestibules were not favored, although steps in the entry were frequent. One house (House 47) was approached by a three-step entry, and several, by two steps. Doubtless a direct expression of the depth of a house below surface level, steps occur from earliest to latest phases.

We have little precise material on structural detail of houses. House posts were identified by the University of Arizona Laboratory of Tree-Ring Research as mesquite and oak. No posts of datable wood were excavated. Inferentially, these main timbers supported a pole framework, with earth covering. Earthen building material, presumably from fallen walls and roof, often covered the floor to a considerable extent.

Floor plans varied from quadrilateral with rounded corners to rectangular and, as in the Gila Basin, there were certain forms best described as elliptical or oblong. No circular houses were found aside from the dubious outside kitchens noted above (Russell 1908: 69).

Details of construction—insofar as we were able to record them—are found below, in the descriptions accompanying individual house plans. Variation in posthole arrangement indicates several different structural plans. Major supports sometimes were centrally spaced within a house, in which case there usually were four, perhaps with auxiliary corner or peripheral posts. Rarely was there a single major post, more or less centrally placed. Two posts aligned with the long axis of a house may have indicated ridge or gable construction. Intramural posts were rare, but did occur. Frequently, postholes circumscribed the floor, either around the periphery or just beyond it. [*Ed. note:* An unnumbered house illustrated in Figure 3.1 shows the remains of numerous posts encircling a pit house floor.] Extramural posts must be assumed for the several floors which lack postholes. In addition to the above, there were houses whose posthole arrangement was scattered. Frequently, a random post or two seemed to have been erected to bolster a sagging roof. With walls and roof earth-covered, the weight must have been very great and sagging the rule, rather than the exception. It is likely that houses were abandoned as collapse threatened, for not more than half the houses showed signs of having been burned.

Orientation of the entry was not constant, although northeast and southwest were preferred. West and northwest consistently were avoided, evidently on account of the winds and dust that swept across the valley.

On the whole, house remains were not well preserved. Many had been disturbed by subsequent house-building. Other features also contributed to the impermanence. First, houses often were built upon trash, a situation at best unstable compared with construction on virgin soil. Second, little discrimination was shown in the selection of building materials. Floors and walls, even those of the more substantial Tanque Verde phase houses, regularly contained a large quantity of rubbish that naturally proved less enduring than a compact clay or caliche base. Houses of the standing-wall and curb-wall types, defined below, generally were better preserved than others: the standing-wall houses, because they belonged to the last occupation and have been spared destruction by later buildings; the curb-wall types, because generally they were built upon hardpan.

CLASSIFICATION

On purely typological grounds, houses may be divided into the five major categories listed in Table 3.1. There are numerous instances of house superposition, summarized in Table 3.2. As a result of this superposition some of the house types can be arranged in chronological order.

The standing-wall house is immediately recognizable as latest in the series. When found in conjunction with other structures, it is invariably uppermost, and it overlies slant-wall, curb-wall, and wall-less houses. Apparently the slant-wall house is next in the series. Although it underlies standing-wall houses, it, in turn, occurs above curb-wall and wall-less types. The latter two may be regarded as earlier, but, as they do not appear in superposition, they cannot on the basis of house stratigraphy be placed with respect to each other.

The pit-wall house occurs both above and beneath the wall-less kind (one case of each). It may be that the pit-wall house was not a true "type" and resulted more from the accident of underlying soil composition than from architectural pattern. Although the curb-wall house generally was dug into the soil, it does not incorporate the walls of the pit into its construction. Furthermore, at Snaketown, houses of pit-wall character were attributable one each to the Vahki and Sacaton phases.

To summarize, to the best of our knowledge, the standing-wall house consistently was latest, with the slant-wall house next youngest. Curb-wall and wall-less types both were earlier, but do not appear in conjunction, and their temporal relationship must rest upon other grounds. The pit-wall house is a dubious "type" and variable in its relationship to the wall-less house.

SUPERPOSITION AND DATING

Figure 3.2 is an interesting example of house superposition. It shows the oldest house excavated, Number 50 (Snaketown). The other houses shown are dated as follows:

TABLE 3.1
House Types

Type	Section	Incidence	Phase Identification
Standing wall: floor bounded by substantial walls		18	16 Tanque Verde
Slant wall: wall a thin plaster coating on fill; slopes back from floor		12	5 Tanque Verde 1 Rincon (?)
Curb wall: floor bounded by low wall or half-rounded rim		8	[Unplaced; some, at least, probably Rillito]
Wall-less: without bounding walls		27	1 Tanque Verde 3 Rincon 1 Rillito-Rincon 3 Rillito 1 Cañada del Oro–Rillito 4 Cañada del Oro 1 Snaketown
Pit wall: excavated into hardpan, walls of excavation serving as lower house walls		3	1 Rillito [1 Cañada del Oro, or earlier; 1 Snaketown, or earlier]
Fragmentary, no data		16	1 Tanque Verde
Total		84	38[a]

[a] Houses mentioned within brackets are not included in this total.

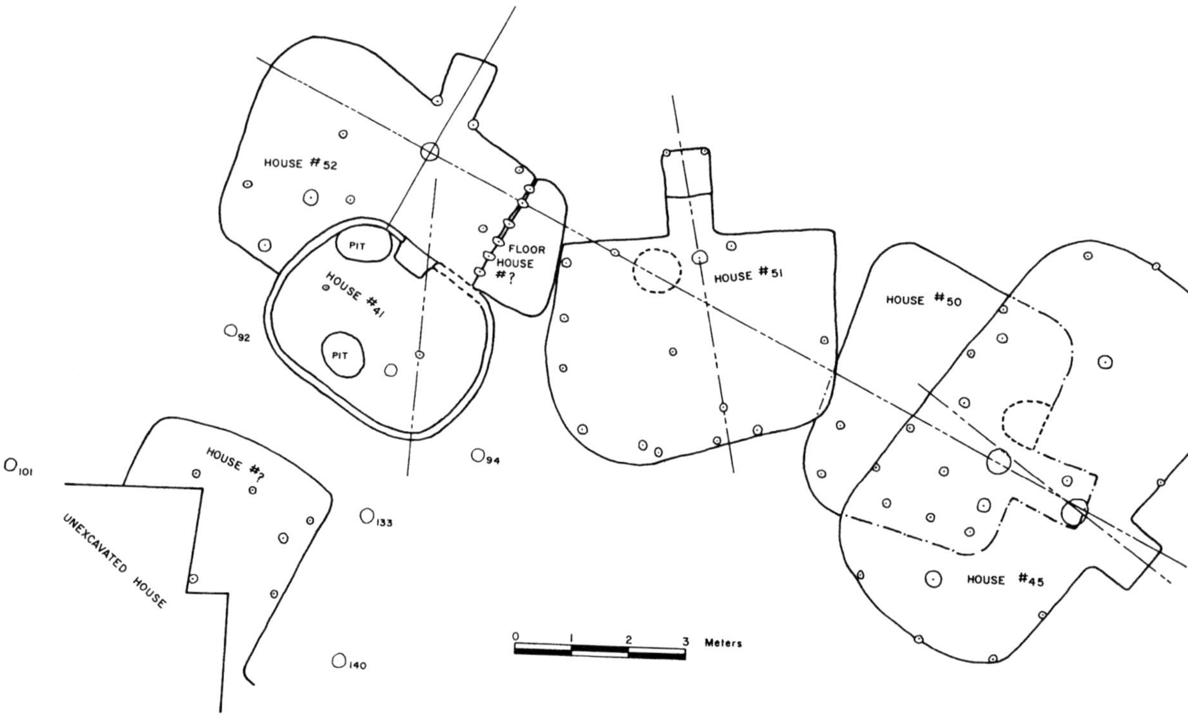

Fig. 3.2 House superposition: Houses 41, 45, 50, 51, and 52

TABLE 3.2

House Superposition

Superposition	Instances	House Numbers	Phases
Standing wall overlies: slant wall	5	11 over 1	Tanque Verde[a] over Tanque Verde
		60 over 69	Tanque Verde over unplaced
		60 over fragment	Tanque Verde over unplaced
		61 over 76	Tanque Verde over probable unplaced
		74 over 75	Tanque Verde over unplaced
curb wall	3	11 over 8	Tanque Verde over unplaced
		42 over 46[b]	Tanque Verde over unplaced
		60 over 68	Tanque Verde over Rillito or earlier
wall-less	2	42 over 43	Tanque Verde over Rillito or earlier
		61 over 64	Tanque Verde over unplaced
Slant wall overlies: slant wall	3	33 cut into 35	Tanque Verde[c] over Tanque Verde
		53 over 54, 84	Tanque Verde over Tanque Verde, unplaced
		72 over 75	Rincon over unplaced
curb wall	2	1 over 2, 8	Tanque Verde over unplaced, unplaced
		48 over 46	Unplaced over unplaced
wall-less	2	54 over 40	Tanque Verde over Cañada del Oro
		53, 54, 84 over 49	Tanque Verde, Tanque Verde, unplaced over unplaced
Curb wall overlies: wall-less	0		
Wall-less overlies: wall-less	5	40 over 49[d]	Cañada del Oro over unplaced
		45 over 50	Rillito over Snaketown
		51 over 50	Cañada del Oro over Snaketown
		59 over 80, 81	Rincon over Cañada del Oro, unplaced
		77 over 79	Unplaced over Rillito
pit wall	1	59, 80, 81 over 83	Rincon, Cañada del Oro, unplaced over unplaced
Pit wall overlies: wall-less	1	41 cut into 52	Rillito over Cañada del Oro

[a] House 11 is Tanque Verde by inference; it overlies a dated Tanque Verde house.

[b] House 46 was not found to be walled, but the floor edge was cupped in a fashion suggesting the former existence of a curb wall.

[c] House 33 was Tanque Verde by inference since it overlies 35, a Tanque Verde house.

[d] Although House 40 overlies 49, it is possible that the latter may be later by virtue of having been cut into the floor of House 40. The floor of the upper house was so broken at the junction that the relationship could not be established with certainty.

Houses 41 and 45, Rillito; Houses 51 and 52, Cañada del Oro.

Although house superposition gives some precise evidence of chronological order of architecture, the relation of the series to ceramic types is much more difficult. Decorated, restorable vessels on a house floor are, of course, incontrovertible evidence; but of the 84 houses cleared, only 19 had such restorable vessels, and these were chiefly of the Tanque Verde phase.

Unfortunately, floor sherds—so useful in other regions—were distinctly unreliable here. For one thing, they were relatively scarce, and we are, therefore, lacking the assurance that comes with strong quantitative evidence. For another, since many houses were built on earlier trash, material from the surrounding rubbish may have washed in after the dwelling collapsed. Thus floor sherds could have come from the surrounding fill, without temporal relationship to the house itself.

As a test case, sherds within 10 cm of the floors of Houses 32, 60, and 80 may be noted. Houses 32 and 60 were determined—on the basis of decorated, restorable vessels—to belong to the Tanque Verde phase. House 80 was assignable to the Cañada del Oro phase on the basis of a decorated vessel on the floor.

The results of the sherd counts are as follows:

Sherds	House 32	House 60	House 80
Tanque Verde	7	41	0
Rincon	15	46	3
Rillito	27	37	6
Cañada del Oro	3	0	3
Snaketown	2	1	1
Sweetwater	1	0	0
Local pottery (unclassified as to type)	4	35	0

It is clear that in Houses 32 and 60 sherds of the Tanque Verde phase are exceeded by those of earlier phases. However, it cannot be assumed that the floor sherds will always be consistently earlier than the house. In House 80, for example, sherds from phases later than Cañada del Oro were found.

Occasionally, sherds from the floor and the overlying fill are so preponderantly of one phase that the house may safely be attributed to that phase. Sherds from beneath an unbroken section of floor naturally give a dependable maximum age. Frequently, however, floors are so broken that the underlying material cannot confidently be assumed to be antecedent. Conversely, floors best preserved are those built on the sterile, red soil with no rubbish underneath.

Of the 84 houses and house fragments cleared, 38 can be identified as to phase (Table 3.3). This allocation rests chiefly upon decorated, restorable vessels from the floor,

TABLE 3.3

Phase Identification of Houses

Phase	Number	House Style	Evidence for Dating
Tanque Verde	1	Slant wall	Restorable vessels
	7	Wall-less	Restorable vessels
	11	Standing wall	Overlies House 1
	12	No data	Restorable vessels
	13	Standing wall?[a]	Restorable vessels
	15	Standing wall?[a]	Restorable vessel
	16	Standing wall	Restorable vessels
	17	Standing wall	Restorable vessels
	19	Standing wall	Restorable vessels
	22	Standing wall	Restorable vessels
	23	Standing wall	Restorable vessels
	28	Standing wall	Tanque Verde sherds under floor
	31	Standing wall	Restorable vessels
	32	Standing wall	Restorable vessels
	33	Slant wall	Post-dates House 35
	35	Slant wall	Large floor sherds, sealed by fallen roof
	42	Standing wall	House type; floor sherds
	53	Slant wall	Floor sherds
	54	Slant wall	Floor sherds
	60	Standing wall	Restorable vessel
	61	Standing wall	Restorable vessel
	73	Standing wall	House type
	74	Standing wall	House type
Rincon	37	Wall-less	Restorable vessels
	55	Wall-less	Sherds: floor fill and sub-floor
	59	Wall-less	Sherds: floor fill and sub-floor
	72	Slant wall	Restorable vessel, probably Rincon, but atypical
Rincon-Rillito (transitional)	65	Wall-less	Restorable vessel
Rillito	41	Pit wall	Sherds: floor fill, underlying pit, next to outer wall
	45	Wall-less	Floor sherds
	63	Wall-less	Sherds: floor fill and sub-floor
	79	Wall-less	Floor sherds
Rillito-Cañada del Oro (transitional)	82	Wall-less	Restorable vessels
Cañada del Oro	40	Wall-less	Sherds: floor and fill
	51	Wall-less	Restorable
	52	Wall-less	Floor sherds
	80	Wall-less	Restorable vessel
Snaketown	50	Wall-less	Floor sherds, sealed by overlying house

[a] Shown as wall-less on Miller's 1936 map; standing wall on his profile.

and upon floor sherds where the evidence is sufficiently strong. Overlying or underlying cremations in several instances are confirmatory, but at best can give no more than a minimum or maximum dating. Only in the Tanque Verde phase is the architectural type sufficiently distinctive to be diagnostic.

TANQUE VERDE PHASE HOUSES

It is obvious at once from Table 3.3 that the Tanque Verde phase is the best-established architectural-ceramic complex. Not only do houses identified as Tanque Verde far outnumber those of other phases, but the allocations rest largely upon restorable vessels and, therefore, are secure. The standing-wall house is confined to the Tanque Verde phase. Its two constant features are a substantial, upright wall and a rectangular floor plan. Other details vary: the walls may be continuous or discrete (Figs. 3.3, 3.4); the entry may be side or end, with or without a step. House width varies from 25 to 95 percent of the length. In posthole arrangement there are almost as many variations as houses. These include a single, central post; four centrally spaced posts; two posts, aligned along the long axis; two, aligned

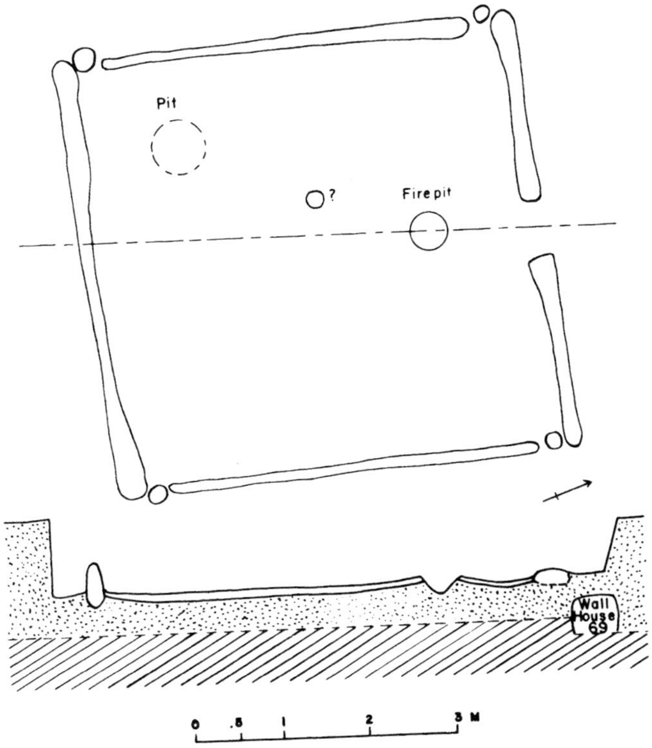

Fig. 3.3 House 60: Tanque Verde phase

Fig. 3.4 House superposition: Houses 60, 61, 67 and 68. Houses 67 and 68 in foreground; House 60 behind and above; House 61 in background. Looking west.

along the short axis; corner posts only; random posts; and no posts (Fig. 3.5).

The only slant-wall houses surely identifiable as to phase are Tanque Verde (Table 3.3; Fig. 3.6) plus one probable Rincon identification. Although on grounds of superposition alone, the standing-wall house seems consistently later than the slant-wall, the Tanque Verde pottery from the two house types is indistinguishable. The slant-wall structure, probably of the Rincon phase, is House 72, from which comes the decorated jar shown in Figure 4.25a. Although not entirely typical, this vessel is closer to Rincon style than anything else. Perhaps, in view of the above evidence, the slant-wall house is best regarded as predominantly Tanque Verde, possibly with roots in the Rincon phase.

Characteristically, the slant-wall house is quadrilateral with rounded corners; occasionally, it is almost oval. Ordinarily, the slant-wall house lacks postholes. One house has two aligned along the long axis; in others, the postholes tend to be peripheral, just inside the base of the wall. The entry generally is on the long side and is unstepped.

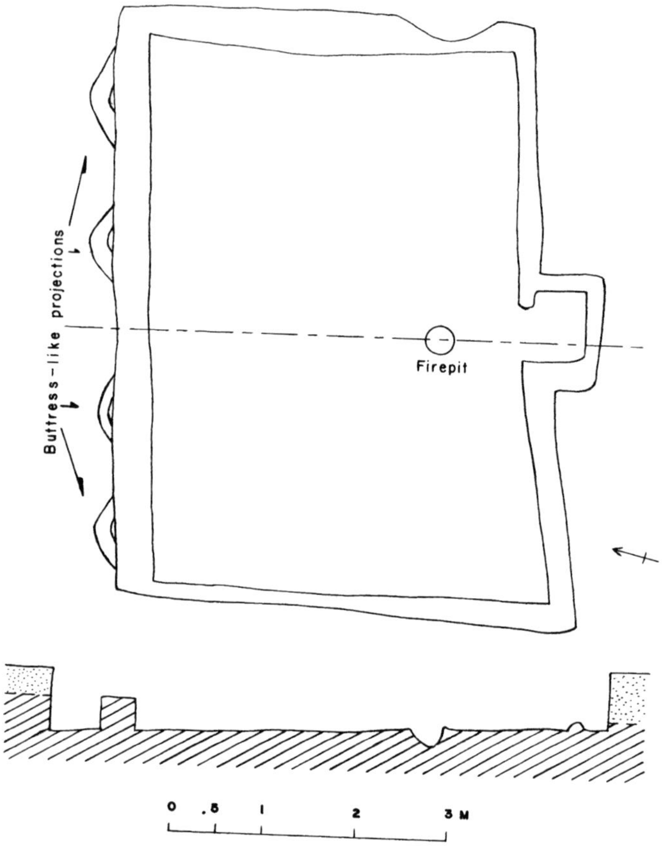

Fig. 3.5 House 23: Tanque Verde phase. Buttress-like projections were noted in Carl Miller's 1936 preliminary report. No further description of them is available. Laurens Hammack suggests these may be "puddling pits" (adobe mixing basins) underlying the house walls.

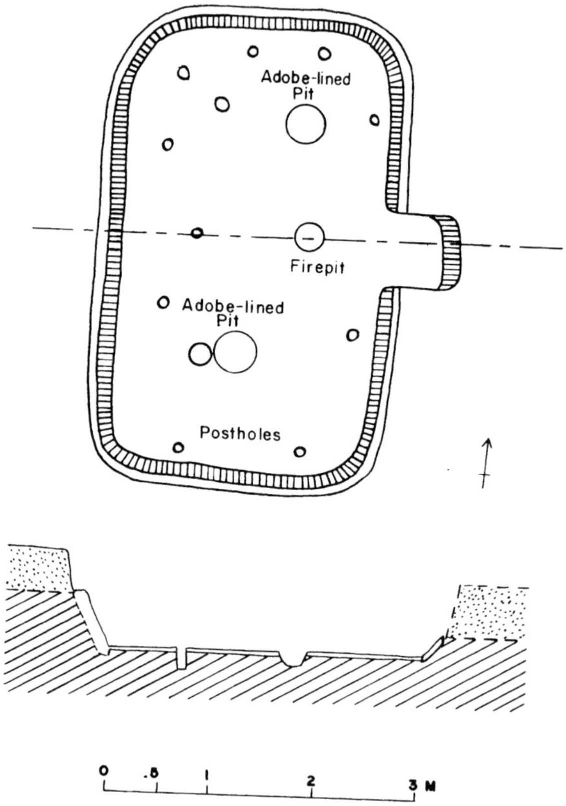

Fig. 3.6 House 33: Tanque Verde phase

RINCON PHASE HOUSES

Except for one probable Rincon phase slant-wall house and one Rillito phase pit-wall structure, all houses identifiable with phases earlier than Tanque Verde lack walls. The wall-less house, therefore, seems to have ranged from the Snaketown phase to the Rincon phase. One wall-less house (House 7) is definitely Tanque Verde. However, this may result from a misinterpretation of Miller's notes. In several instances houses were represented on his map as wall-less, although the profiles were drawn with standing walls. House 7 is wall-less in both recordings, but there exists the possibility of a misunderstanding.

Aside from the slant-wall house referred to above, the Rincon phase is represented only by Houses 37, 55, and 59 (Figs. 3.7, 3.8, 3.9). All are wall-less; all lack steps. The shape is quadrilateral with rounded corners, although one floor (House 37) is so skewed as to be nearly round. House width in proportion to length varies from 65 to 95 percent. Posthole arrangement is variable and consists of four interior holes, poorly spaced; four centrally spaced holes, as well as a full series of peripheral ones; and peripheral holes only. The entry is not consistent: that of House 59 has a dubious fan-shaped attachment; that of House 55 is slightly graded. The bulbous entry frequently found in the Gila Basin Sacaton phase does not occur.

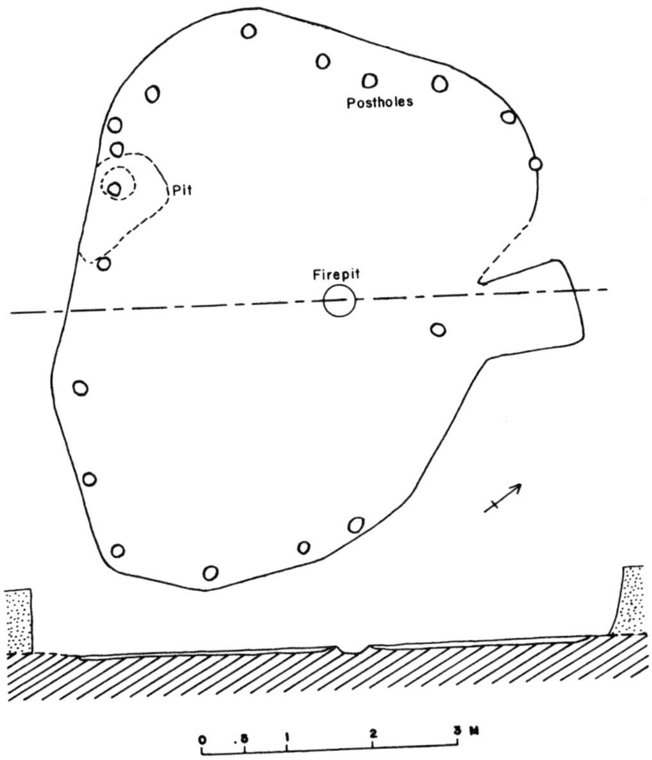

Fig. 3.7 House 37: Rincon phase

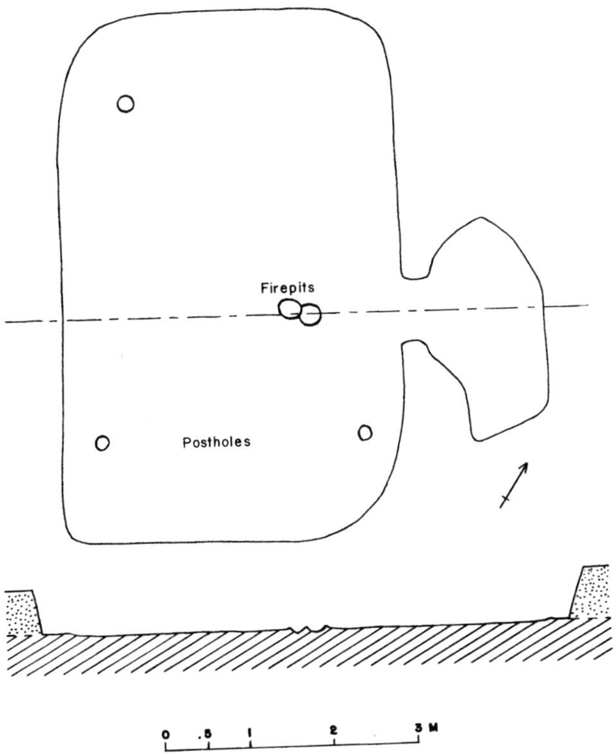

Fig. 3.9 House 59: Rincon phase

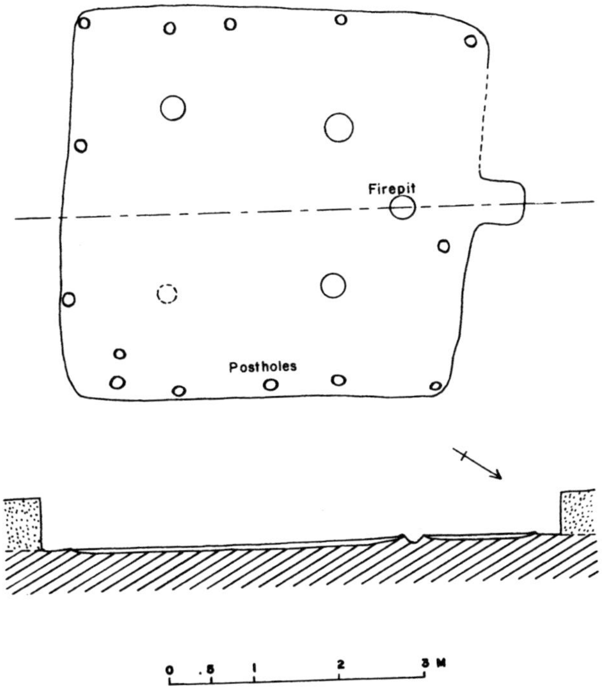

Fig. 3.8 House 55: Rincon phase

RILLITO PHASE HOUSES

Except for House 41, which is an oval pit wall house, Rillito phase houses are wall-less and without steps. Proportion of width to length varies from 50 to 85 percent, which is somewhat narrower on the average than that of the Rincon phase and comparable to Gila Basin trends. House 79 has a single off-center posthole; another, House 45, has two central posts along the long axis, with a full series of peripheral postholes on two sides. House 65, whose one restorable vessel is transitional between the Rillito and Rincon phases, is oval, with peripheral postholes outside the floor (Fig. 3.10).

The pit-wall structure attributable to the Rillito phase is House 41 (Fig. 3.11). It is small and oval, with two postholes on the long axis. The southern and western sides were dug into hardpan and were plastered to form the walls. But on the north the house cut into House 52, and there walls were made (Fig. 3.2). They are badly broken but seem to have been structurally similar to the slant-wall type, although more nearly vertical. A unique feature of this house is the lack of a vestibule and the low step on the floor inside the doorway.

The curb-wall house may be mentioned here, for although not definitely placed, there are strong indications

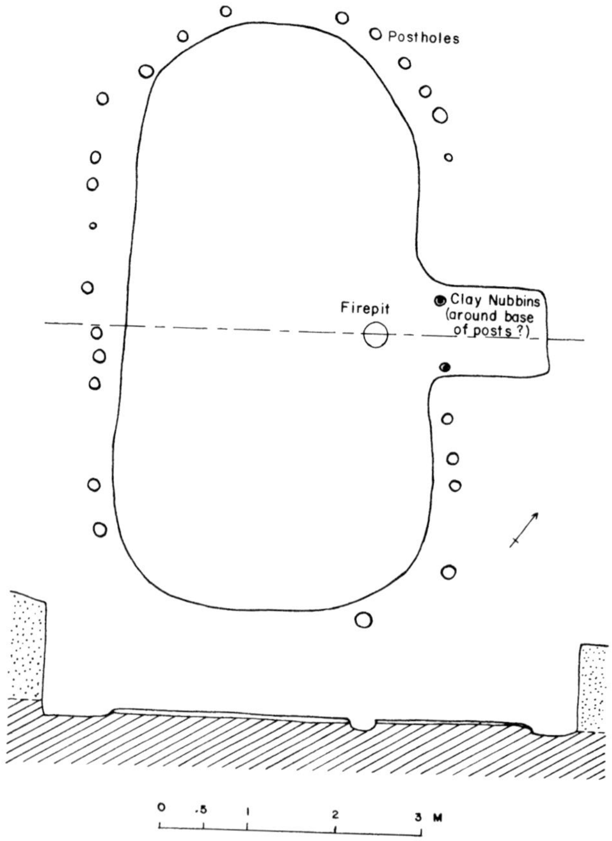

Fig. 3.10 House 65: Transitional between Rillito and Rincon phases

that it belongs to the Rillito phase. It is, however, peculiarly elusive in its dating because of paucity of floor sherds and lack of restorable vessels. However, House 68, a curb-wall structure, was overlain by a Rillito phase cremation, which places the floor as Rillito or earlier. Moreover, from beneath the floor of House 56 (a small fragment of a curb-wall structure) came a Rillito sherd. This house, therefore, should be regarded as Rillito or later. The implication is that the curb wall was present in the Tucson Basin during Rillito times.

In the Gila Basin the homologous house type was confined to the Sacaton phase, the equivalent of the Rincon phase. It might be suggested on these grounds that in the Tucson Basin the curb-wall house came into vogue during the Rillito phase and probably (on the strength of Gila Basin evidence) continued into the Rincon phase. Of the latter suggestion, however, we have no decisive local evidence. If this interpretation is correct, the curb-wall house appeared subsequent to the first wall-less houses and the two continued concurrently.

The curb-wall house tends, more than any other style, to be somewhat elongate, with an end rather than a side entry. The rim-like wall usually encloses the entry, which may or may not have been stepped. House 47 is unique in its three-step entry (Figs. 3.12, 3.13). Three of the eight curb-wall houses have no postholes; three are fragmentary or incompletely excavated. The two remaining houses are divided between axial with peripheral postholes, and peripheral alone.

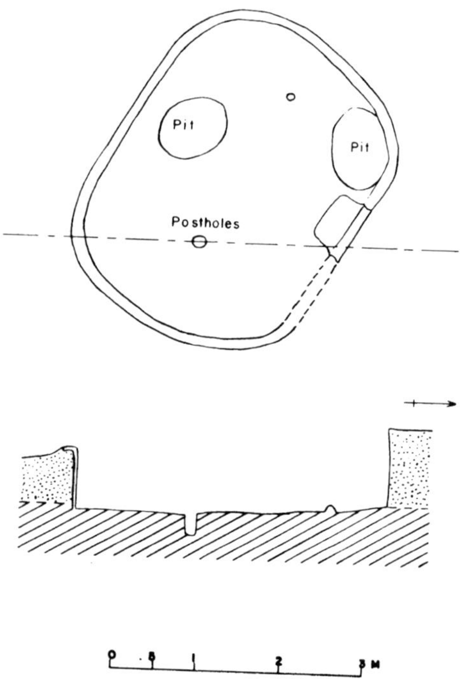

Fig. 3.11 House 41: Rillito phase

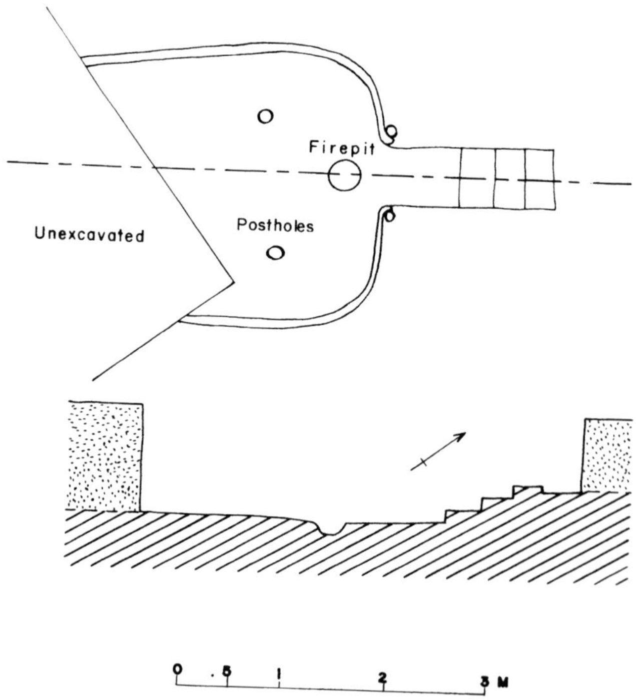

Fig. 3.12 House 47: Unplaced, three-step entry

Fig. 3.13 House 47: View of three-step entry

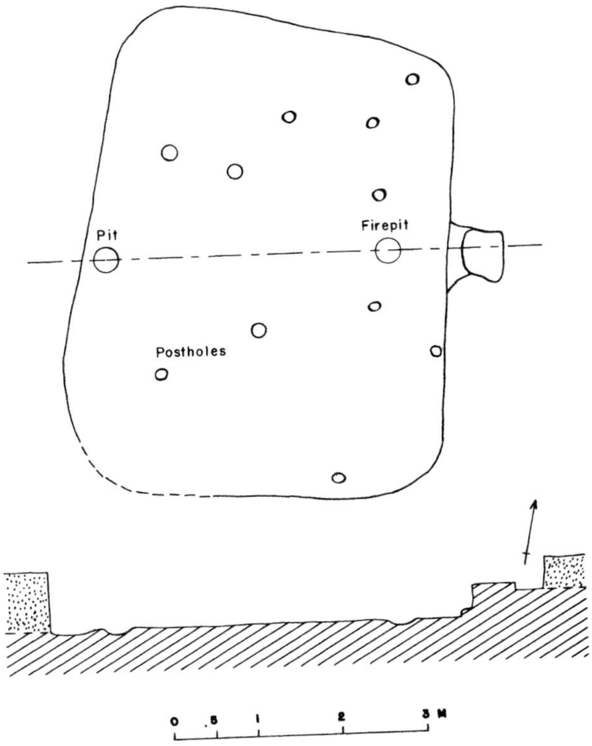

Fig. 3.14 House 40: Cañada del Oro phase

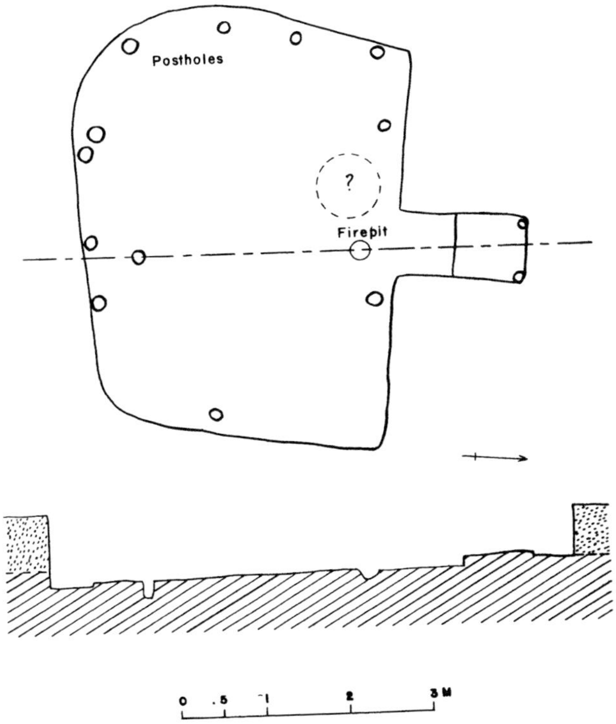

Fig. 3.15: House 51: Cañada del Oro phase

CAÑADA DEL ORO PHASE HOUSES

We are fortunate in having four floors (Houses 40, 51, 52, 80) identifiable as Cañada del Oro (Figs. 3.14, 3.15, 3.16, 3.17). At Snaketown only one house was attributed, doubtfully, to the equivalent Gila Butte phase. All our examples are wall-less, which seems to be the one common feature. Proportion of width to length is greater than in Rillito, averaging between 75 and 80 percent. Entries are side rather than end, with one off-center and two badly skewed. Two are stepped. Postholes seem to follow no set pattern; House 80 has two on the long axis, but in the other houses postholes appear to have been randomly placed.

House 82, transitional between the Cañada del Oro and Rillito phases, is so fragmentary that little can be said of it.

SNAKETOWN PHASE HOUSES

The one floor (House 50) attributable to the Snaketown phase is not especially distinctive (Fig. 3.18). Quadrilateral with rounded corners, it has a rather long side

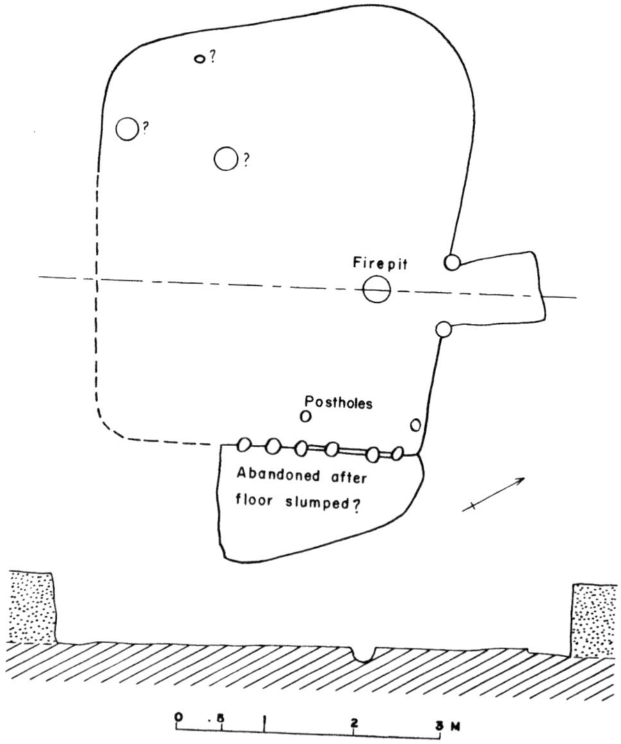

Fig. 3.16 House 52: Cañada del Oro phase

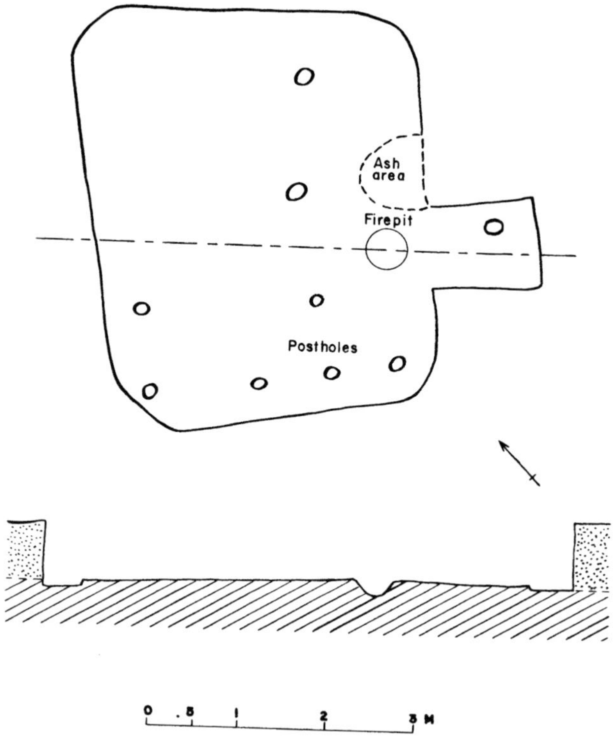

Fig. 3.18 House 50: Snaketown phase

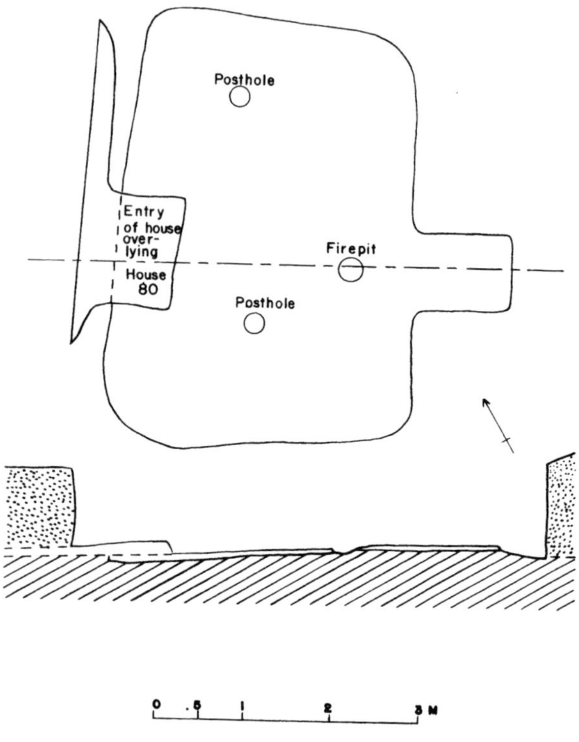

Fig. 3.17 House 80: Cañada del Oro phase

entry that is somewhat off-center. Postholes are along the southern edge of the floor, with two randomly spaced in the northern half. The firepit is not well defined, but there is a shallow, broken, ash-filled area in the floor immediately opposite the entry.

Here, mention should be made of the two pit-wall houses that remain. House 38 (Fig. 3.19) underlay a Snaketown phase cremation; hence, it must have been Snaketown or earlier. The other (House 83) was beneath a well-placed Cañada del Oro phase house, so it must have been of the Cañada del Oro phase or earlier. Floor sherds were so scanty as to be useless. The implication is strong that both these pit-wall houses belonged to the Pioneer period, although within it they cannot be definitely assigned to any phase and are therefore not listed in Table 3.3

SUMMARY OF STRATIGRAPHIC EVIDENCE FROM HOUSE SUPERPOSITION

It is clear from the foregoing that, although there are numerous instances of house superposition, many of the structures cannot be identified as to phase. Obviously, in order to provide phase stratigraphy, two or more houses of the series must be identifiable. The last column of Table 3.2 summarizes the phase affiliation of superimposed houses.

Fig. 3.19 House 38: Snaketown phase or earlier

This can be restated as follows, taking only those instances of surely identifiable structures:

Tanque Verde over Rillito, or earlier
Tanque Verde over Cañada del Oro
Rincon over Cañada del Oro
Rillito over Cañada del Oro
Rillito over Snaketown
Cañada del Oro over Snaketown

Tanque Verde overlies Cañada del Oro; and, in two cases, Tanque Verde overlies houses placed as Rillito or earlier. But Rillito overlies Cañada del Oro and both overlie Snaketown. The sequence therefore reads: Tanque Verde, Rillito, Cañada del Oro, Snaketown. Rincon overlies Cañada del Oro but cannot be placed with respect to Rillito; nor, for that matter, to Tanque Verde. The sequence just outlined above is entirely in agreement with that of the Gila Basin. That being the case, it seems justifiable to insert Rincon between Tanque Verde and Rillito, on the basis of its obvious relationship to the Sacaton phase of the Gila Basin.

The conjunction of houses and cremations adds little; it merely emphasizes the relationship between the Tanque Verde phase and the Rillito phase. A Rillito phase cremation (Number 162) in part underlies House 42, which belongs to the Tanque Verde phase; and a Tanque Verde phase cremation (Number 14) overlies Rillito House 63.

4. CERAMICS

Because of the typologically close resemblance, ceramic types from Hodges and from the Gila Basin can be equated phase by phase during the Pioneer period. The earliest phases from the Hodges site, Sweetwater and Snaketown, are indistinguishable from their Gila Basin homologues; hence the Gila Basin phase names have been retained for them. Affinities with Mogollon ceramics are also present but are less easily demonstrable.

Below is a description of the ceramic material from the Hodges site. In the Snaketown report (Gladwin and others 1937), pottery was described in order from the latest to the earliest phases, presumably for the sake of progression from the known to the unknown. Thanks to the Snaketown study, the earlier material now is well established. We may, therefore, begin with the earliest phase and proceed chronologically to the latest.

TABLE 4.1
Pottery Types Found at the Hodges Site

Period	Phase	Pottery Type
Classic	Tanque Verde	Tanque Verde Red-on-brown
		Casa Grande Red-on-buff
		San Carlos Red
		Gila (?) Red
		Plainware
		Corrugated
Sedentary	Rincon	Rincon Red-on-brown
		Sacaton Red-on-buff
		Rincon Red
		Plainware
Colonial	Rillito	Rillito Red-on-brown
		Picacho Red-on-brown
		Santa Cruz Red-on-buff
		Plainware
	Cañada del Oro	Cañada del Oro Red-on-brown
		Gila Butte Red-on-buff
		Plainware
Pioneer	Snaketown	Snaketown Red-on-buff
		Miscellaneous redwares
		Plainware
	Sweetwater	Sweetwater Red-on-gray
		Plainware (presumptive)

The descriptions that follow are based upon restorable and near-restorable vessels, supplemented by all available sherds except those from floors, which have been kept separate. A sketch of vessel forms, accompanied by a table of incidence, is provided for each phase. The latter indicates to what extent the source material consists of restorable vessels and to what extent of sherds.

An effort has been made, as in the Snaketown report (Gladwin and others 1937), to apply the design criteria and terminology suggested by Amsden (1936). Because of the relative scarcity of whole vessels and large sherds, the major design scheme was consistently difficult to determine; moreover, some of the instances merge and overlap. Doubtful cases have, of necessity, been omitted. Moreover, the Amsden scheme was designed to fit specifically the Colonial and Sedentary periods of the Gila Basin and is somewhat less applicable to the Pioneer and Classic periods.

The various pottery types found at the Hodges site are listed in Table 4.1. In addition is a small series of trade sherds that will be enumerated in a later section. In the presentation to follow, decorated types will be treated first, followed by red and plainwares.

PAINTED POTTERY

Pioneer Period: Sweetwater Red-on-gray

Little can be said concerning the Sweetwater phase at the Hodges site. The ceramics consist of a handful of sherds (24) and four restorable or near-restorable vessels. The material is not only scanty but scattered. In spite of intensive testing it was not possible to find a concentration of Sweetwater ceramics either in pure trash, in cremations, or in association with house floors.

COLOR

Color is brown to tan to gray; decoration is often obliterated by firing clouds. There is no indication of polychrome as in the Gila Basin.

SHAPE

Various bowl forms, as well as beakers and jars, are shown in Figure 4.1 and are listed in Table 4.2. There is no evidence of scoops or of effigy vessels.

TABLE 4.2

Sweetwater Red-on-Gray: Statistics of Vessel Form

Form	Fig. 4.1 (part)	Approximate Diameter[a] (cm)	Scored (No.)	Sherds (No.)	Restorable Vessels (No.)	Total[b]
Hemispherical bowls	*a*, *b*	25	0	0	2	2
Outcurved bowls	*c*, *d*, *e*	9, 20–25	0	2	1	3
Seed bowl	*f*	7	0	1	0	1
Beaker	*g*	Not estimated	1	1	0	1
Jars	*h*, *i*	16 (body)	0	1	1	2
Indeterminate form			16	19	0	19
Total			17	24	4	28

[a] Dimensions in this and similar tables of this chapter refer to diameter at the rim unless otherwise noted. Individual numbers refer to individual vessels (often exceptional); ranges refer to diameters estimated from sherds.

[b] In this and similar tables of this chapter, the total refers to the total of represented vessels, that is, "Sherds" plus "Restorable Vessels."

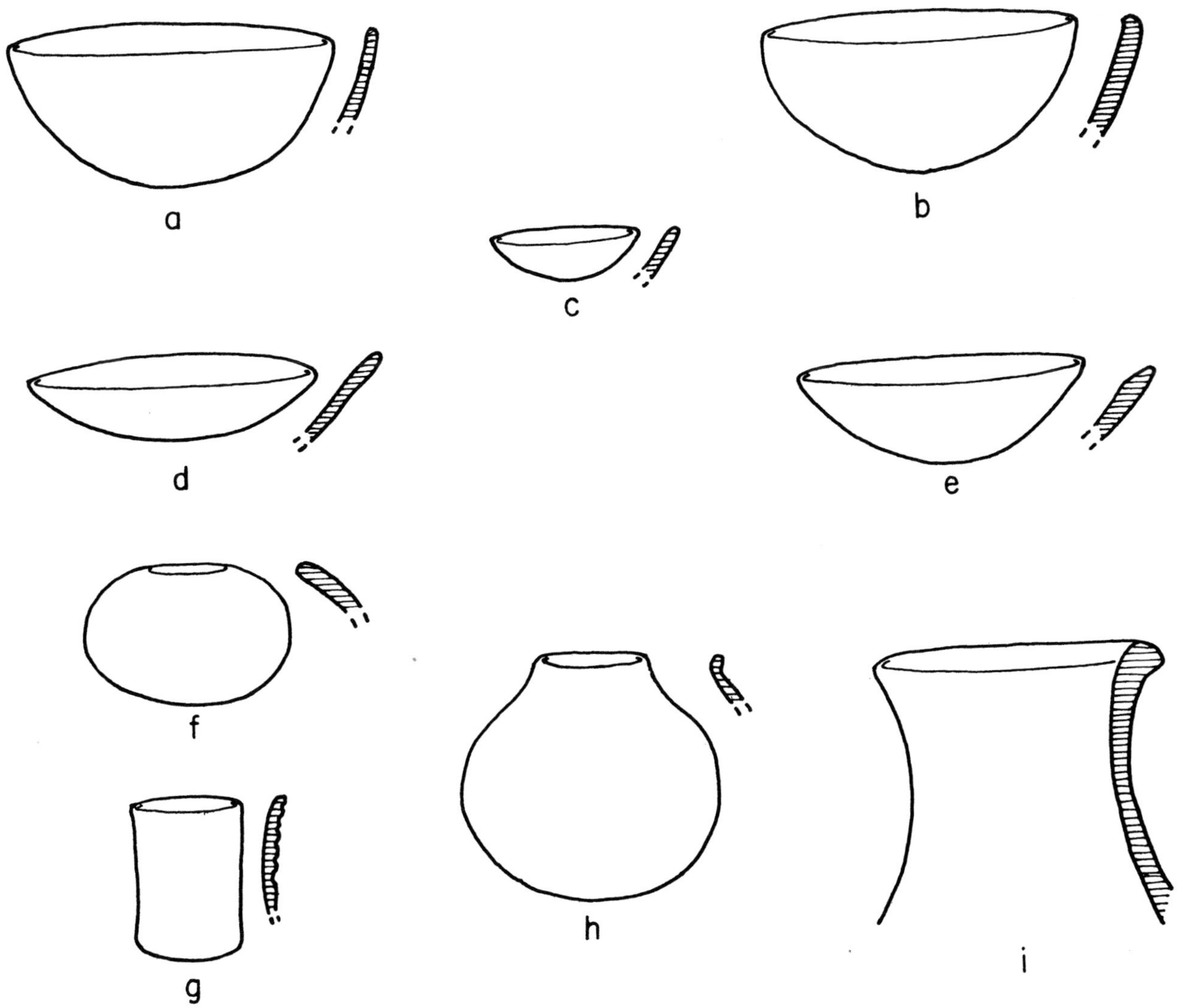

Fig. 4.1 Sweetwater Red-on-gray: Vessel forms. *a*, *b*, hemispherical bowls; *c–e*, outcurved bowls; *f*, seed jar; *g*, beaker; *h*, *i*, jars.

DESIGN

Design is mostly indeterminate because of the small size of sherds. Of interior decorated bowls, only one has an identifiable design arrangement:

Half band (Fig. 4.2*b*) (*Ed. note*: The figures in this chapter illustrate examples of design layouts and elements. Only the best examples are cited in the figure references. Other repetitious or borderline cases are generally not cited.)

Jars and other exterior decorated vessels:

Banded, continuous (Fig. 4.2*d*?)

Banded, vertically panelled (not illustrated)

DESIGN ELEMENTS

Ornamentation is essentially linear and is dominated by open hatch. There is no occurrence of scrolls, keys, or small elements, unless Figure 4.2*h* be so considered. In all lists of design elements below, motifs of notable frequency are single-starred; diagnostic elements are double-starred, even in the case of a single occurrence, provided the trait is restricted to a given phase. For the Sweetwater phase, the material is so scanty that it is impossible to judge diagnostic traits, or even common elements. Motifs are as follows:

Triangles with open hatch fill (Fig. 4.2*a*, right)

Wavy hatch (not illustrated)

Cross hatch Fig. 4.2*b*)

Chevron hatch (Fig. 4.2*d*)

*Fringed lines and panels (Fig. 4.2*a*, left); but fringe is distinct from that of Rillito and Rincon.[1]

SURFACE TREATMENT

Surfaces are unslipped and are heavily sprinkled with fine mica particles. They are also well smoothed with a sheen resulting from mica content rather than from polishing. The exteriors of the one beaker (Fig. 4.2*e*) and of most of the fragments of indeterminate form are heavily scored, either regularly or patterned (Gladwin and others 1937: Plate CLXXXV). It is impossible to determine if regular scoring is spiral or concentric, inasmuch as vessel bottoms are lacking. Two sherds are punctate (Gladwin and others 1937: Plate CLXXXV*u*). Occasionally painted ornamentation is superimposed on the scored surface.

REMARKS

The preceding material includes everything attributable to the Sweetwater phase. The series is so small that it cannot be representative. Incurved bowls and certain specialized forms (oval vessels, heavy-walled vessels, and

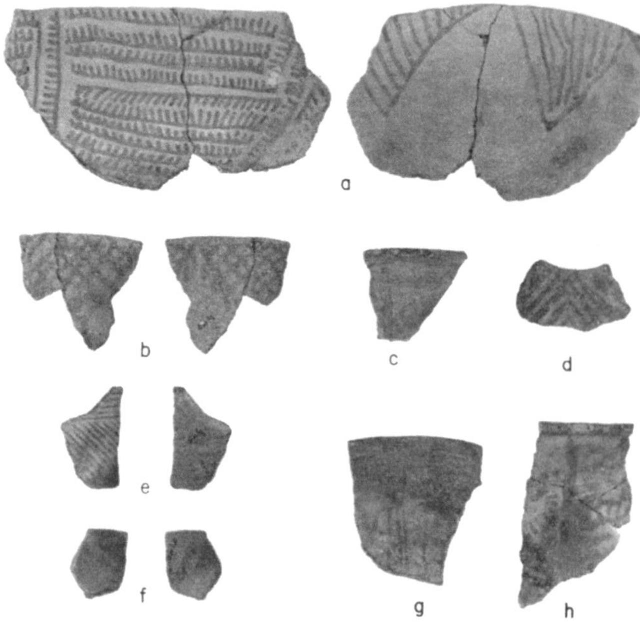

Fig. 4.2 Sweetwater Red-on-gray: Interior and exterior decoration. *a* left, fringed lines and panels; *a* right, triangles with open hatch fill; *b*, half band (this is the only layout that can be determined); *c*, indeterminate; *d*, chevron hatch; *e*, scoring; *f*, indeterminate; *g*, *h*, possibly figured and repeated. Maximum dimension of *a*, 17.5 cm.

effigies) that occur in the Gila Basin Sweetwater phase are not present. In the Hodges collection as a whole, oval vessels do not occur, except in isolated instances, even in the later, more heavily represented phases; and heavy-walled vessels of local manufacture occur not at all.

There are minor differences in bowl form and jar contour between the Tucson and Gila Basin Sweetwater phases, but on the whole, the resemblance is marked. In weight, in micaceous content, in polish, and in characteristic heavy exterior scoring of bowls, the pottery is indistinguishable from that of the Gila Basin. In regard to design placement, our sherds are too few and too small to permit valid comparison. There may be real differences in motif—our fringed lines and wavy hatch seem to be without Gila Basin counterparts; conversely, the hatched scroll and squared scroll are wanting in the Tucson assemblage. By and large, however, our material could be fitted satisfactorily into the range embraced by the Gila Basin Sweetwater phase.

Pioneer Period: Snaketown Red-on-buff

This type is also indistinguishable from its Gila Basin counterpart.

COLOR

Color is tan to brown, to gray and black; firing clouds are prominent.

SHAPE

There are various bowl forms, scoops, beakers, jars, and odd shapes, as indicated in Figure 4.3 and Table 4.3.

[1]Throughout the descriptions in this chapter, a single asterisk (*) designates frequent motifs, a double asterisk (**) diagnostic elements.

TABLE 4.3

Snaketown Red-on-Buff: Statistics of Vessel Form

Form	Fig. 4.3 (part)	Approximate Diameter (cm)	Exterior Scored (No.)	Sherds (No.)	Restorable and Semi-Restorable Vessels (No.)	Total
Hemispherical bowls	*a, b*	11–16	4	4	0	4
*Outcurved bowls	*c–f*	16, 17, 28–35	20	31	1	32
*Flare-rim bowls	*g*	18–36	19	27	2	29
Semi-flaring rim bowls	*i, k*	18–26	0	3	0	3
Incurved bowls	*l*	10–16, 26	3	7	3	10
Seed bowl	*h*	Not estimated	1	1	0	1
Bowl sherds, shape indeterminate			32	45	0	45
Scoops	*j*	12 x 18, 14 x 18	3	3	2	5
*Beakers	*m*	15–22	9	7	2	9
Jars	*p*	Not estimated	7	21	1	22
Miniature jars	*n*	5–7	0	2	0	2
Sherds, exterior decorated, presumably jars			4	7	0	7
**Eccentric forms: Gourd-shaped	*o*	25 (max. length)	0	0	1	1
Total			102	158	12	170

*Frequent motifs.

**Diagnostic elements.

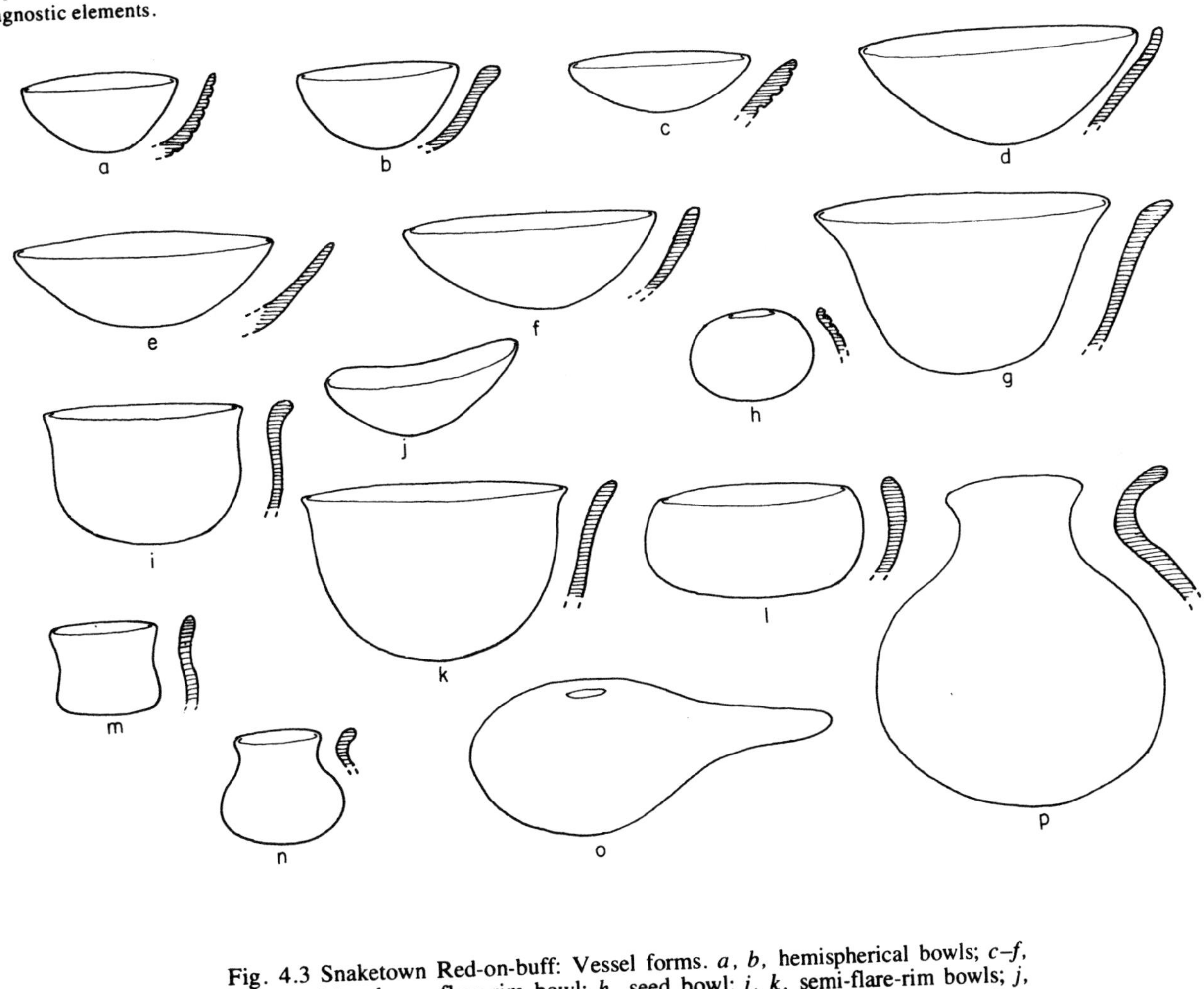

Fig. 4.3 Snaketown Red-on-buff: Vessel forms. *a, b,* hemispherical bowls; *c–f,* outcurved bowls; *g,* flare-rim bowl; *h,* seed bowl; *i, k,* semi-flare-rim bowls; *j,* scoop; *l,* incurved bowl; *m,* beaker; *n,* miniature jar; *o,* gourd-shaped vessel; *p,* jar.

The gourd-shaped vessel shown in Figure 4.3*o* is aberrant and has been classed as Snaketown phase because of its decorative treatment. It may conceivably be later; if so, it must be of the Tanque Verde phase, the only other phase with predominantly angular ornament. This supposition is strengthened by the fact that the specimen in question comes from a cremation, in an area used extensively for Tanque Verde interments. Nevertheless, typologically, it is closer to the Snaketown phase than to the Tanque Verde.

DESIGN

Again, design is difficult to determine, but bowl interiors include at least the following:

All-over patterned (Fig. 4.4*b*)
*Half band (Fig. 4.4*c*)
Circling, continuous (Fig. 4.5*f*)
Cross banded (Fig. 4.6*a*)
Figured (Fig. 4.4*a*, interior view)

In addition, several vessels (Fig. 4.5*c*, for example) are irregular and suggest an elaborate and perhaps asymmetrically interlocked arrangement not covered by Amsden's (1936) categories.

Jars are so fragmentary that there is no clue to design placement. Exterior ornament on other vessels includes:

Half band (not illustrated)
Banded, continuous (Fig. 4.6*a*)
Figured and repeated (Figs. 4.4*a*)

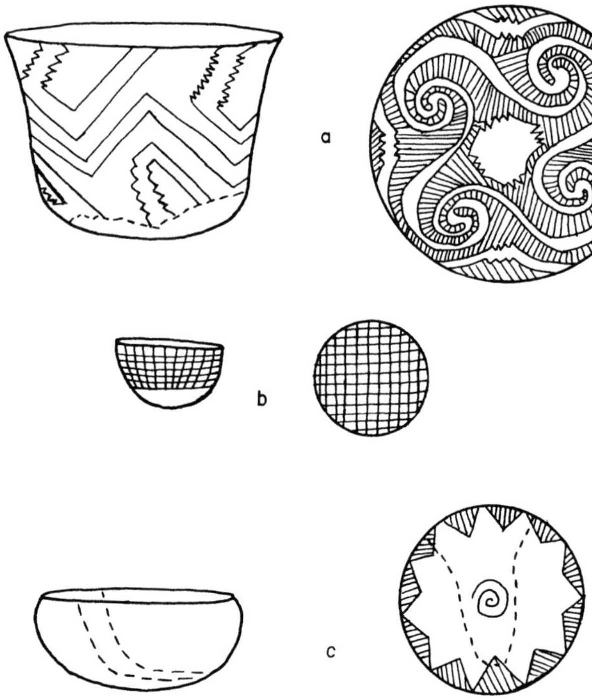

Fig. 4.4 Snaketown Red-on-buff: Vessel designs. *a*, figured and repeated; *b*, all-over patterned; *c*, half band.

DESIGN ELEMENTS

The entire decorative scheme is dominated by close hatching. Motifs:

**Serrated scrolls, close hatched, mostly interlocking (Figs. 4.4*a*, interior; 4.5*i*)
**Serrated square scrolls, close hatched, interlocking (Figs. 4.4*a* exterior; 4.5*j*; 4.6*b*)
*Triangles, hatched (Fig. 4.4*c*)
Bands and indeterminate angular figures, hatched (Figs. 4.5*j-o*; 4.6*a*, *c*)
Wavy hatch (not illustrated)
Cross hatch (4.4*b*)
Chevron hatch (Fig. 4.5*h*); apparently confined to painting over scored exterior

SURFACE TREATMENT

Surfaces are unslipped and are moderately polished save for interior of vessels with constricted mouth. As in the Sweetwater phase, mica flecking is characteristic. Bowl exteriors are frequently (about 60 percent) scored, often with painted design added after incision. Unscored bowl exteriors are usually painted with parallel lines, hatched triangles, or other hatched figures. Beakers are consistently scored. Jar exteriors are less frequently scored (about 30 percent) than bowls. All scoring is moderate to light and is noticeably less deep than in the Sweetwater phase. Patterned scoring is rare and is confined to bowls and scoops. Regular scoring, so far as determinable, is spiral, except for one sherd, which is concentric.

REMARKS

The decorative pattern of the Snaketown phase, as an outgrowth of the Sweetwater phase, retains various forms of hachure, as well as exterior scoring of bowls, often with supplementary painting. But the diagnostic hatched and serrated scrolls, either single, double, or square double, are departures from the Sweetwater pattern.

Haury (Gladwin and others 1937: Fig. 89) shows hatched scrolls of the Sweetwater phase. Typologically most of these differ little from the Snaketown phase, and doubtless have been identified as Sweetwater on the basis of their association with material of pronounced Sweetwater characteristics. At the Hodges site, we have so little pure trash that our classification necessarily has been typological. Therefore, although hatched scrolls may have come in during the Sweetwater phase, on typological grounds we have regarded them as Snaketown.

Colonial Period: Cañada del Oro Red-on-brown

The first marked divergence from the decorated types of the Gila Basin comes at the beginning of the Colonial period. At the site of Snaketown this is represented by the Gila Butte phase; at the Hodges site we have called the equivalent Cañada del Oro.

In the Gila Basin the red-on-buff style has become crystallized, with its porous paste, cream wash, and fugitive pigment. The Tucson equivalents lean toward Mogollon types, with a fine-grained paste, a suggestion of polish, and an absence of slip. In ornament, however, Tucson adheres closely to the Gila Basin pattern—the diagnostic motif is the serrated scroll, and serration generally. Bowl exteriors are faintly scored, with overpainted pattern, or are painted without scoring. Shapes are much the same as in the Gila Basin, but there are specialized local forms in both areas.

COLOR

Color is brown to cream, to gray, to black. Firing clouds are prominent, but smudging evidently is not deliberate.

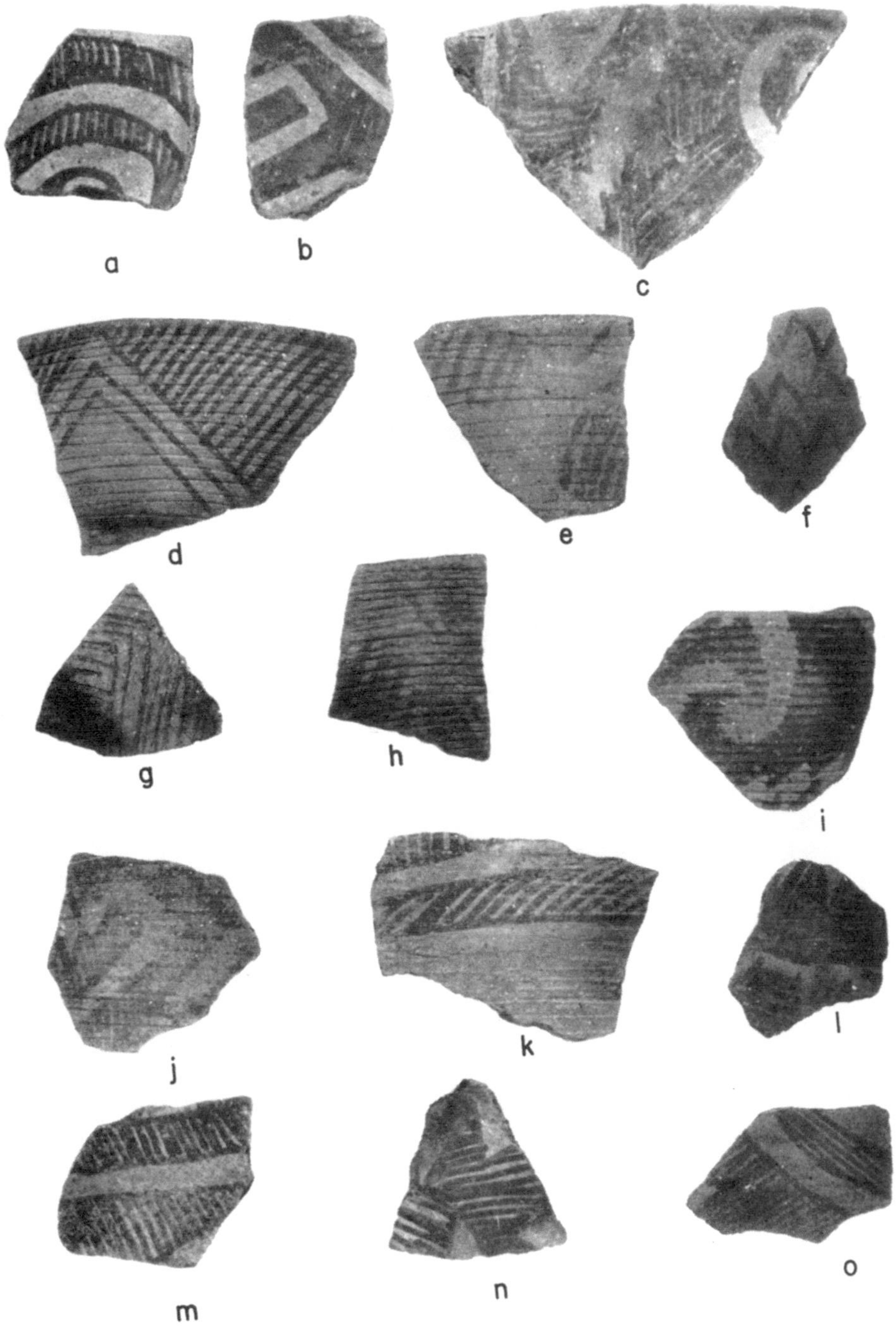

Fig. 4.5 Snaketown Red-on-buff: Design elements. *a–c*, bowl interiors; *d–g*, bowl exteriors; *h*, beaker exterior; *i–o*, jar exteriors. Maximum dimension of *m*, 8 cm.

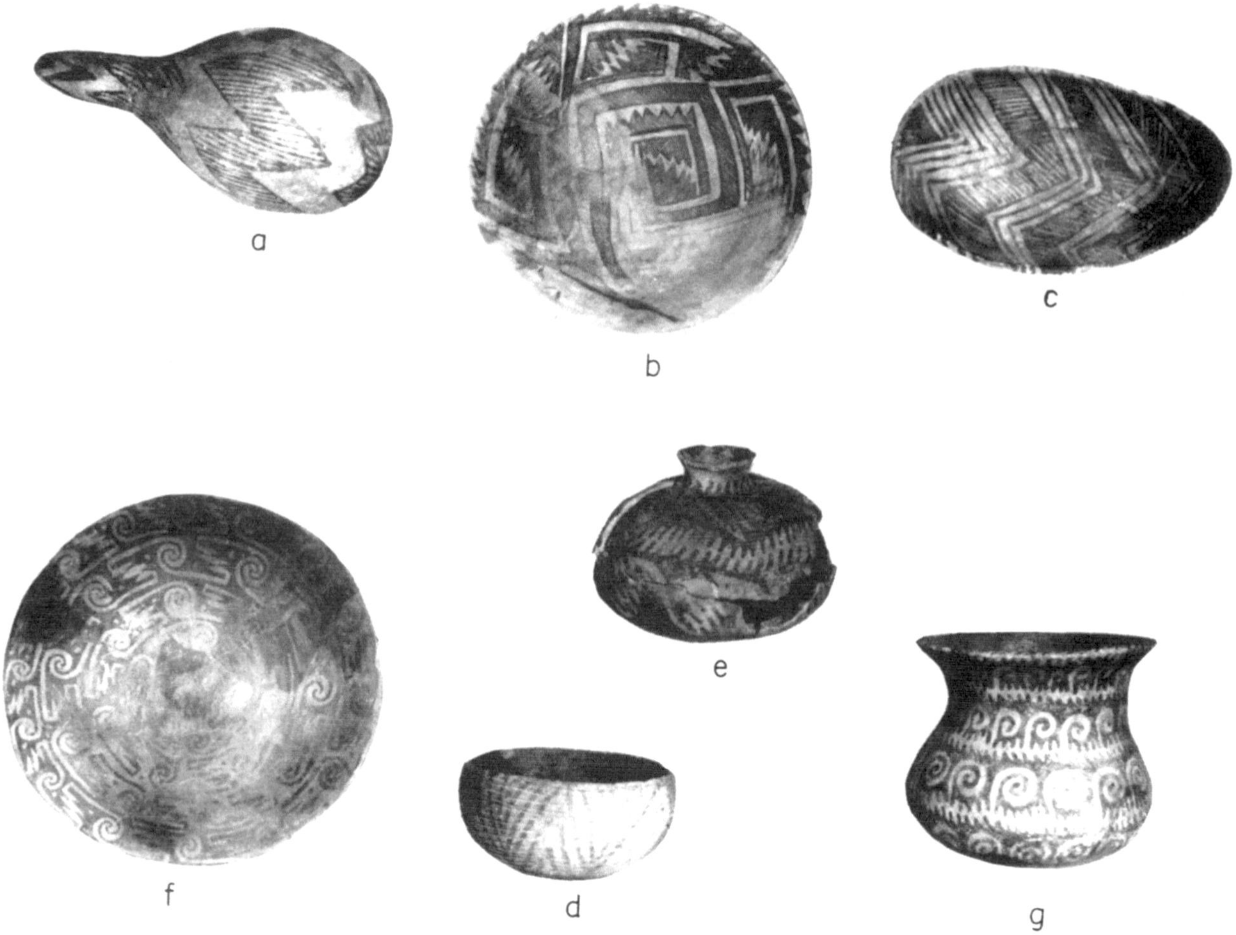

Fig. 4.6 Snaketown Red-on-buff and Cañada del Oro Red-on-brown: Vessels. *a–c*, Snaketown; all others, Cañada del Oro. *a*, *c*, dippers; *b*, flare-rim bowl; *d*, small hemispherical bowl; *e*, bottlenecked jar; *f*, plate; *g*, flare-rim jar. Rim width of *f*, 32.5 cm.

SHAPE

Shapes are shown in Figures 4.6*d–g* and 4.7 and are listed in Table 4.4. Bowls are overwhelmingly predominant, with flare-rimmed bowls the most prominent (Fig. 4.7*d–i*); sherds are too small to permit estimate of vessel proportions except for the few itemized in Table 4.4.

DESIGN

Design is difficult to determine because of the paucity of whole vessels and large sherds. Bowl interiors are:

All-over patterned (Fig. 4.8*b*, *h*)

Cross banded (not illustrated)

Circling, continuous (Fig. 4.9*d*; possibly also Figs. 4.8*g*, 4.9*c*, *e*)

Circling, repeated (possibly Fig. 4.10*a*); rare

Quartered and figured (Fig. 4.11); skewed quartering, rare; Figure 4.11 is the only determinable instance of sectoring of any sort

*Figured and repeated (Figs. 4.6*f*; 4.8*a*,*c*) probably would prove highly characteristic were sherds larger

Design arrangements of jars and other exterior decorated vessels include:

Banded, continuous (Figs. 4.6*g*; 4.8*i*,*n*)

**Banded, vertically paneled (not illustrated)

Banded, figured and repeated (Fig. 4.6*e*)

DESIGN ELEMENTS

Serration, in particular the serration of double scrolls, dominates the entire complex (Fig. 4.12)

**Double scroll, solid, serrated (Figs. 4.8*a*,*c*,*d*; 4.12*e*,*f*)

Single scroll, serrated (Fig. 4.6*g*)

**Double square scroll, solid, serrated (Figs. 4.8*e*; 4.12*d*)

**Lines and solids serrated (Figs. 4.6*e*; 4.8*f*,*g*; 4.9*g*,*i*; 4.12*a*, *b*)

*Wavy hatch (Cañada del Oro specimens not suitable for reproduction, but similar to Rillito specimens Fig. 4.15*b*, *c*, *d*); especially on exterior decorated bowls

Cross hatch (Fig. 4.9*b*)

TABLE 4.4

Cañada del Oro Red-on-Brown: Statistics of Vessel Form

Form	Fig. 4.7 (part)	Approximate Diameter (cm)	Exterior Scored (No.)	Sherds (No.)	Restorable and Semi-Restorable Vessels (No.)	Total
Hemispherical bowls	*a*	22–28 cm	3	3	0	3
Outcurved bowls	*b, c*	17, 27–41	17	26	1	27
Flare-rim bowls:						
Medium	*d*	10–12; most, 17–32	3	17	2	19
Shallow, plate-like	*e, f*	17, 33	0	1	2	3
Deep	*g, h*	23, 31–33	2	3	3	6
Recurved	*i*	37	1	1	0	1
Sherds, proportions indeterminate			14	65	0	65
Incurved bowls	*j*	8–28	3	6	2	8
Seed bowls	*k*	18 (body)	1	0	1	1
Bowl sherds, shape indeterminate			23	42		42
Scoops	*l*	Mouth width: 14	0	2	1	3
Beakers	*m*	11, 17	1	1	1	2
Jars:						
Bottle neck	*n*	15 (body)	1	0	1	1
Open, flare-rim	*o*	12 (rim)	0	1	1	2
Normal	*p*	30 (body)	0	2	1	3
Sherds, probably jars, shapes indeterminate			15	28	0	28
Sherds, exterior decorated, shapes indeterminate			4	9	0	9
Total			88	207	16	223

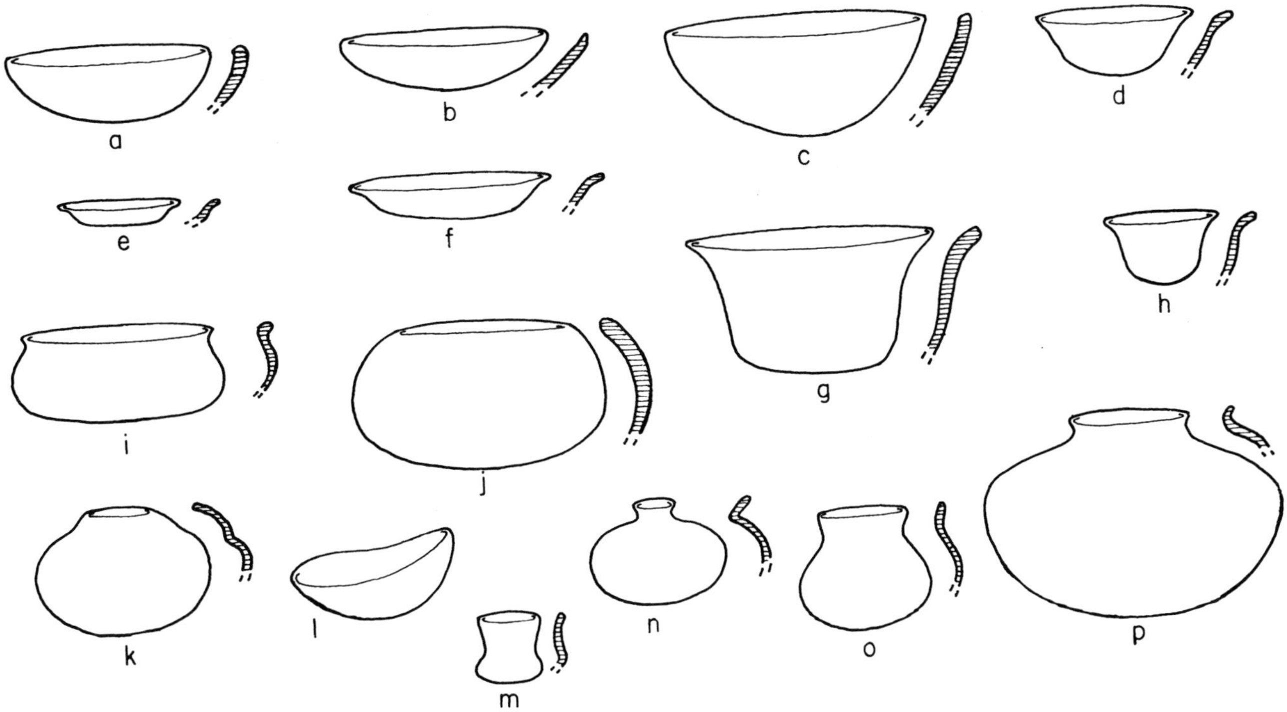

Fig. 4.7 Cañada del Oro Red-on-brown: Vessel forms. *a*, hemispherical bowl; *b, c*, outcurved bowls; *d–i*, flare-rim bowls; *j*, incurved bowl; *k*, seed bowl; *l*, scoop; *m*, beaker; *n–p*, jars.

Fig. 4.8 Cañada del Oro Red-on-brown: Design elements. *a–h*, bowl interiors; *i–l*, bowl exteriors; *m–t*, beaker and jar exteriors. Maximum dimension of *q*, 6.9 cm.

Chevron hatch (not illustrated; chevrons without hatching are shown in Fig. 4.6*d*)
Bands and geometric areas hatch-filled (Fig. 4.9*e*,*f*)
*Checkerboard (Fig. 4.8*h*)
Staggered lines (Fig. 4.9*h*)
Bull's-eye (not illustrated)
Small elements (Fig. 4.9*c*,*e*)
Life forms (some negative) (Fig. 4.10*a*–*d*)

SURFACE TREATMENT

There is considerable variation in surface treatment. Ordinarily sherds are unslipped, but a few have a suggestion of surface wash. In porosity some fragments suggest Gila Basin ceramics. On the whole, the material from this phase has a close-grained surface, moderately good finish, with polish variable. There is little mica compared with the decorated types of the Pioneer period.

Seldom are bowl exteriors unadorned. They may be lightly scored, with superimposed painting in the form of trailing lines (Fig. 4.8*j*), rarely of triangles (Fig. 4.8*k*), chevron hatch (not illustrated), or paneled hachure (not illustrated). Scoring on bowl exteriors has declined in popularity (39 percent of bowls) and in excellence and is being replaced by painting alone. The painting, for the most part, is limited to hatched triangles (Fig. 4.8*l*) or closely spaced trailing lines (not illustrated).

In the case of vessels whose exterior constitutes the chief decorative field—jars, beakers, and some bowls—scoring is more common (about 47 percent of such forms) and the superimposed painting more elaborate (Figs. 4.6*d*, *e*; 4.8*m*–*t*).

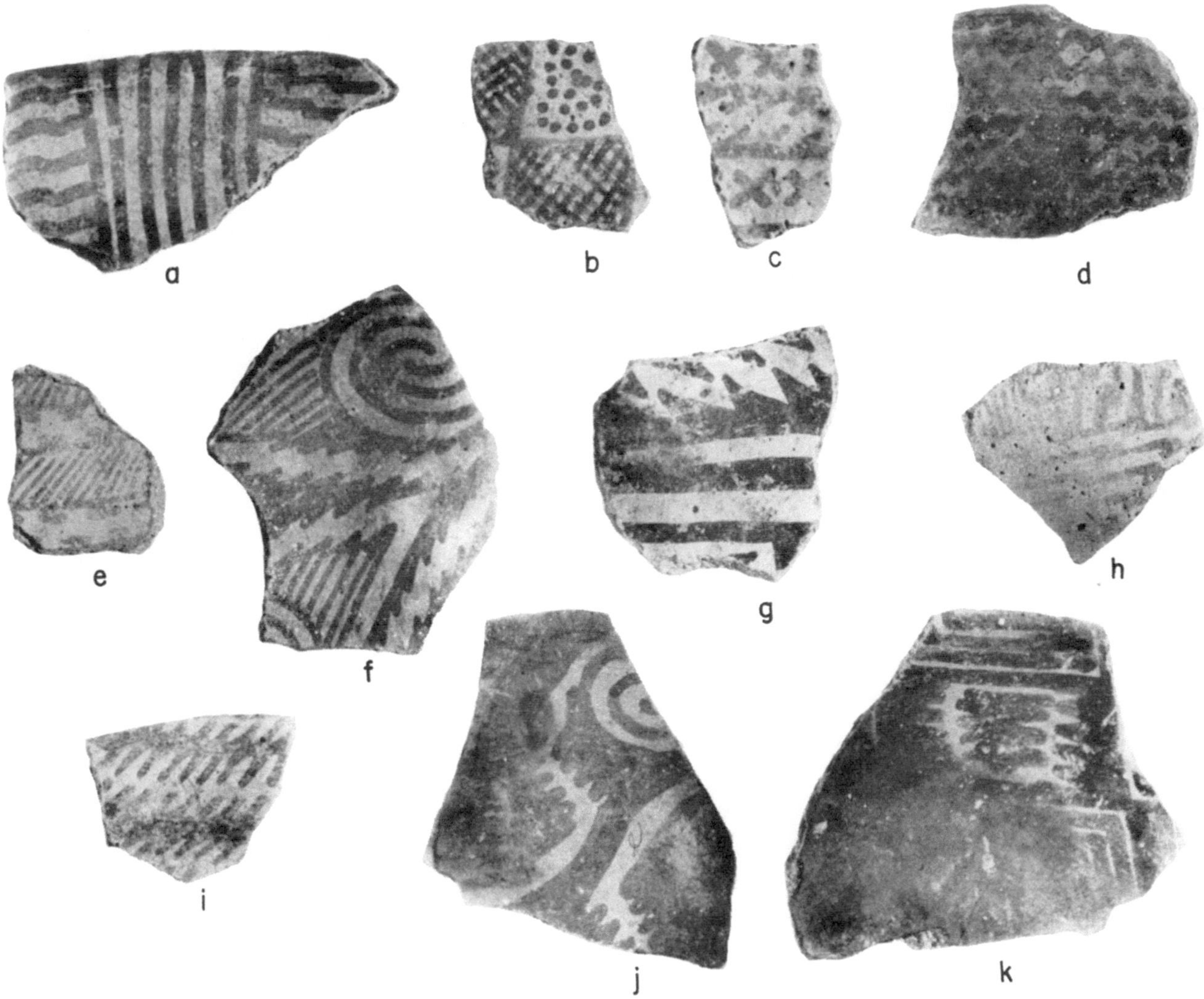

Fig. 4.9 Cañada del Oro Red-on-brown: Design elements. Bowl interiors. Maximum dimension of *j*, 11 cm.

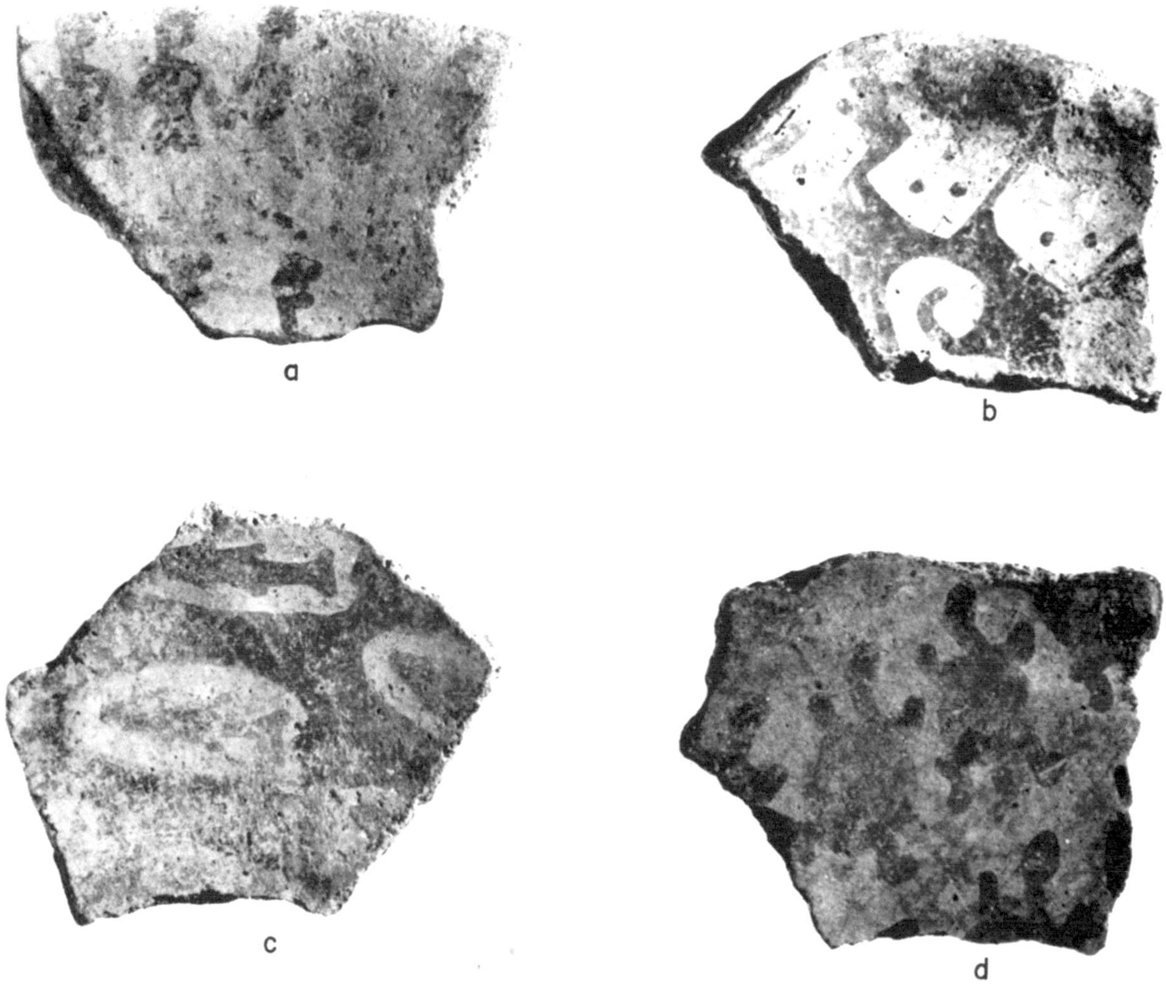

Fig. 4.10 Cañada del Oro Red-on-brown: Life forms. Maximum dimension of *c*, 7.4 cm.

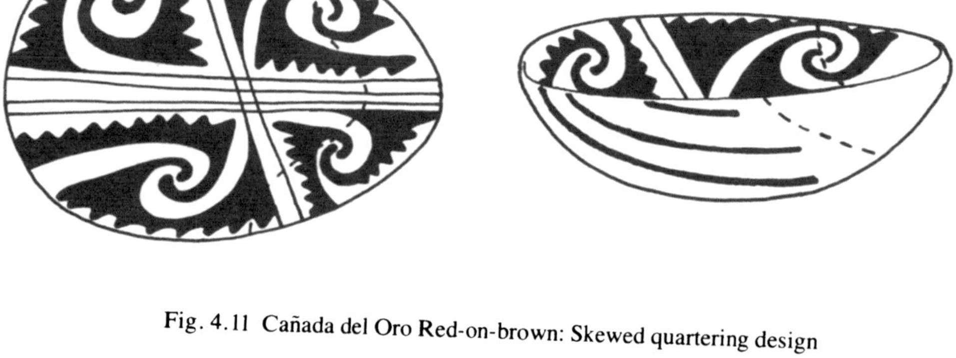

Fig. 4.11 Cañada del Oro Red-on-brown: Skewed quartering design

REMARKS

In many respects Cañada del Oro ceramics may be regarded as an outgrowth of Snaketown phase ceramics, although there is an infusion of new elements. Basic bowl forms continue, with some specialization; jar forms are more varied. In design placement, there is a continuation from the Snaketown phase, although circling of bowls by repeated small elements is new. This is, however, infrequent in Cañada del Oro and is but a weak foreshadowing of an arrangement that reaches its peak in the Rillito phase. Banding of exterior-ornamented vessels is more pronounced. A specialized form of vertical paneling makes a brief appearance, then dies out without continuing into the Rillito phase. In number and range of motifs there is a sharp increase over the Snaketown phase, a situation paralleled precisely in the Gila Basin with the shift from the Pioneer to the Colonial period. Hachure continues, with some new forms. Scrolls also continue, invariably serrated, but they are solid instead of hatched. Bull's-eyes, small elements, and life forms appear for the first time, as does negative design. Scoring of bowl exteriors weakens; the incision is faint and the trailing lines appear to be at least as important as the scoring. Some bowl exteriors are painted but not scored; in these cases the ornament consists of hatched triangles, or of trailing lines, which are either closely spaced or clustered. In the following sections it will be seen that this tendency is carried to its logical conclusion, for in the Rillito phase scoring disappears entirely, and by Rincon phase times, even trailing lines are losing favor.

It has been noted already that with Cañada del Oro comes the first appreciable divergence from the Gila Basin. Except for the difference in surface finish, Gila Butte Red-on-buff is very similar to Cañada del Oro Red-on-brown. No legged vessels, plates, or effigy scoops are known from the Hodges site for this phase, but otherwise there is marked agreement in shape. Moreover, the two types are in complete accord in both design arrangement and in explicit motifs on both jars and bowls. In short, save for the difference in paste, slip, and polish, there is little to differentiate Cañada del Oro Red-on-brown from Gila Butte Red-on-buff.

Colonial Period: Rillito Red-on-Brown

The decorated ceramics of the Rillito and succeeding phases adhere to the precedent established in the Cañada del Oro phase; over-all appearance and surface treatment favor Mogollon types, while shape, motif, and design placement parallel the Gila Basin.

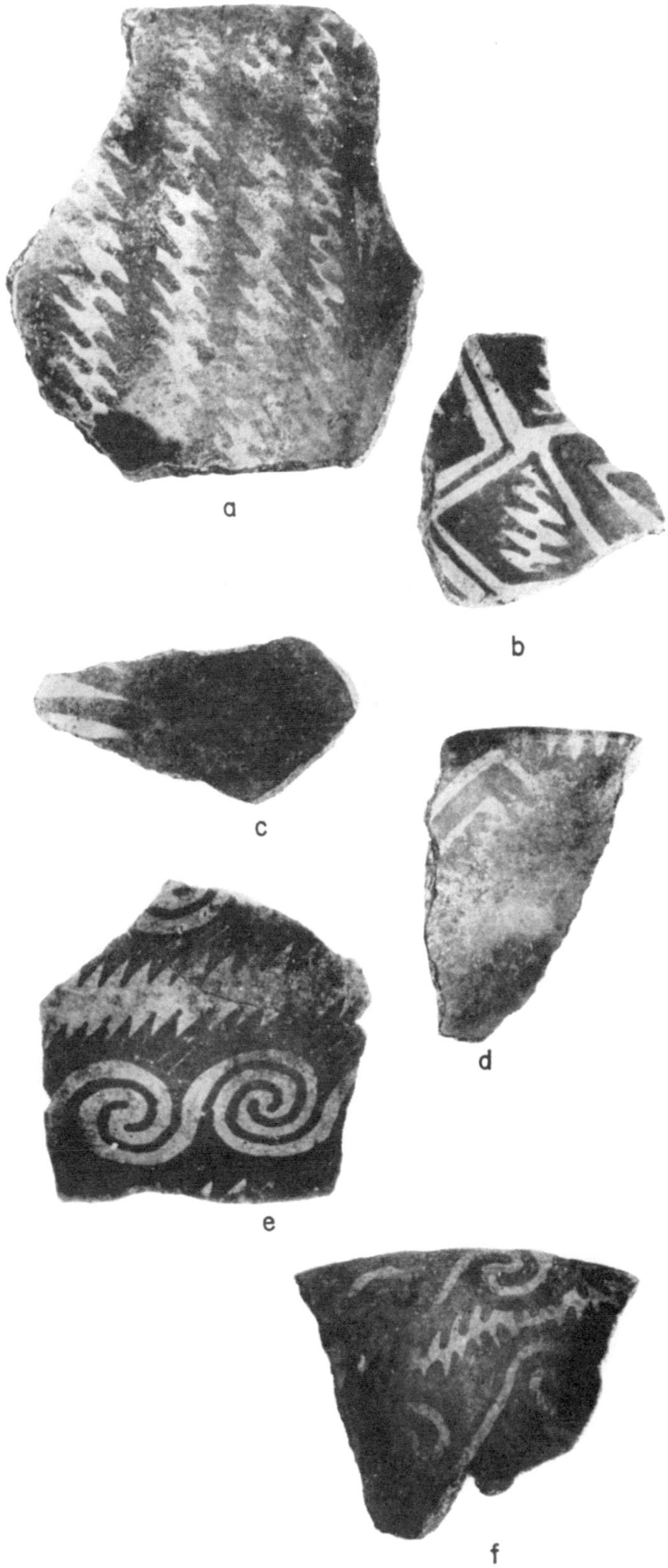

Fig. 4.12 Cañada del Oro Red-on-brown: Serration. Maximum dimension of *f*, 8.2 cm.

COLOR

Color ranges from brown to cream, to orange, to gray. Firing clouds frequently obscure the design, but there is no indication of deliberate smudging. Pigment tends to weather somewhat, although it is less fugitive than that of the Gila Basin.

SHAPE

Shapes are shown in Figures 4.13 and 4.14. Vessel statistics are provided in Tables 4.5 and 4.6. Approximately 80 percent of the vessels of identifiable form are bowls, among which the flare-rim is overwhelmingly predominant. Jars have compressed globular

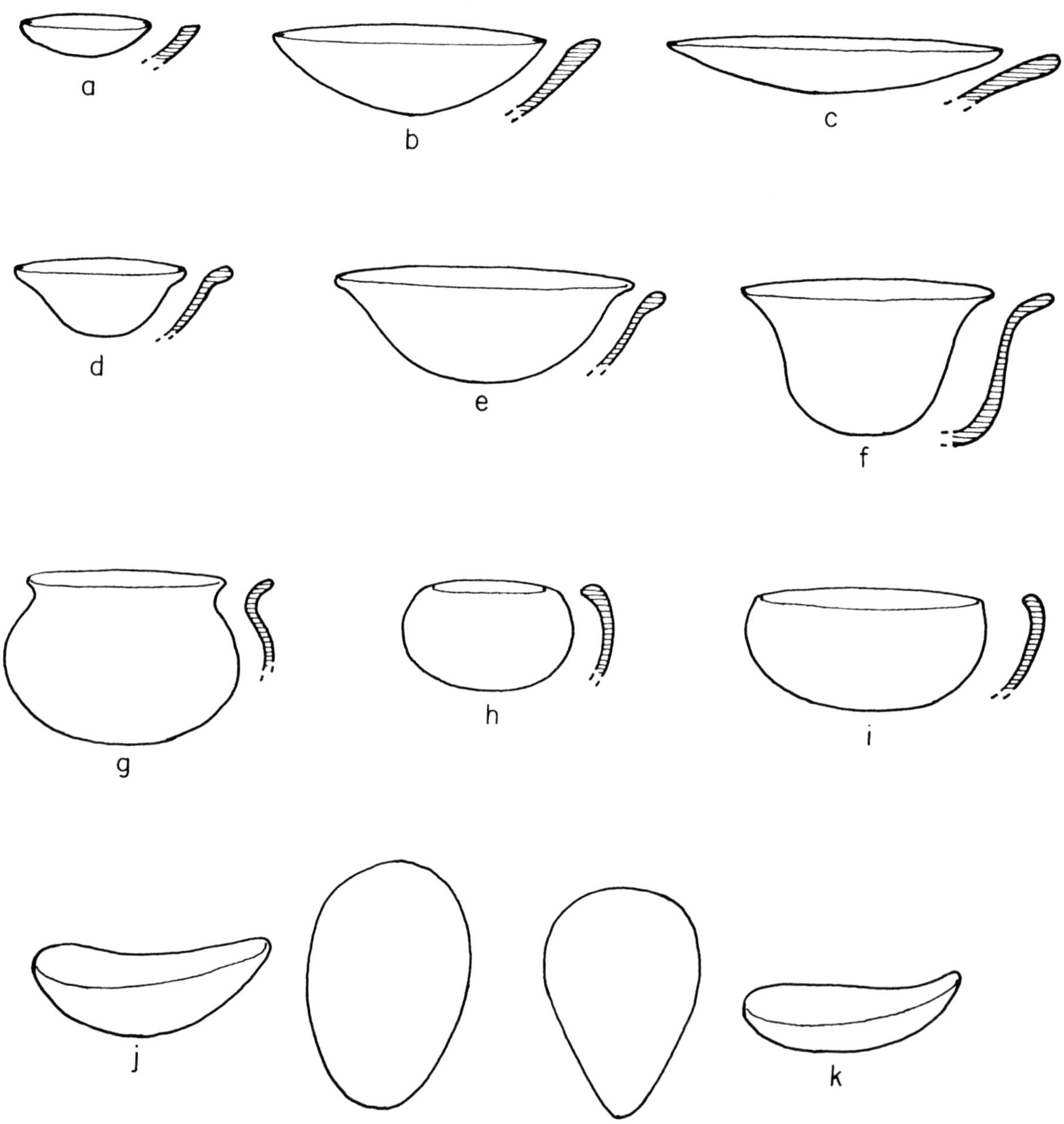

Fig. 4.13 Rillito Red-on-brown: Bowl and scoop forms. *a–c*, outcurved bowls; *d–g*, flare-rim bowls; *h*, *i*, incurved bowls; *j*, *k*, scoops.

TABLE 4.5

Rillito Red-on-Brown: Statistics of Vessel Form (bowls and scoops)

Form	Fig. 4.13 (part)	Approximate Diameter (cm)	Sherds (No.)	Restorable and Semi-restorable Vessels (No.)	Total
Outcurved bowls:					
Small	*a*	9–16	3	1	4
Medium	*b*	21–41	8	0	8
Plate-like	*c*	25–32	2	0	2
*Flare-rim bowls:					
Medium	*d, e*	10–15, 18–35	5	20	25
*Deep	*f*	22–38	14	7	21
Recurved	*g*	20.5	0	1	1
Sherds, proportions indeterminate			167	0	167
Incurved bowls	*h, i*	12–21	3	2	5
Bowls, indeterminate shape			39	0	39
Scoops	*j, k*	12.5 × 17, 14 × 19	0	2	2
Total			241	33	274

*Frequent motifs.

bodies and flaring rims. Seed jars and vases are extremely rare, with the latter confined to the Rillito phase. Effigy vessels are lacking except for four sherds, two of which suggest a form similar to that shown in Figure 4.14*k*.

DESIGN

As usual, design is difficult to determine from sherds. Bowl designs include the following:

All-over, patterned (Fig. 4.15*a*; 4.16*f*)

Cross-banded (not illustrated)

*Circling, continuous (Figs. 4.15*d*; 4.19*o*)

**Circling, repeated (Fig. 4.19*a*, *f*, *g*, *l*)

Circling, alternate bands continuous (Figs. 4.17*e*, *h*; 4.18*c*, *i*)

Quartered (not illustrated), a unique offset variant of quartered; doubtless quartering would be more common were whole vessels available

Trisected (not illustrated); rare

*Figured (Fig. 4.16*a*)

*Figured and repeated (Fig. 4.17*c*, *k*, *m*; probably Fig. 4.18*d*, *f*, *g*, *h*)

Jars are consistently banded:

Banded, continuous (Fig. 4.16*e*, *g*)

**Banded, repeated elements (Fig. 4.16*c*, *d*)

Banded, alternate bands continuous, repeated (Fig. 4.19*c*)

**Banded, figured and repeated (Fig. 4.19*k*)

DESIGN ELEMENTS

*The double scroll (Fig. 4.18*b*, *f*, *g*, *i*, *j*) is highly characteristic although not diagnostic

Abutting scroll (single or double scrolls in close proximity) (Fig. 4.18*b*, *d*, *e*, *f*, *g*, *i*)

**Scroll-hachure assemblages (Fig. 4.17*c*; 4.18*a*, *d*, *f*, *g*), sometimes with chevron hatch

Hachure: straight, wavy, mixed, cross (Figs. 4.15*b*, *c*, *d*; 4.17; 4.19*o*)

Chevron hatch, plain and mixed; includes:

*Triangular (Figs. 4.16*g*; 4.17*b*, *c*, *h*, *l*; 4.18*h*)

**Cuneiform (Figs. 4.16*a*, *e*; 4.17*k*, *m*)

Checkerboard (Fig. 4.19*h*)

**Line and stagger (Figs. 4.16*b*, *f*; 4.17*f*)

Lines, serrated (Fig. 4.15*e*)

Lines, fringed (Fig. 4.18*h*)

*Fringe, free-standing (Figs. 4.18*i*; 4.19*f*, *k*, *l*, *m*)

Bull's-eye (Fig. 4.19*d*, *o*, *q*)

Animal motifs, positive (not illustrated)

Animal motifs, negative (Fig. 4.19*b*, *j*)

Zigzag, negative (Fig. 4.17*e*)

**Small elements: all-over; between fringe bands; in bull's-eyes (Figs. 4.16*c*, *d*; 4.19*a*, *f*, *g*, *k*, *l*, *m*)

SURFACE TREATMENT

Vessels are unslipped save for a few specimens which may bear a self-slip. A moderate polish is common; micaceous content is negligible except in isolated instances.

TABLE 4.6

Rillito Red-on-Brown: Statistics of Vessel Form
(jars, vases, and effigies)

Form	Fig. 4.14 (part)	Approximate Diameter (cm)	Sherds (No.)	Restorable and Semi-Restorable Vessels (No.)	Total
Flare-rim jars	*a*	7	0	1	1
	b	9	0	1	1
	c	9–10	0	3	3
	d	11	0	1	1
	e	10.5	0	1	1
	f	11.5–13.5	1	3	4
	g	12.5	0	1	1
	j	22	0	1	1
Seed jar	*l*	11.5	0	1	1
Presumably jar sherds, shape indeterminate			49	0	49
**Vases	*h,i*	7, 11	0	2	2
Effigies	*k*		4	0	4
Total			54	15	69

** Diagnostic elements.

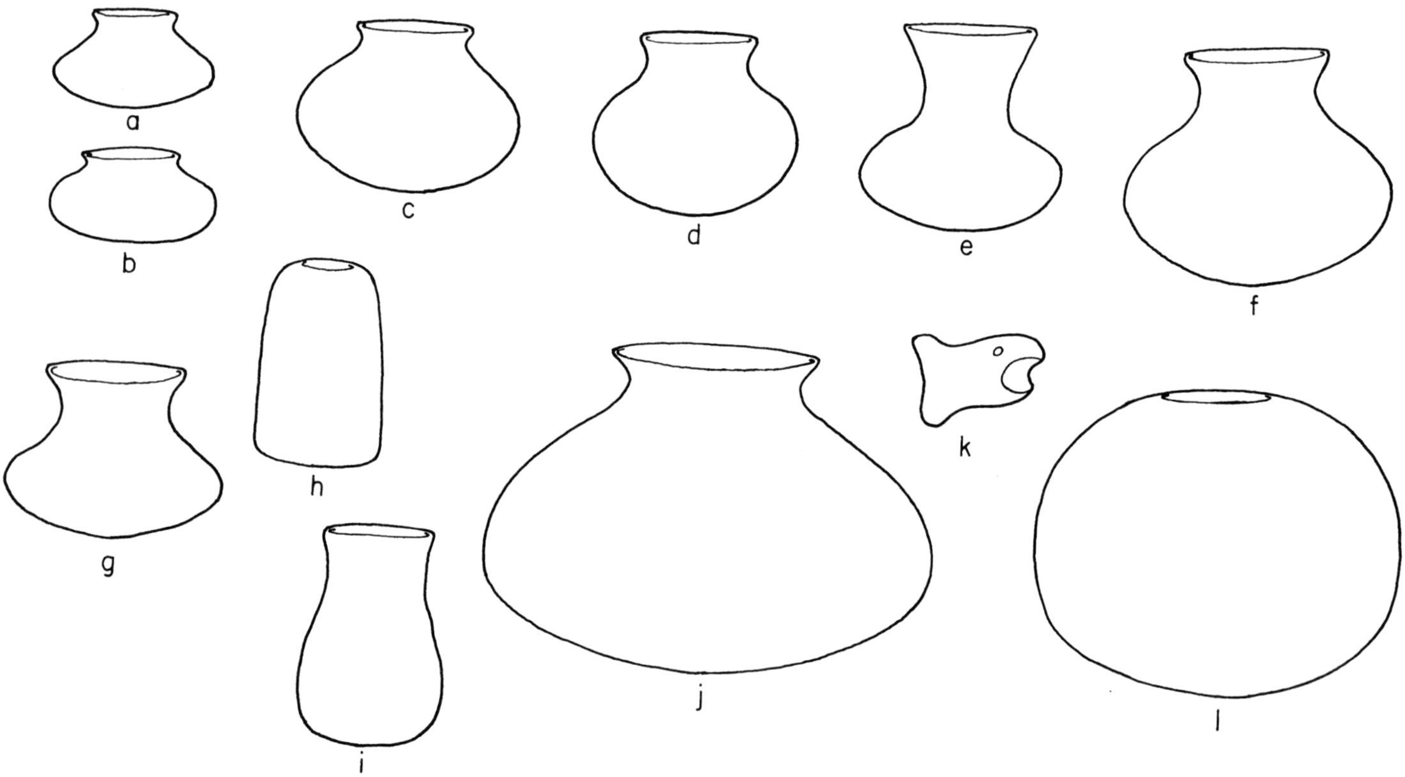

Fig. 4.14 Rillito Red-on-brown: Jar, vase, and effigy forms. *a–g*, *j*, flare-rim jars; *h*, *i*, vases; *k*, effigy; *l*, seed jar.

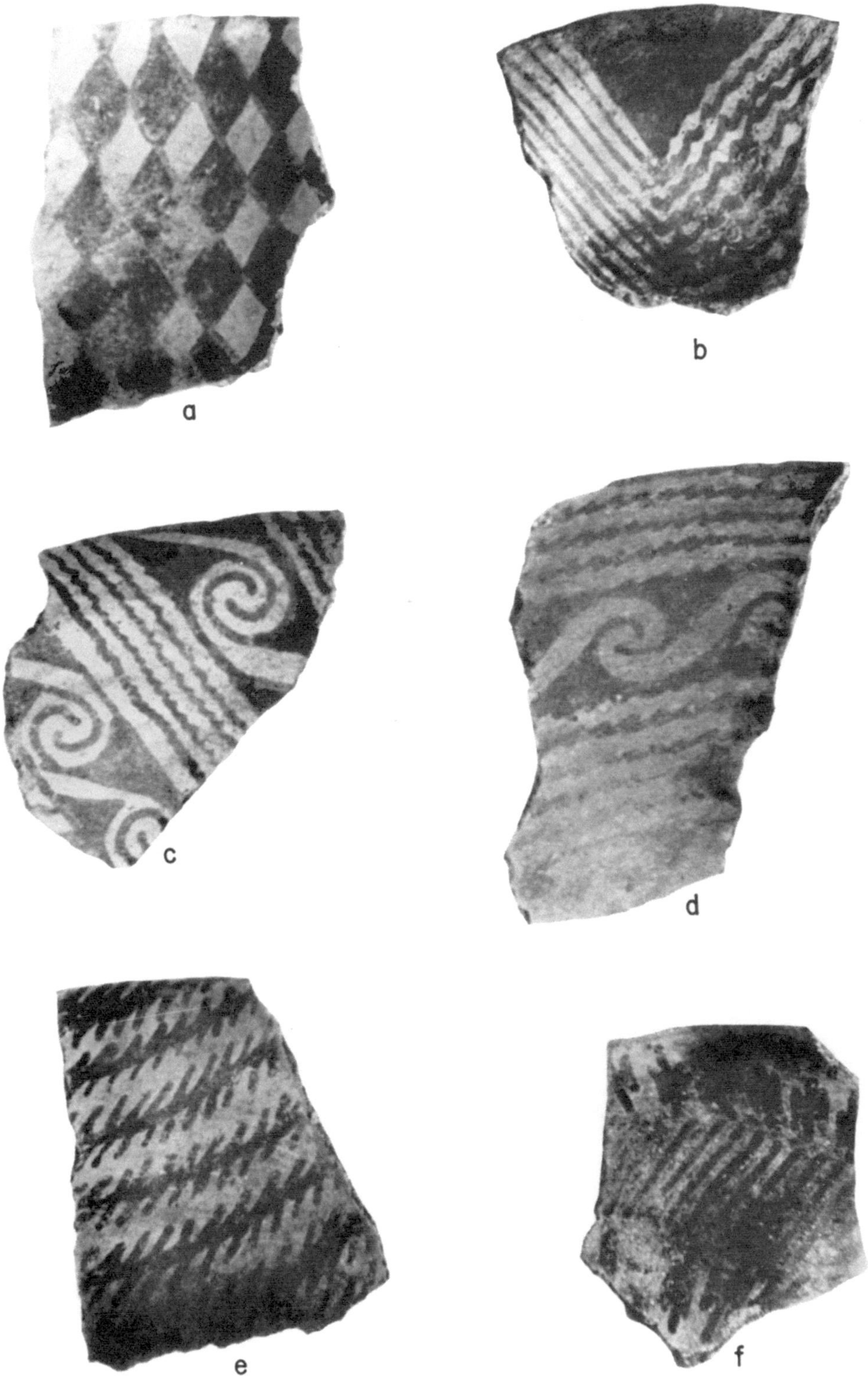

Fig. 4.15 Rillito Red-on-brown: Design elements. *a–e*, flare-rim bowls; *f*, incurved bowl. Maximum dimension of *a*, 6.3 cm.

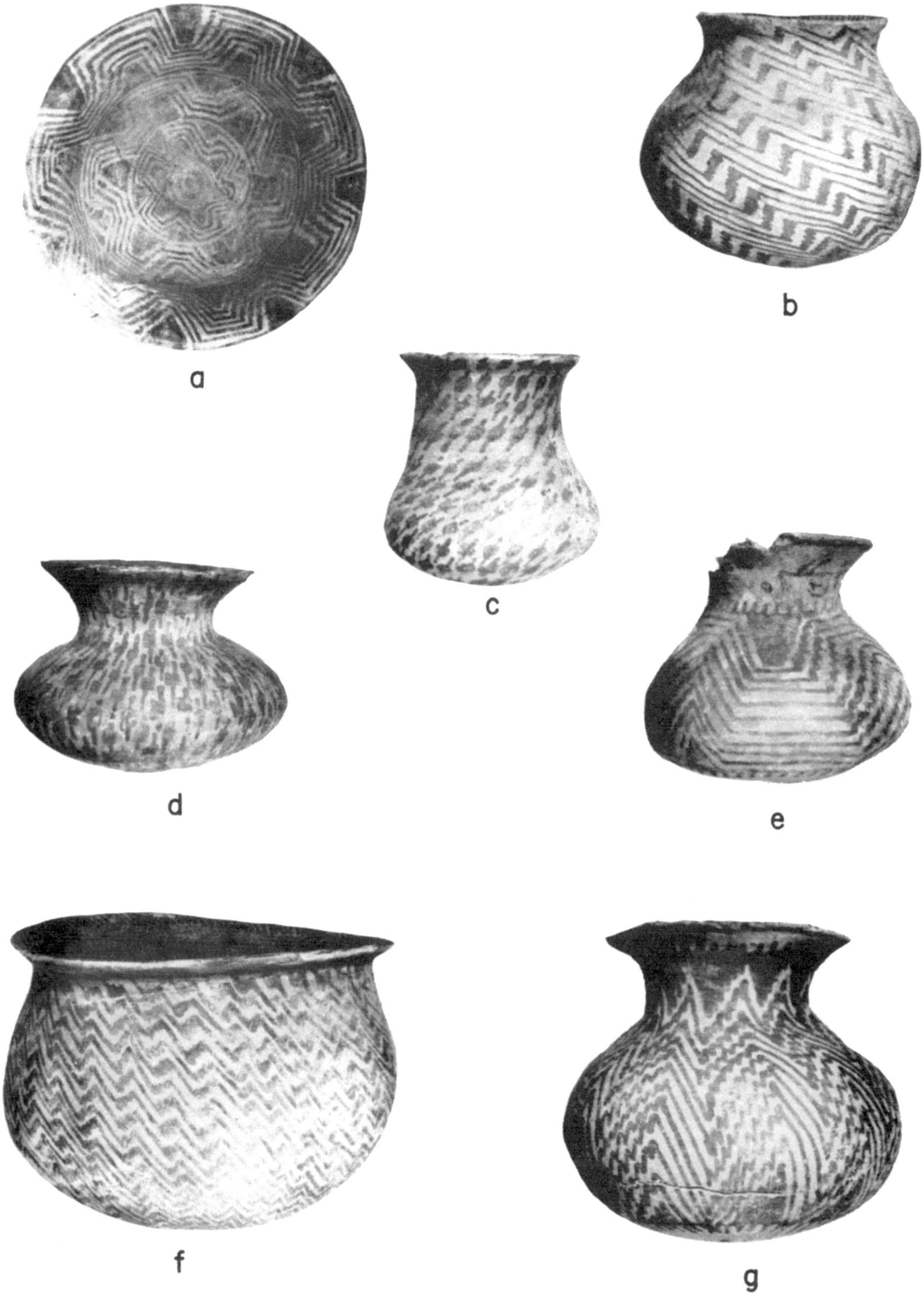

Fig. 4.16 Rillito Red-on-brown: Bowls and jars. *a*, outcurved bowl; *b–e*, *g*, flare-rim jars; *f*, recurved flare-rim bowl. Greatest diameter (non-rim) of *a*, 20 cm.

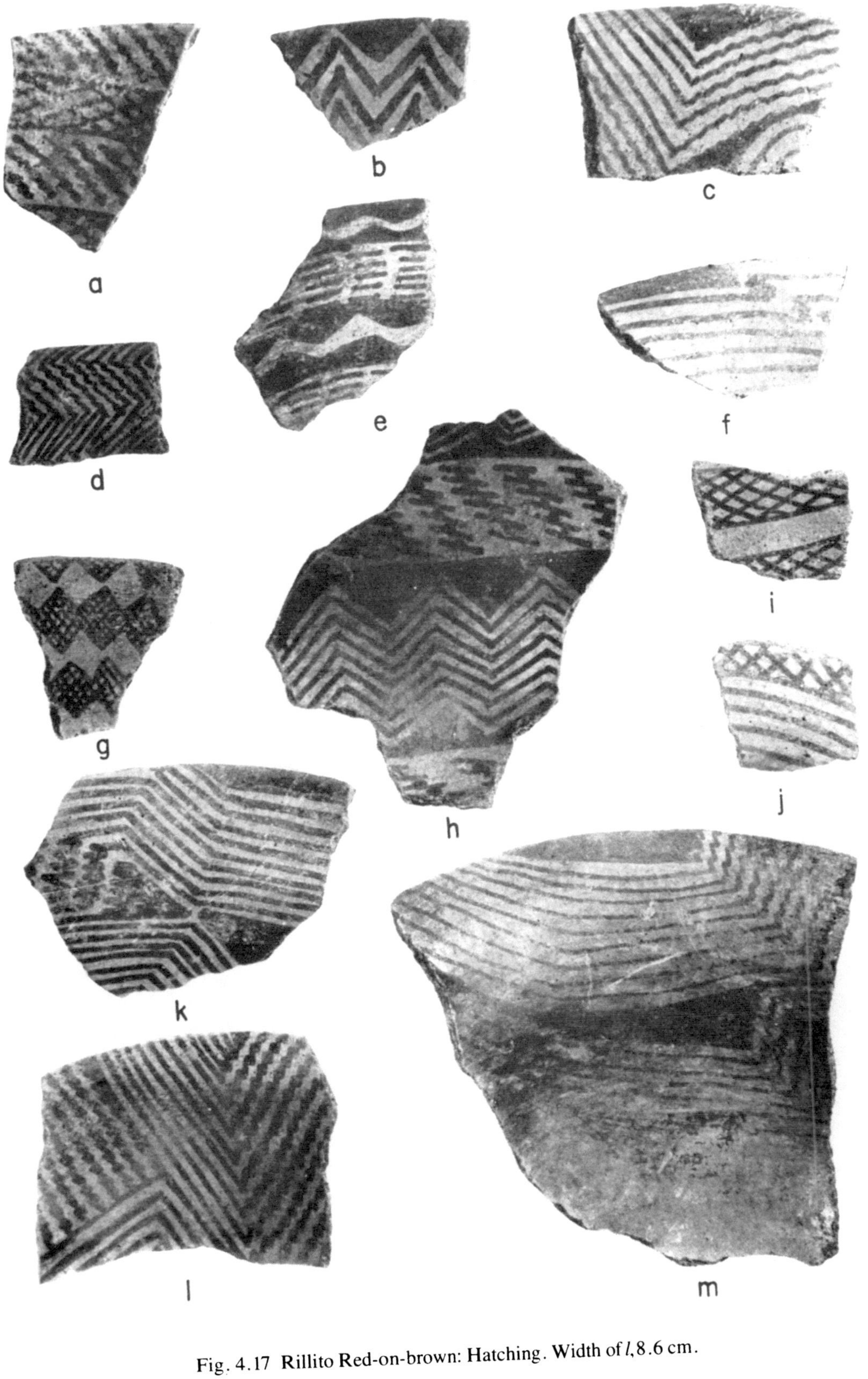

Fig. 4.17 Rillito Red-on-brown: Hatching. Width of *l*, 8.6 cm.

Fig. 4.18 Rillito Red-on-brown: Scrolls. All sherds are from bowl interiors. Width of *i*, 14 cm.

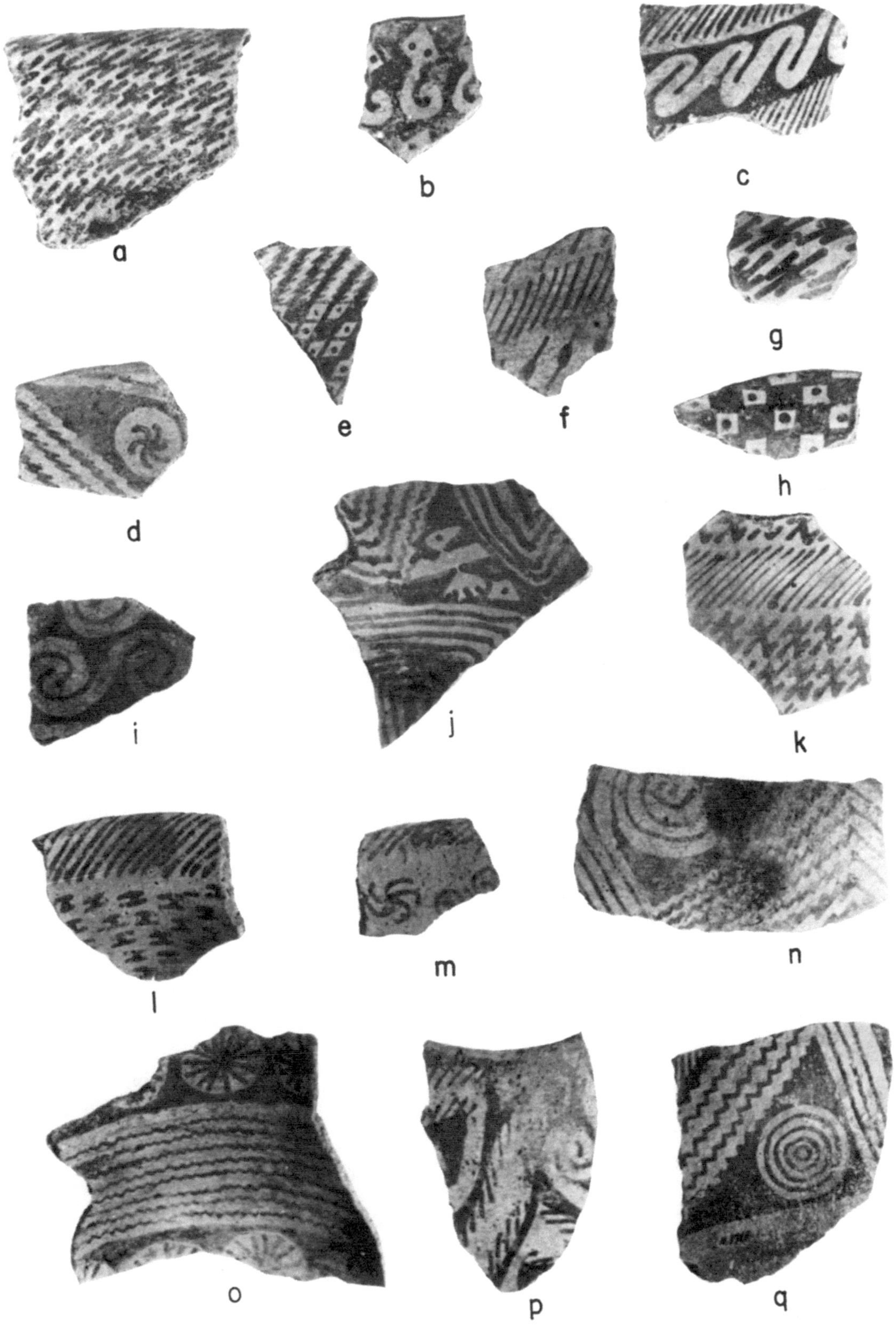

Fig. 4.19 Rillito Red-on-brown: Various design elements. *a, b, d, e–h, j, l, m, o,* bowl interiors; the remainder, jar exteriors. Width of *p*, 9.6 cm.

Bowl exteriors are no longer scored. Spaced trailing lines occur on 60 percent of Rillito interior decorated bowls.

REMARKS

The Rillito heritage from the Cañada del Oro phase is pronounced in nearly all respects. Basic vessel forms continue but are enriched, bowls and jars alike. Flare-rimmed vessels of various proportions are dominant among bowls; jars vary more than in the Cañada del Oro phase, with the introduction of vase-like affairs and low-bellied jars with flaring rims. The beaker has died out; effigy fragments are present but not abundant.

Design arrangement continues from the Cañada del Oro phase, but with a particular fondness for a layout that is difficult to place in Amsden's (1936) scheme. It has elements of his figured, his continuous circling, and might also be regarded as what he calls incomplete sectoring (Fig. 4.16*a*, for example). The specimen just cited has been classed as figured; it must be noted, however, that when a comparable design occurs on a jar exterior, inconsistently enough, it has been regarded as continuous banding (Fig. 4.16*e*). Sectoring increases,but neither in the Rillito phase nor in other local phases does it approach its strength in the Gila Basin. Circling, of repeated small elements, is highly characteristic of Rillito; and circling, with alternate bands continuous and repeated, enjoys a certain vogue. Jar decoration favors bands consisting of repeated small elements; this is a Rillito diagnostic. Also diagnostic are figured and repeated designs that usually involve scroll-hachure assemblages.

Motifs are largely a carry-over from the Cañada del Oro phase, but with minor alteration and amplification. Chevron and cuneiform mixed hatch are greatly favored; the cuneiform variety is new and confined to the Rillito phase; mixed chevron hatch makes a weak first appearance in the Cañada del Oro phase, but is highly characteristic of the Rillito phase. The line and stagger probably is an outgrowth of mixed chevron hatch. Scrolls undergo some changes, being as often fringed as serrated; generally, they are consolidated into a scroll-hachure complex that again is a Rillito diagnostic. Scrolls also are worked into an all-over figured and repeated design, by means of a motif that may be called the abutting scroll (Fig. 4.18*b*, *d*, *e*, *f*, *g*, *i*). This occurs occasionally in the Cañada del Oro phase, is primarily Rillito, but survives into Rincon times.

Fringing is extremely strong in the Rillito phase; it may be added to lines, scrolls, or to solids, but in diagnostic form it occurs free. Bull's-eyes, small elements, and life forms continue from the Cañada del Oro phase.

Both fringing and small elements are highly characteristic of the Rillito phase, and are relatively more frequent on jars than on bowls. Comparable data from the Gila Basin are not available, but the same may hold there. In the Rillito phase, for the first time, our series is sufficiently large to permit comparison between jar and bowl ornamentation. Although most designs and design elements are about equally distributed among the various vessel forms, the differences listed below seem to be significant (percentages are based on 274 bowls and 69 jars; see Tables 4.5 and 4.6):

Design Placement	Percent of Bowls	Percent of Jars
Band, repeated elements		25
Circling, repeated elements	5	

In structure, these are equivalent, banding being applied to exterior jar ornament, circling to interior bowl ornament.

Design Elements	Percent of Bowls	Percent of Jars
Wavy hatch (regardless of association)	14	8
Cross hatch	4	0
Plain chevron hatch	5	11
Mixed chevron hatch	14	6
Line and stagger	1	8
Fringe	8	22
Small elements	11	20

There is no obvious reason why cross hatch is confined to bowls, nor why fringe is nearly three times as frequent on jars as on bowls. Probably the correlation rests upon an arbitrary, formal pattern rather than upon a logical or functional basis, but it is precisely such arbitrary patterns that give pottery its significance in permitting the formulation of ceramic styles and the development of relative dating through the changes that occur in such styles.

Parallels between the Rillito phase and the Santa Cruz phase of the Gila Basin are manifest throughout. On the whole, vessel shapes are similar; at least in both areas the flare-rimmed bowl, with trailing lines, and the compressed globular jar, with flaring rim, are characteristic. There are, however, some differences. At the Hodges site, bowls outnumber jars four to one; in the Gila Basin, eight to one. Moreover, the Hodges site lacks some of the eccentric forms of the Santa Cruz phase such as rectangular vessels, compound vessels, beakers, handled scoops, thick-walled vessels (Gladwin and others 1937: Figs. 72, 75).

In design treatment certainly the most striking difference is the weak development of life forms at the Hodges site. Human representation, diagnostic of the Santa Cruz phase, scarcely occurs at all, except on Gila Basin trade ware (only three local sherds have human representation, one each from the Cañada, Rillito, and Rincon phases). Other life forms occur but are weak numerically. Of the approximately 350 sherds and restorable vessels upon which our Rillito description is based, there are but 11

Fig. 4.20 Picacho Red-on-brown: Plate. Diameter, 33 cm.

instances of animal representation, two in positive painting, the remainder negative.

Colonial Period: Picacho Red-on-brown[1]

As Picacho Red-on-brown we have designated a small lot of material which intergrades with Rillito Red-on-brown but which, at the same time, shows minor divergences in paste and finish. The pottery is cream and unslipped. A high micaceous content, combined with polish, gives the surface a lustrous sheen. Brush work is consistently precise and well controlled. One or two sherds equate stylistically with Cañada del Oro Red-on-brown, but the remainder, in shape and all decorative aspects, belong with the Rillito–Santa Cruz phase complex.

Picacho Red-on-brown is sparsely represented in our series. Except for one restorable plate (Fig. 4.20), it is represented by sherds only. The exact provenience of this type is not known, but it may have come from some locality intermediate between Tucson and the Gila Basin, perhaps the lower Santa Cruz. A number of Gila Pueblo site collections from the general area of Picacho have an appreciable quantity of sherds of this type. Therefore, for convenience, we have designated the type as Picacho Red-on-brown.

Sedentary Period: Rincon Red-on-brown

The Tucson equivalent of the Sacaton phase we have called Rincon. In part its pottery may be regarded as a direct outgrowth of Rillito Red-on-brown; some new elements are involved, and these will be reviewed below. Features that carry into the Rincon phase from the Rillito phase are readily recognizable. On the whole, however, the type is heavier, designs often are cursive, and brush work frequently is slap-dash. In short, Rincon Red-on-brown shows signs of the same decadence that in the Gila Basin marks the change from Santa Cruz Red-on-buff to Sacaton Red-on-buff.

COLOR

Color is the same as in Rillito Red-on-brown, save for the prevalence of smudging. Firing clouds are prominent, as before, but smudging evidently has become deliberate. It occurs on 61 percent of jar interiors and 30 percent of bowl interiors. Bowl interiors may be smudged regardless of whether the design is exterior or interior. With interior decorated bowls, painting is sometimes obliterated by smudging; the resulting color scheme is often essentially red-on-gray or red-on-black.

---

[1] *Ed. Note:* Picacho Red-on-brown is no longer considered a valid type.

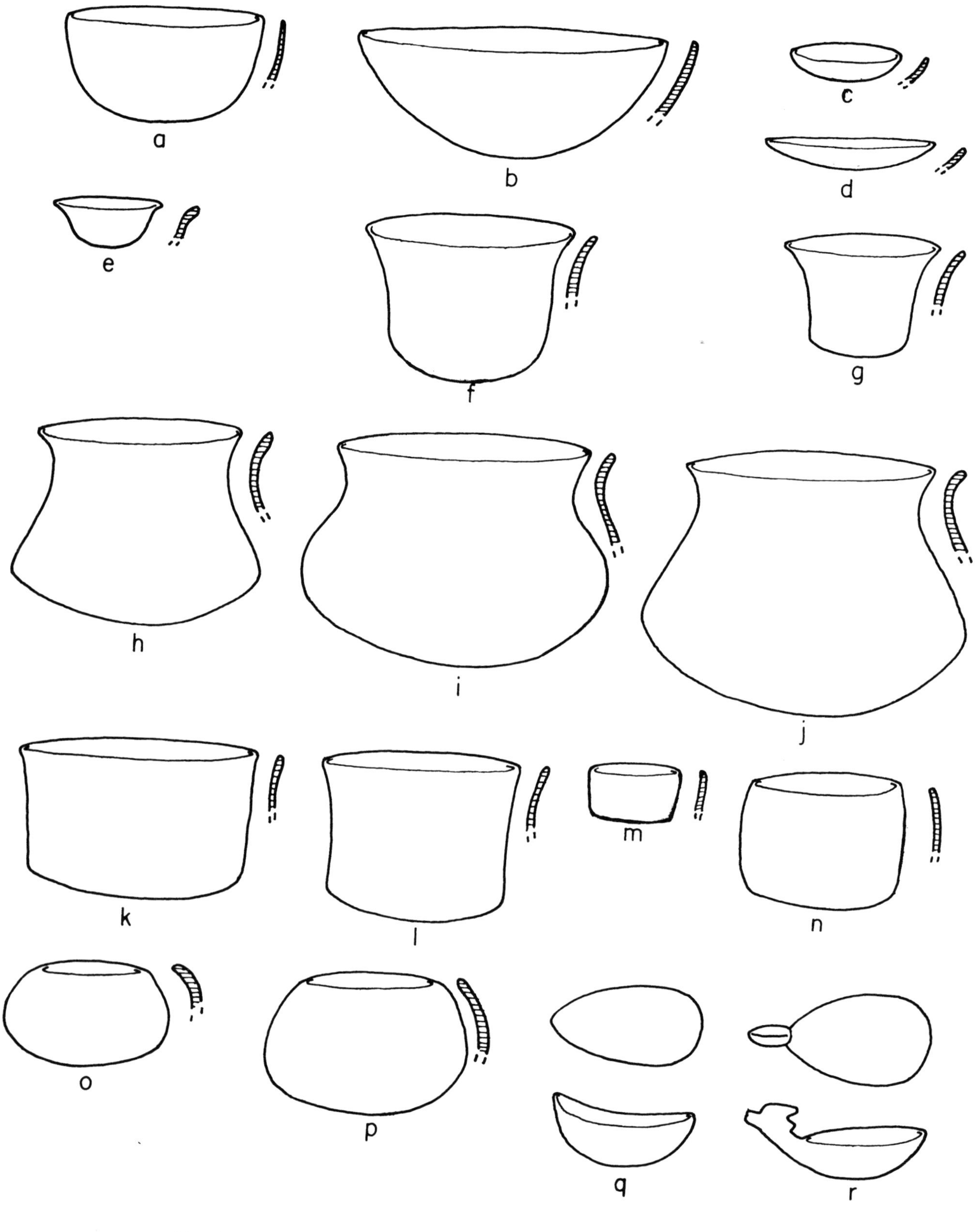

Fig. 4.21 Rincon Red-on-brown: Bowl and scoop forms. *a*, hemispherical bowl; *b–d*, outcurved bowls; *e–j*, flare-rim bowls; *k, l*, semi-flare-rim bowls; *m, n*, straight-sided bowls; *o, p*, incurved bowls; *q*, scoop; *r*, effigy bowl.

TABLE 4.7

Rincon Red-on-Brown: Statistics of Vessel Form (bowls and scoops)

Form	Fig. 4.21 (part)	Approximate Diameter (cm)	Sherds (No.)	Restorable and Semi-Restorable Vessels (No.)	Total
Hemispherical bowls	*a*	19–34	14	9	23
Outcurved bowls: Normal	*b*	30–54	50	12	62
Sherds, presumably normal outcurved			59		59
Small, shallow[a]	*c*	14.5–21	10	1	11
Plate-like	*d*	23–26	1	3	4
Flare-rim bowls: Round bottom	*e, f*	13–22, 26–37	0	12	12
Flat bottom	*g*	17, 26 (2 measurable)	0	4	4
Flare-rim bowls, precise shape not determinable			30	0	30
Recurved	*h–j*	16.5, 30–37	47	6	53
Semi-flare-rim bowls	*k, l*	22–27	1	4	5
Straight-sided bowls	*m, n*	13–19	3	3	6
Incurved bowls	*o, p*	8–18	4	5	9
Bowl sherds, shape indeterminate			116		116
Scoops	*q*	12 x 15 (1 example)	9	1	10
Effigy[b]	*r*		0	1	1
Total			344	61	405

[a]Small sherds may be confused with scoop fragments.

[b]In addition, one unpainted effigy scoop.

SHAPE

Shapes are shown in Figures 4.21 and 4.22 and are tabulated in Tables 4.7 and 4.8. Bowls continue to account for about 80 percent of all vessels of identifiable forms, excluding special shapes, such as effigies and scoops, and sherds with exterior decoration which might be either jars or large flare-rim bowls (Table 4.8). Flare-rim bowls are not so popular as in Rillito times and comprise less than 30 percent of the bowls, in contrast to nearly 80 percent during the Rillito phase. Rincon flare-rims tend to be relatively deep. A new feature is the large recurved flare-rim, often with a shoulder (Fig. 4.21*h, j*). Correlated with the decline in flare-rim forms is a renaissance of the hemispherical bowl, which seems not to occur in the Rillito phase, although it is found in the Cañada del Oro phase. Also correlated is a tremendous increase in outcurved bowls which, during the Rincon phase, account for nearly half the bowls of identifiable shape.

Jar shapes are variable. Bodies are globular to squat (Fig. 4.22*a,e*); some are shouldered (Fig. 4.22*e,f,g*). Rims are flaring to sharply returned. There are four instances of effigies (Figs. 4.23*e,g;* 4.24*b,d*), two of which (Figs. 4.23*e*; 4.24*d*) are unpainted. Two are scoops (Figs. 4.23*g*; 4.24*d*); one is a sherd, apparently with an arm modeled in relief (Fig. 4.24*b*); the fourth is a vessel with human features in relief (Fig. 4.23*e*). The sherd shown in Figure 4.24*f* is not an effigy but is of unique contour.

DESIGN

Bowl layouts include the following:

** Plaited band (illustrated only on bowl exteriors)

The plaited band is found more frequently on jars than on bowls. Probably it is equivalent structurally to offset quartering but is expanded because of the larger design field offered by jars. Bowls with plaited-band arrangement also are offset quartered, but the resulting sectors are subdivided into bands.

All-over, patterned (not illustrated)

All-over, spiral (Fig. 4.23*b*)

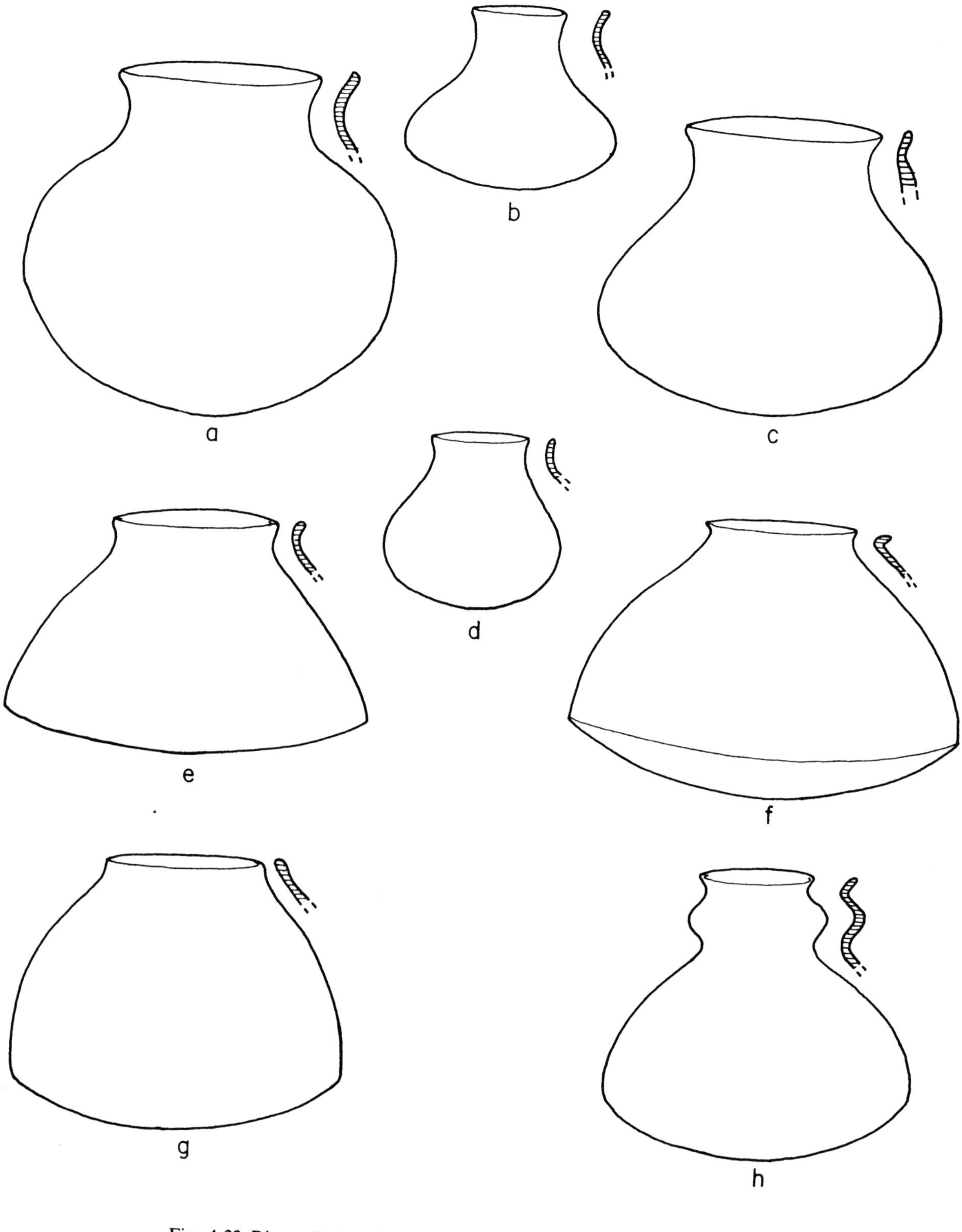

Fig. 4.22 Rincon Red-on-brown: Jar forms. *a–c*, flare-rim jars; *d*, low returned rim, low bellied; *e*, low returned rim, shouldered; *f*, sharply returned rim, shouldered; *g*, rimless, low bellied; *h*, expanded neck, low bellied.

TABLE 4.8

Rincon Red-on-Brown: Statistics of Vessel Form (jars)

Form	Fig. 4.22 (part)	Approximate Diameter (cm)	Sherds (No.)	Restorable and Semi-Restorable Vessels (No.)	Total
Flare-rim, globular bodied jar	*a*	20	0	1	1
Flare-rim, low bellied	*b*	9	0	1	1
	c	20–21	0	3	3
Sherds, flare-rim, body indeterminate		18–30	14	0	14
**Low returned rim, low bellied	*d*	10–11	0	2	2
**Low returned rim, shouldered	*e*	18–19	0	2	2
Sherds, low returned rim, body indeterminate		15–18	5	0	5
*Sharply returned rim, shouldered	*f*	15–26	0	3	3
Sherds, sharply returned rim		12–24	5	0	5
Rimless, low bellied	*g*	16	0	1	1
Expanded neck, low bellied	*h*	15	0	1	1
Sherds, body fragments			68	0	68
Sherds, exterior decorated: either jars or large flare-rim, recurved bowls			98	0	98
Total			190	14	204

*Frequent motifs.
**Diagnostic elements.

All-over, figured and repeated (Fig. 4.23*c*)

Quartered, hatched (quartering by hachure alone rare) (not illustrated)

Quartered, figured (Fig. 4.23*a*, *g*)

**Quartered, offset (Figs. 4.23*i*)

Trisected (Fig. 4.23*f*)

Circling, continuous (not illustrated)

Circling, repeated (extremely rare) (not illustrated)

Circling, alternate bands continuous, repeated (not illustrated)

Jars and bowls with exterior decoration are, with the exception of Figure 4.25*a*, consistently banded:

All-over, patterned (Fig. 4.25*a*)

Banded, continuous (Figs. 4.23*h*; 4.25*c*)

Banded, alternate bands continuous, repeated (Figs. 4.24*e*; 4.25*b*)

Banded, figured and repeated (Fig. 4.23*j*); the repeated element is usually abutting scrolls rather than scroll-hachure assemblages as in the Rillito phase.

**Banded, diamond subdivision (Figs. 4.23*d*; 4.25*g*)

**Plaited band (Fig. 4.25*d*)

DESIGN ELEMENTS

*Double scroll (Figs. 4.23*a*, *c*, *d*, *g*, *j*; 4.24*c*, *e*, *g*; 4.25*d*,*e*,*f*)

**Single scroll (Figs. 4.23*i*; 4.24*a*)

*Abutting scroll (Fig. 4.23*c*, *j*)

Square scroll (Fig. 4.24*f*)

Square scroll, locked (Fig. 4.25*d*)

**Meander (Fig. 4.25*g*)

Scroll-hachure assemblages (Figs. 4.23*c*; 4.24*a*) (Hatch less frequently chevron-shaped than in the Rillito phase)

*Hachure: straight, wavy, mixed, cross (Figs. 4.24*c*; 4.25*d*, *g*)

*Chevron hatch (triangular only; no cuneiform) (Figs. 4.23*c*, *d*, *f*, *h*; 4.24*a*; 4.25*c*, *f*, *h*)

**Hatched band (4.24*e*)

Checkerboard (Fig. 4.25*g*)

Line and stagger (extremely rare; not illustrated)

Lines and panels, serrated (Figs. 4.23*i*; 4.25*d*, *e*)

Fringe: lines, panels, and free standing (Figs. 4.24*f*; 4.25*b*)

Bull's-eye (Figs. 4.23*f*; 4.25*a*, *g*)

Life forms, positive (2 examples only: Fig. 4.23*f*; other example not illustrated)

Animal motifs, negative (Fig. 4.23*c*; 4.24*f*; 4.25*b*)

Zigzag, negative (not illustrated)

Zigzag, positive, capped (rare, but confined to Rincon; not illustrated)

Small elements (chiefly panel fillers) (Fig. 4.25*h*)

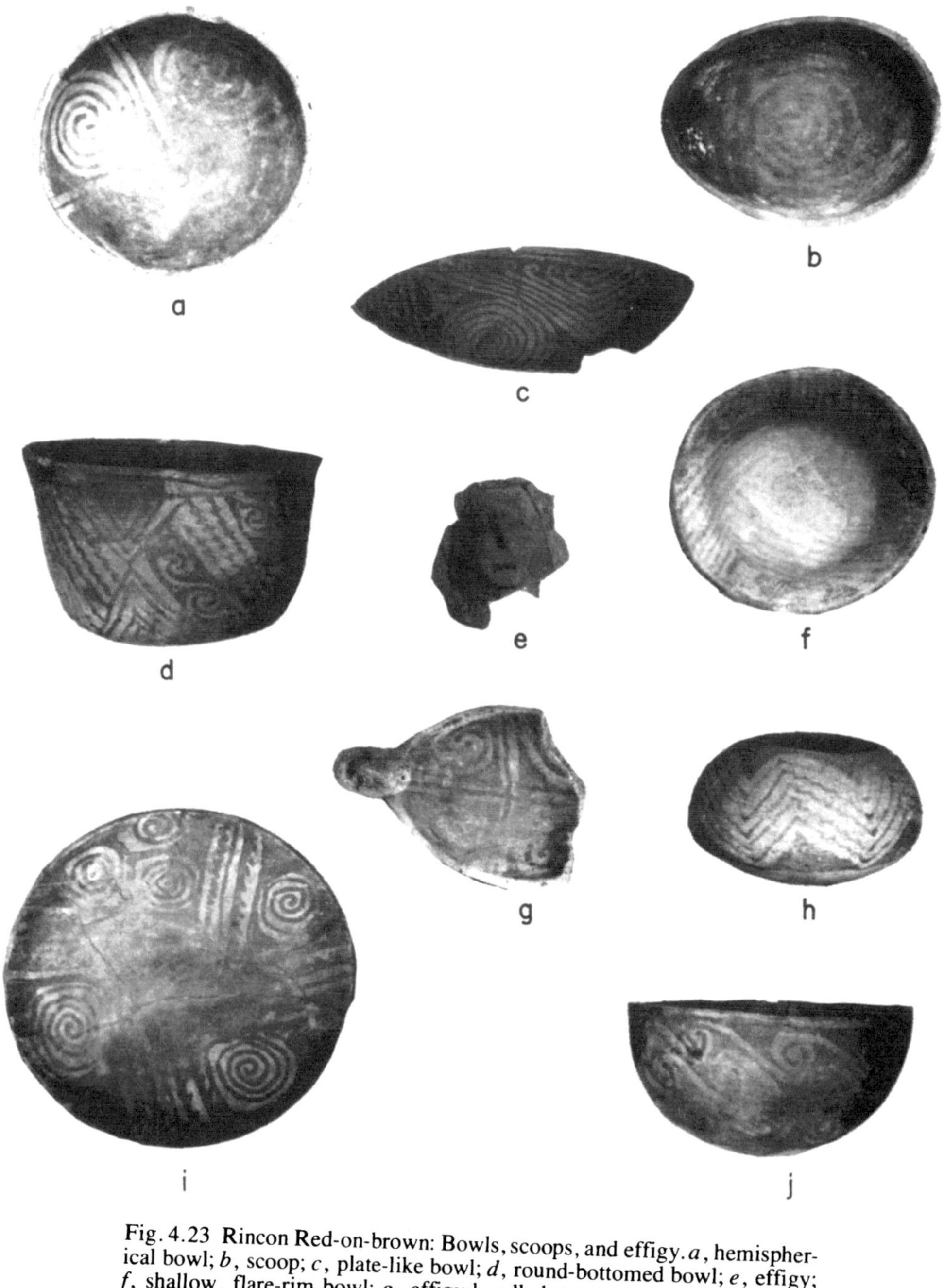

Fig. 4.23 Rincon Red-on-brown: Bowls, scoops, and effigy. *a*, hemispherical bowl; *b*, scoop; *c*, plate-like bowl; *d*, round-bottomed bowl; *e*, effigy; *f*, shallow, flare-rim bowl; *g*, effigy-handled scoop; *h*, incurved bowl; *i*, plate-like bowl; *j*, hemispherical bowl. Maximum diameter of *a*, 14.5 cm.

SURFACE TREATMENT

Slip is not characteristic, but occurs in roughly 10 percent of Rincon ceramics; it is divided equally between bowls and jars. In most cases it is apparently a self-wash and definitely not the chalky slip of the Gila Basin. Despite the slip, the surface finish continues to be polished rather than matte.

Exterior trailing lines on bowls are less common than in the Rillito phase. This characteristic is evidently dying out; 16 percent of interior decorated bowls exhibit trailing lines in contrast to 60 percent in Rillito specimens. As would be expected, they are more frequent on flare-rim vessels than on other bowl forms. Lines are frequently paired; otherwise, they are more widely spaced than in the Rillito phase. There are isolated cases of a trailing zigzag.

Fig. 4.24 Rincon Red-on-brown: Bowl, jar, and effigy sherds. *a*, interior decorated bowl; *b*, effigy vessel with (?) in relief; *c*, interior decorated bowl; *d*, unpainted effigy scoop; *e*, neck-decorated jar; *f*, uniquely contoured jar; *g*, exterior decorated bowl. Note use of interlocking scrolls in *a*, *c*, *e*, *f*, *g*. Maximum dimension of *f*, 19.1 cm.

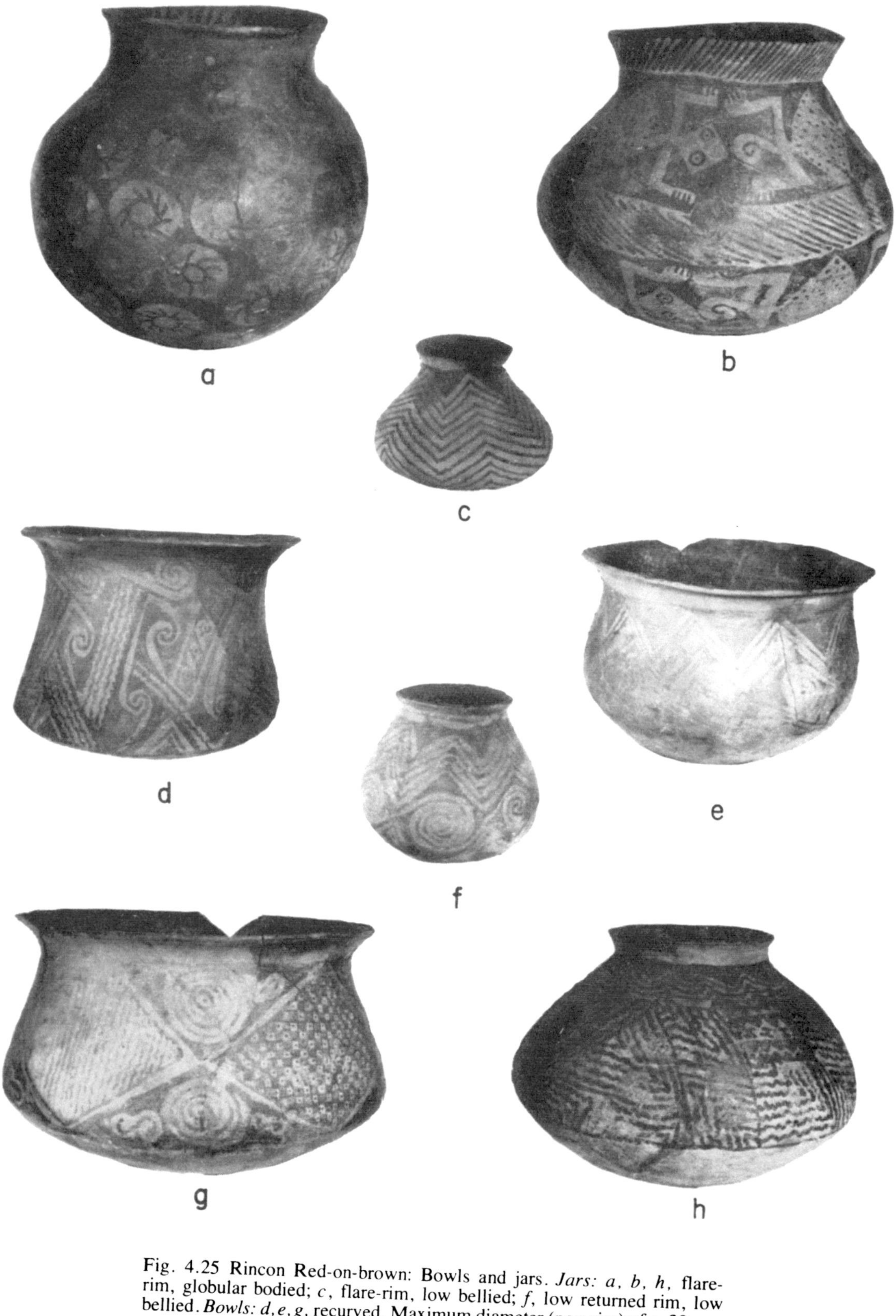

Fig. 4.25 Rincon Red-on-brown: Bowls and jars. *Jars: a, b, h,* flare-rim, globular bodied; *c,* flare-rim, low bellied; *f,* low returned rim, low bellied. *Bowls: d,e,g,* recurved. Maximum diameter (non-rim) of *g*, 39 cm.

Fig. 4.26 "Cortaro Red-on-brown": Bowl interior

REMARKS

It has been noted above that as Sacaton Red-on-buff has a Santa Cruz heritage, so at the Hodges site, Rincon Red-on-brown has a Rillito heritage. At the same time, as in the Gila Basin, certain new elements appear. At Hodges, the outcurved bowl with interior painting, and often with interior smudging, largely replaces the flare-rim bowl. Jars remain in part globular bodied, with flaring collars, but at the same time, the shoulder and sharply returned neck, so characteristic of the Gila Basin Sacaton phase, appear. Associated with this cluster of new forms is the occasional use of a slip, more gray than buff, and more polished and more enduring than the Gila Basin slip. Likewise associated is the plaited-band arrangement, and, in motif, an increase in fringed lines and panels, in hatched bands, and in single scrolls as compared with interlocking scrolls.

Rincon Red-on-brown is, therefore, a somewhat heterogeneous assemblage. It has not been possible to subdivide it into more than one phase, because the various features which survive from the Rillito phase and those which have just been noted as innovations both occur associated in cremations. Three large sherd cremations (Nos. 161, 169, 182) constitute our largest individual Rincon phase series. These were checked carefully for stylistic elements. Ceramically, two of the cremations were predominantly a carry-over from Rillito; the third lot showed similar heritage, but at the same time there was a noticeable increase in what may be called intrusive elements. It must be emphasized that here these new elements do not occur in isolation but in association with the essentially Rillito heritage of Rincon.

Such heterogeneity may be regarded as yet another expression of the exceedingly close relationship to the Gila Basin. There Sacaton Red-on-buff manifestly contains a strong Santa Cruz ingredient; at the same time, its chief diagnostic features are the Gila shoulder, the sharply returned jar collar, and the interwoven band design.

Our Rincon phase ceramics may contain still another ingredient, and one which is more difficult to isolate. Again in association with perfectly normal Rincon Red-on-brown, if such a varied style can be so described, are several vessels which show a divergence in an over-simplification of design (not illustrated). Counterparts can be found within the very considerable range embraced by Gila Basin Sacaton Red-on-buff (see especially Gladwin and others 1937: Fig. 69*c-e*; Plates CXXXIV and CXXXVIII). Under the circumstances there seems to be little point in designating them as a thing apart from Rincon Red-on-brown.

This, however, brings up the problem of a transition between Rincon and the next succeeding phase, Tanque Verde. At the start of the work at the Hodges site, on the basis of a few sherds, but largely upon theoretical grounds, Harold Gladwin envisaged a phase designated as Cortaro which would bridge the gap between the more or less curvilinear style of Rincon and the essentially angular treatment of Tanque Verde, between Rincon interior bowl decoration and Tanque Verde exterior ornamentation. Hypothetically, this would be an interior decorated bowl, its design verging on the Tanque Verde angular. Logically there is need of a transition, but we found few sherds of such description and only one restorable vessel (Fig. 4.26). Nor did this material occur pure. For these reasons, we are not warranted in isolating a Cortaro style on the basis of evidence from the Hodges site. However, at the University Ruin, near Tucson, Emil Haury found a considerable quantity of material that answers these theoretical demands. There, however, the Cortaro type occurs *later* than our Tanque Verde, in association with polychrome; hence, it must be regarded as derivative of Tanque Verde rather than antecedent. So far there is no material that satisfactorily bridges the very real gap between the Sedentary and the Classic periods.

It may be noted that the same stylistic hiatus holds for the Gila Basin. It is a far cry from Sacaton to Casa Grande, and the break parallels precisely the situation at the Hodges site. Doubtless the Classic complex was not evolved on the spot, either at Hodges or at any of the Gila Basin sites so far excavated. [*Ed. note*: see Doyel (1974) and Hammack (1969) for discussions of the transition from the Sedentary period to the Classic period in the Gila Basin.]

Classic Period: Tanque Verde Red-on-brown

The Tanque Verde phase is the local equivalent of the Soho phase of the Gila Basin; therefore, it marks the beginning of the Classic period. A later phase of the Classic, not found at the Hodges site, is represented in the Tucson area at the Martinez Hill Ruin and the University Ruin.

Tanque Verde pottery constitutes a sharply defined and compact ceramic complex which departs from the old traditions in both shape and decoration. Its relationship to the pottery of the earlier phases will be discussed below, following the description of Tanque Verde Red-on-brown.

COLOR

Color has substantially the same range as that of the immediately preceding phases, although more frequently with a pronounced orange cast. Firing clouds continue; interior smudging, especially of bowls, is prevalent.

SHAPE

Shapes are shown in Figures 4.27 and 4.28 and are tabulated in Tables 4.9 and 4.10. The sample is rather small but suggests a very slight gain in jar strength. Excluding effigy vessels and exterior decorated sherds, which might be from either bowls or jars, bowls comprise about 77 percent of the total. More than a third of these bowls are moderately large hemispherical vessels with exterior decoration. Recurved bowls, with rounded bodies, are present, and incurved bowls, some of considerable size, occur in

TABLE 4.9
Tanque Verde Red-on-Brown: Statistics of Vessel Form (bowls)

Form	Fig. 4.27 (part)	Approximate Diameter (cm)	Sherds (No.)	Restorable and Semi-Restorable Vessels (No.)	Total
Hemispherical bowls, exterior decorated with interior borders:					
Small	*b, d*	16–18		6	6
**Large	*a*	22–36	19	36	55
Outcurved bowls, semi-flare-rim	*c, f*	14.5, 32		2	2
Recurved bowls:					
**Tall	*g*	15		1	1
*Normal	*e*	19–29	5	4	9
Incurved bowls:					
Tall	*h, i*	9.5		2	2
*Medium	*j, l*	9–17		10	10
**Large	*k*	20–31	5	6	11
Proportions indeterminate			4		4
Oval bowl	*m*	19.5 × 23		1	1
Bowl sherds, shape indeterminate			66		66
Other sherds, exterior decorated, either bowls or jars			107		107
Total			206	68	274

*Frequent motifs.
**Diagnostic elements.

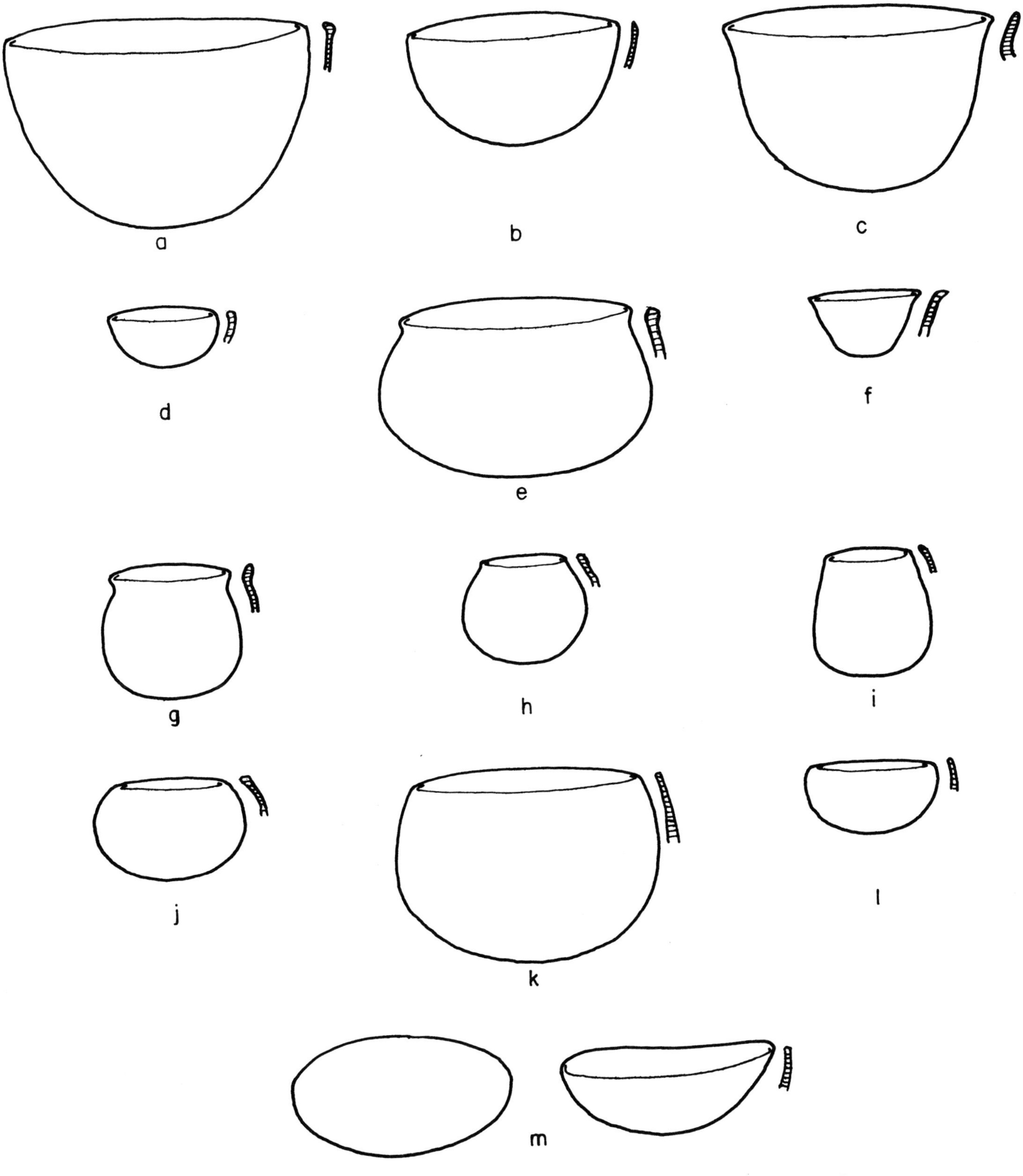

Fig. 4.27 Tanque Verde Red-on-brown: Bowl forms. *a, b, d,* hemispherical bowls; *c, f,* outcurved, semi-flare-rim bowl; *e, g,* recurved bowls; *h–l,* incurved bowls; *m,* oval bowl.

Fig. 4.28 Tanque Verde Red-on-brown: Jar and effigy forms. *a, b,* unshouldered jars; *c, f,* Tanque Verde shoulder, tall collar; *d,* shouldered, short collar; *e,* Tanque Verde shoulder, short collar; *g–i,* animal effigy vessels.

TABLE 4.10

Tanque Verde Red-on-Brown: Statistics of Vessel Form (jars and effigies)

Form	Fig. 4.28 (part)	Approximate Diameter (cm)	Sherds (No.)	Restorable and Semi-Restorable Vessels (No.)	Total
Jars:					
Unshouldered	*a, b*	7, 13	0	2	2
**Shouldered, short collar	*d*	11	0	1	1
**Tanque Verde shoulder, short collar	*e*	14–15	0	3	3
**Tanque Verde shoulder, tall collar	*c, f*	9–18	0	6	6
Jar sherds:					
Short collar			1	0	1
Tall collar			7	0	7
Tanque Verde shoulder			6	0	6
Shape indeterminate			24	0	24
**Animal effigy vessels	*g–i*		0	3	3
Total			38	15	53

** Diagnostic elements.

appreciable number. Outcurved and flare-rim bowls are absent, as are scoops, seed jars, and seed bowls.

Jar collars tend to be vertical, either short or tall (Figs. 4.29*b*; 4.30*a*, *e*, *f*, *g*; exception, Fig. 4.30*c*). Jar bodies vary from globular (rare, Fig. 4.30*c*) to shouldered and sub-conic (Fig. 4.28*d*, *e*), for example. The shoulder current during Tanque Verde times is distinct from the so-called Gila shoulder, which comes invariably at the point of greatest vessel diameter. In contrast, the shoulder of Tanque Verde vessels occurs well below the point of maximum diameter. Moreover, immediately below the angle is a slight concavity which gives a mammiform contour to the vessel base (Figs. 4.28*c*, *e*; 4.29*a*, *b*). This type of shoulder may prove to be characteristic of the Soho phase as well; at least several jars in the Gila Pueblo collection show it. Should this be the case, this shoulder might well be designated as the Classic shoulder, to distinguish it from the Gila shoulder.

Animal effigy forms (Fig. 4.31) are confined to the Tanque Verde phase. A fragment of a human effigy (Fig. 4.32), unpainted, comes from the floor of a Tanque Verde phase house (House 42), but as the associated floor sherds are Rillito to Tanque Verde, the specimen cannot be placed precisely.

DESIGN

Amsden's (1936) categories of design placement used heretofore require minor modification to fit the Tanque Verde complex. Bowl and jar ornament alike is contained in a horizontal band that encircles the exterior of the vessel. Save for rims, there is but one instance in the Tanque Verde series of an interior decorated bowl (not illustrated). In the

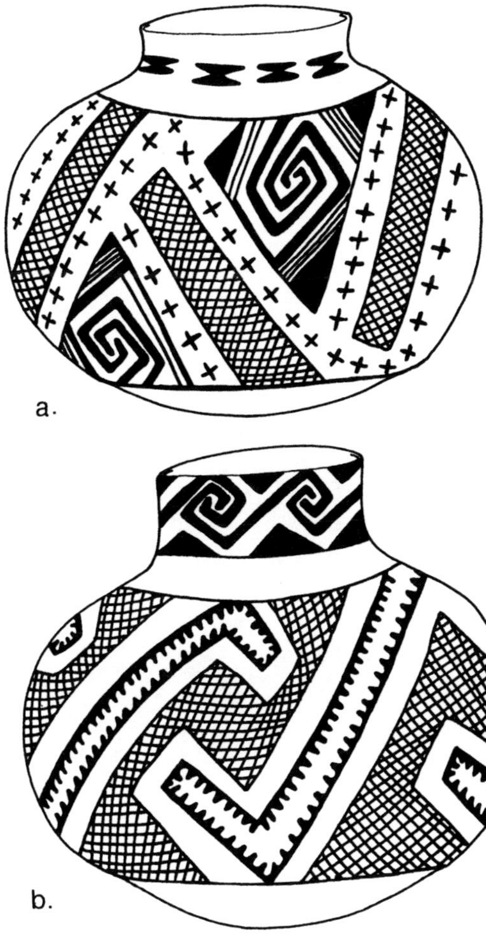

Fig. 4.29 Tanque Verde Red-on-brown: Jars. *a*, short collar, Tanque Verde shoulder, banded, opposed pendant; *b*, tall collar, Tanque Verde shoulder, banded, figured and repeated, interlocking.

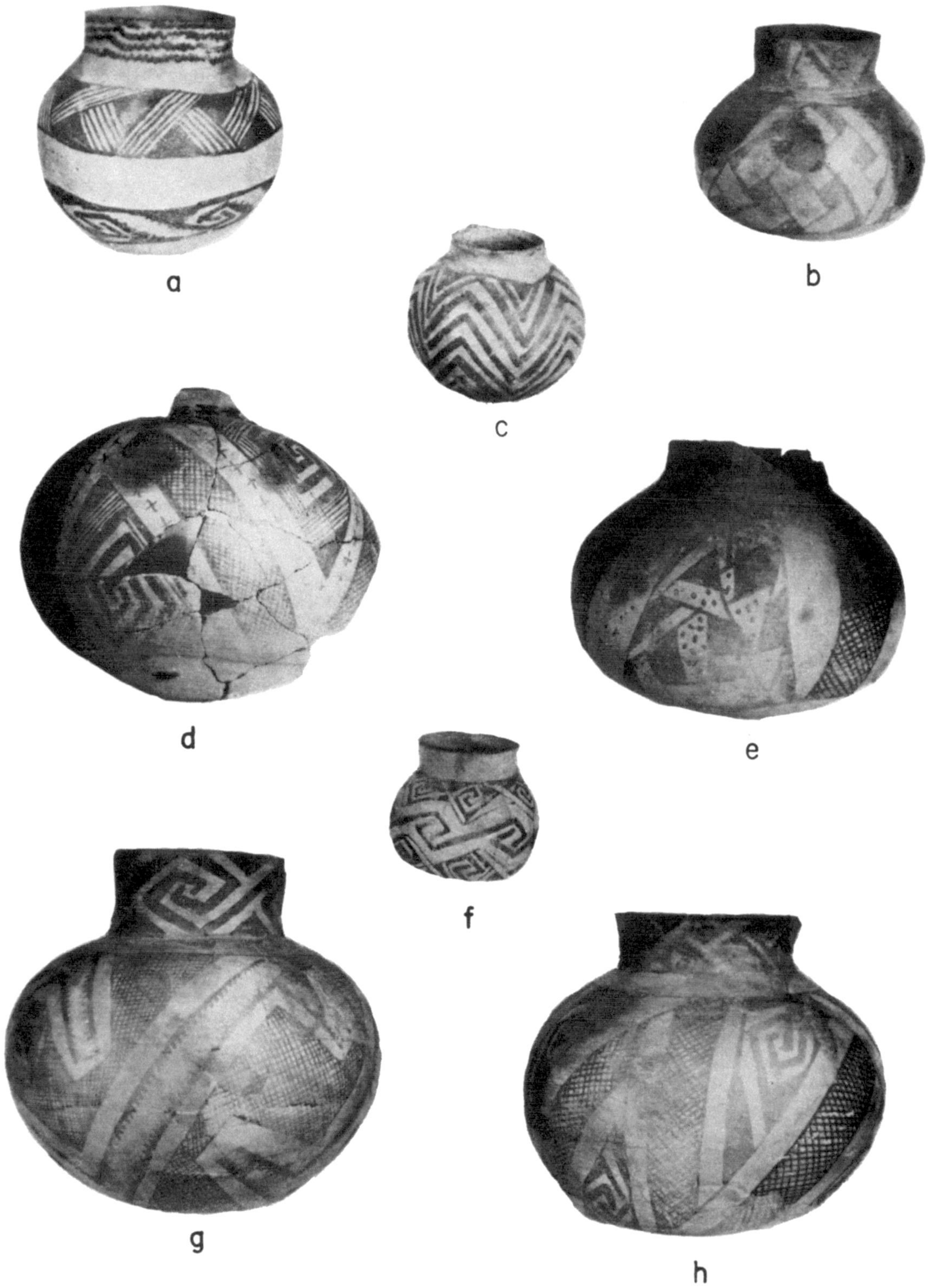

Fig. 4.30 Tanque Verde Red-on-brown: Jars. Maximum diameter (non-rim) of *g*, 39 cm.

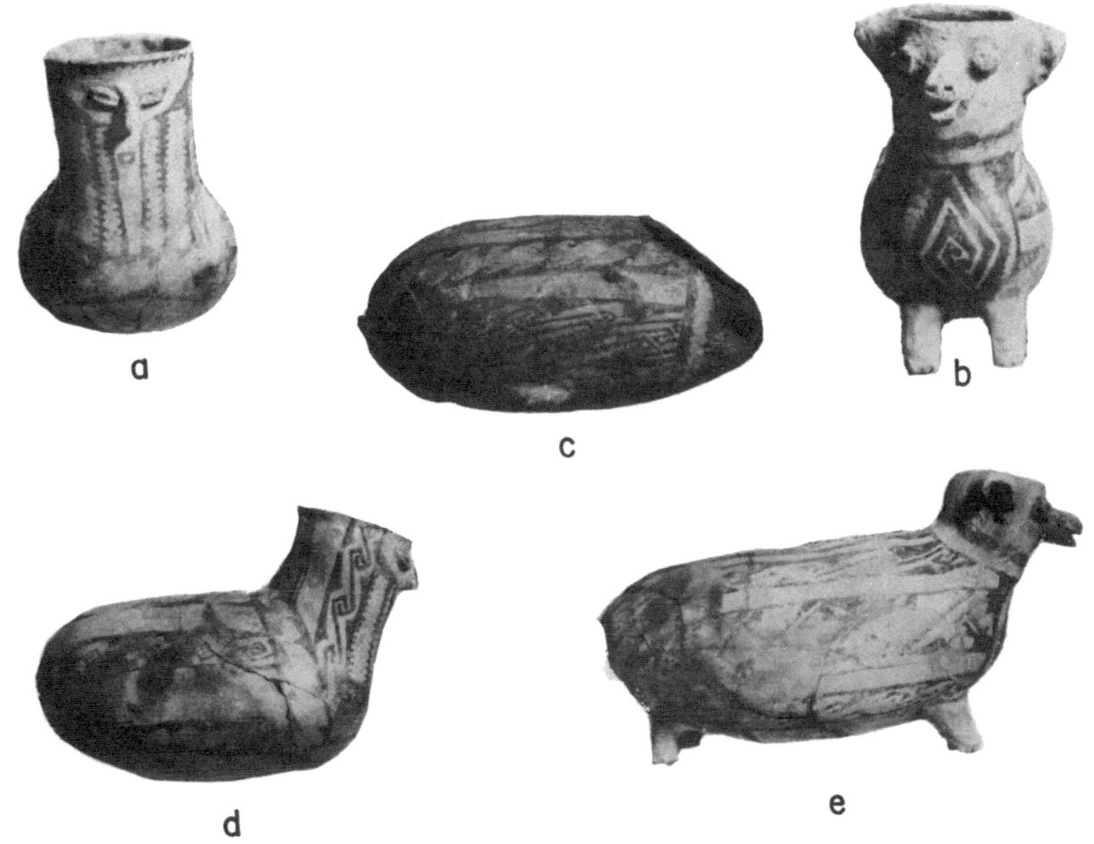

Fig. 4.31 Tanque Verde Red-on-brown: Effigy vessels. *a* and *b* are frontal views of *d* and *e* and are not at the same scale as *c, d, e. d* measures 28 cm from breast to tail.

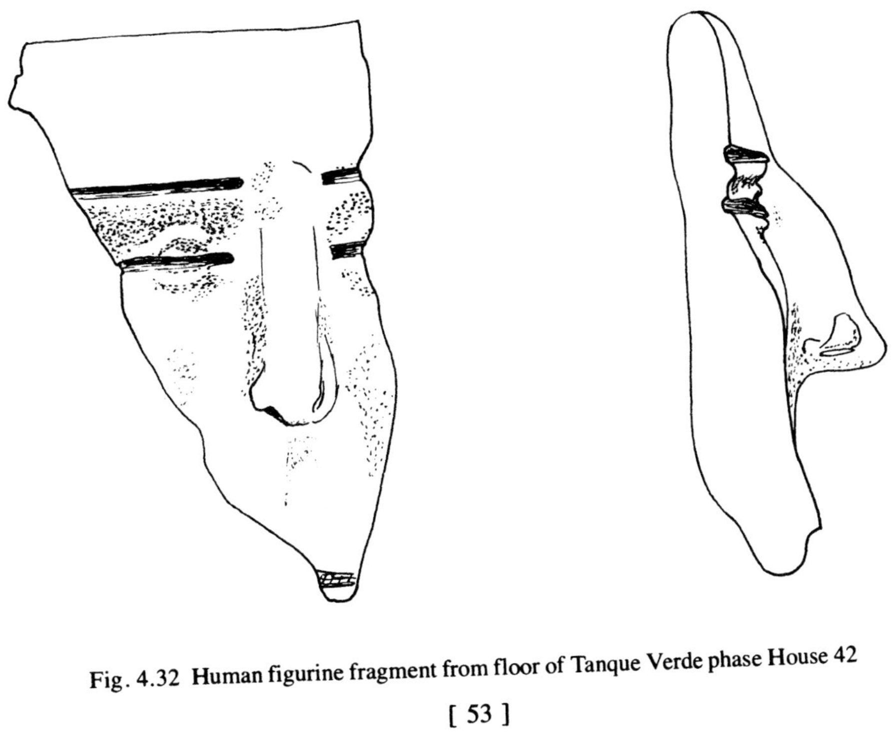

Fig. 4.32 Human figurine fragment from floor of Tanque Verde phase House 42

subdivision of this band two additions to Amsden's (1936) design series may be suggested.

These two additions may be termed banded, opposed pendants; and banded, opposed pendants overlapping. Banded, opposed pendants (Fig. 4.33*a*) are a strong Tanque

Fig. 4.33 Tanque Verde Red-on-brown: Band designs. *a*, banded, opposed pendants; *b*, banded, opposed pendants overlapping; *c*, banded, figured and repeated, interlocking.

Verde diagnostic found on 34 percent of all Tanque Verde phase vessels. Banded, opposed pendants overlapping (Fig. 4.33*b*) are a Tanque Verde diagnostic found on 24 percent of all Tanque Verde phase vessels. These layouts obviously relate to and intergrade with the plaited band; they may result from reduction in the number of repeats. Were the plaited band not known to precede these layouts, they might be thought of as prototypes of the plaited band. Evidently, however, they represent a simplification rather than an ancestor.

Otherwise, the design placement categories used previously continue to be applicable. Figured and repeated designs are not frequent, but always assume a characteristic interlocking form (Fig. 4.33*c*). Inasmuch as all Tanque Verde phase vessels are exterior decorated and the design field is approximately equivalent, there is no need to distinguish between bowls and jars as far as layout is concerned.

Quartered, offset (rare, 1 instance only) (not illustrated)

Banded, all-over patterned (rare, 1 instance only) (Fig. 4.35*a*)

Banded, continuous (Figs. 4.30*a*, *c*; 4.35*c*)

**Banded, figured and repeated, interlocking (Figs. 4.29*b*; 4.36*b*; 4.37*b*)

**Banded, opposed pendants (Figs. 4.29*a*; 4.30*f*, *h*; 4.35*b*, *f*, *g*, *h*; 4.36*a*; 4.37*a*)

**Banded, opposed pendants overlapping (Figs. 4.34*d*, *e*, *f*, *g*, *k*)

*Plaited band (Fig. 4.34*a*, *b*, *h*)

DESIGN ELEMENTS

Contained within triangular zone of pendant:

**Square scroll, interlocking (Figs. 4.29*a*; 4.30*f*, *h*; 4.34*a*, *b*, *c*, *i*, *j*, *k*; 4.35*b*, *d–i*; 4.36*a*; 4.37*a*)

Wavy hatch (rare) (Fig. 4.34*g*)

Cross hatch (Fig. 4.35*b*)

Triangle with chevron hatch (rare) (not illustrated)

Checkerboard (Fig. 4.34*d*)

**Plaited band as a filler (Figs. 4.30*b*, *e*; 4.34*e*)

Contained within band of pendant:

Square scroll, interlocking (Fig. 4.35*f*)

Hatch, longitudinal (Fig. 4.34*c*, *e*, *i*, *k*)

Hatch, diagonal or horizontal (Fig. 4.35*h*)

*Cross hatch (Figs. 4.29*a*; 4.30*d*, *e*, *h*; 4.35*b*, *g*, *i*; 4.36*a*)

Checkerboard (not illustrated)

*Lines picoted, ticked (Fig. 4.34*d*)

*Lines barbed (Fig. 4.34*g*, *i*, *k*)

*Lines barbed, with fret fill (Fig. 4.34*h*)

*Lines, flagged or plumed triangles (Fig. 4.35*h*)

**Lines strung with small elements (Fig. 4.37*a*)

Small elements free or as band fillers (rare) (Fig. 4.29*a*)

Not associated with pendant arrangement:

Square scroll, interlocking (Figs. 4.30*a*, *g*; 4.34*a*, *b*; 4.37*b*)

Hachure: plain, wavy, plain chevron, offset, and cross (Figs. 4.29*b*; 4.30*a*, *c*, *g*; 4.36*b*; 4.37*b*)

Checkerboard (Fig. 4.35*a*)

Lines picoted, ticked (Figs. 4.29*b*; 4.31*d*; 4.34*a*, *b*, *d*, *h*)

*Lines barbed (Fig. 4.34*g*)

*Lines barbed, with fret fill (Fig. 4.31*c–e*)

**Lines, flagged triangles (Figs. 4.31*c*; 4.36*b*)

**Plaited band as a motif (Fig. 4.30*a*)

Fringe: on square scrolls (Fig. 4.37*b*)

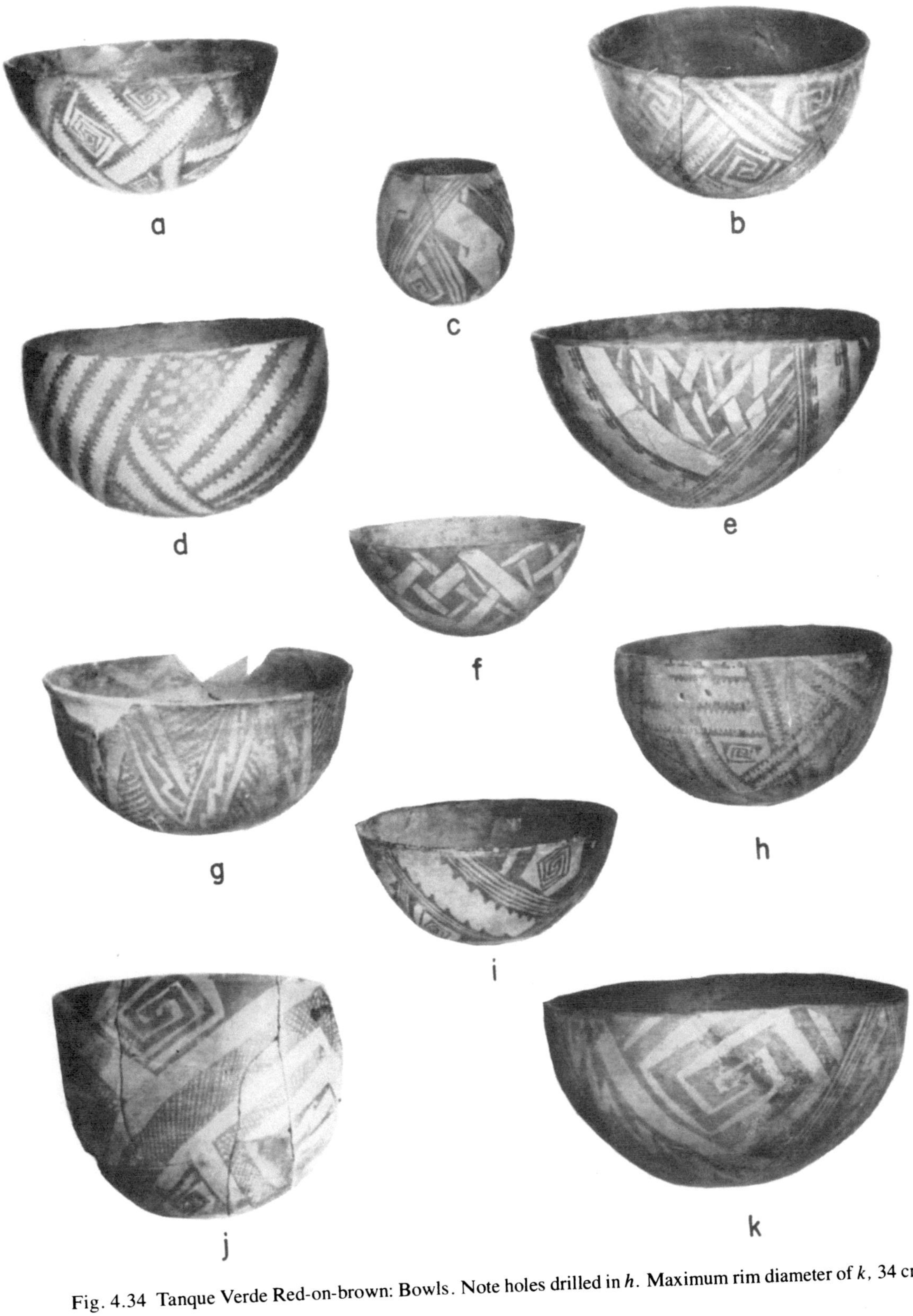

Fig. 4.34 Tanque Verde Red-on-brown: Bowls. Note holes drilled in *h*. Maximum rim diameter of *k*, 34 cm.

Fig. 4.35 Tanque Verde Red-on-brown: Bowls. Note use of square and interlocking scrolls and opposed pendants. Maximum rim diameter of *i*, 36 cm.

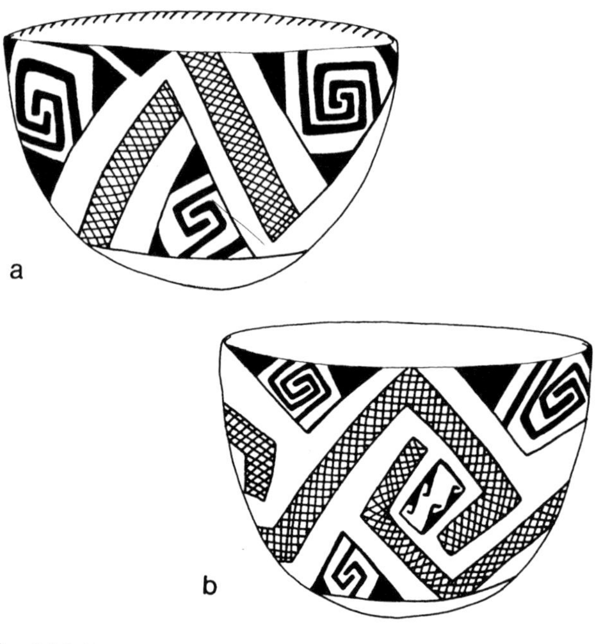

Fig. 4.36 Tanque Verde Red-on-brown: Bowls. *a*, banded, opposed pendants; *b*, banded, figured and repeated, interlocking.

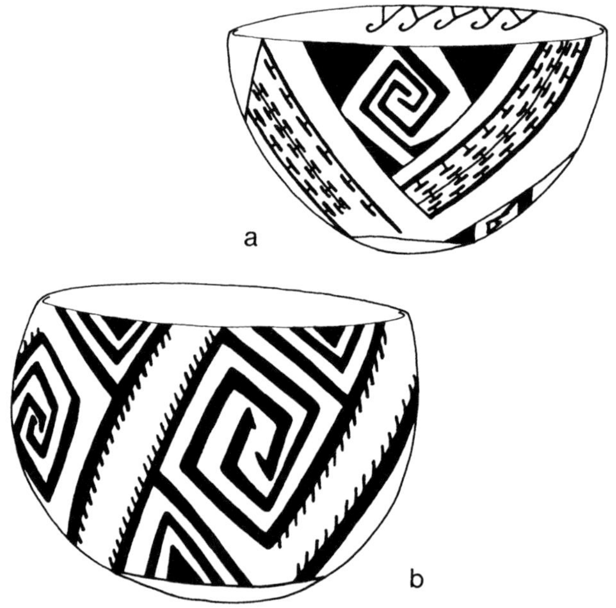

Fig. 4.37 Tanque Verde Red-on-brown: Bowls. *a*, banded, opposed pendants; *b*, banded, figured and repeated, interlocking.

SURFACE TREATMENT

Surfaces are unslipped and polished. Bowl decoration has shifted completely from the interior to the exterior, automatically eliminating trailing lines and other subsidiary exterior treatment. Save for borders, there is but one example of interior bowl decoration (not illustrated), and this specimen also is exterior decorated. Bowl interiors are characteristically (62 percent) smudged, frequently with narrow to medium-width interior painted borders. A series of the latter, comprising almost the complete range, is shown in Figure 4.38.

Interior jar finish is variable; smudging is less frequent than on bowls, appearing deliberate on about 25 percent of

Fig. 4.38 Tanque Verde Red-on-brown: Interior bowl borders

jars. Sometimes jar interiors are well smoothed; sometimes they are left rough, with anvil depressions noticeable. Interiors of jar necks are normally undecorated. Because of height, exteriors of jar necks offer a ready field for banded designs. They are painted in characteristic Tanque Verde motifs, but on a smaller scale than major body decoration (Fig. 4.39).

REMARKS

Stylistically there is evident discontinuity between Tanque Verde Red-on-brown and preceding pottery styles. This break may be summarized as follows: certain changes in vessel form, a shift from interior to exterior decorated bowls, and a wholesale angularization of motif.

In shape the most obvious innovation is the large hemispherical bowl, exterior decorated, with interior border and interior smudging. The recurved bowl of Tanque Verde differs in proportions and in lack of shoulder from that of the Rincon phase. Incurved bowls become, for the first time, prominent. Scoops are lacking, as are outcurved bowls and normal flare-rimmed bowls. Jar shapes are modified. The shoulder continues, but in distinctive form. Jar collars show a minor cluster of new traits; often they are vertical, exterior ornamented, and lack interior rim painting. Animal effigies appear.

In design there is also divergence. Tanque Verde decoration is essentially angular, with asymmetrical elements skillfully juxtaposed. The shift to the angular is abrupt and only mildly foreshadowed in the Rincon phase. There is scarcely a survival of the heretofore dominant scroll, and then only occasionally, as the plumed tip of a triangle. Despite a sharp reduction in the actual number of motifs, the design itself becomes, if anything, more complex, more highly integrated and formalized.

Nevertheless, there is ample precedent in earlier phases for the fundamental pendant unit of the Tanque Verde complex, inasmuch as a similar form results naturally from the sectoring of bowl interiors (Fig. 4.23*a*, *i*, for example). The pendant-shaped element of the Rillito and Rincon phases usually is scroll-filled and is flanked by

Fig. 4.39 Tanque Verde Red-on-brown: Exterior jar necks. Interior of jar necks characteristically undecorated.

chevron hatch, while in Tanque Verde Red-on-brown the scroll is squared and a band replaces the hachure. It has been noted above that opposed and overlapping pendant arrangements relate to the general pattern of offsetting, which appears in the Rincon phase, with offset quartering and the plaited band. Therefore, upon closer inspection, the fundamentals of Tanque Verde phase ornament are to be found in the Rincon phase.

Tanque Verde Red-on-brown has broad stylistic parallels in Casa Grande Red-on-buff of the Gila Basin. There, too, a shift from curvilinear to rectangular takes place, with some resemblance in precise motif: barbed lines, longitudinally hatched bands, and square scrolls. But the prevailing Tanque Verde Red-on-brown vessel form, the hemispherical bowl, is without counterpart in the Gila Basin; indeed, no bowl forms are known from the Soho phase (Gladwin and Gladwin 1933: 22). Jars in both cases have vertical collars; Tanque Verde jars are perhaps more consistently shouldered, a trait which appears to be dying out in the Soho phase. On the whole, from what little is known of Soho, its red-on-buff type appears as poor and decadent, while Tanque Verde Red-on-brown is without question still a vigorous ceramic style.

However, the most striking Tanque Verde resemblances are found, not in Casa Grande Red-on-buff, of the Soho and Civano phases, but in San Carlos Red-on-brown. In certain typical shapes and in design treatment the resemblance amounts to virtual identity, except for the fact that San Carlos vessels invariably are smaller than Tanque Verde and that the designs and brush work accordingly are more delicate. At first sight San Carlos appears a miniature version of Tanque Verde Red-on-brown. Upon closer inspection, however, San Carlos Red-on-brown proves to include a wider range of shapes, but the typical Tanque Verde jar is represented and, among bowls, hemispherical shapes are dominant. The latter are proportionately shallower than Tanque Verde; they have the same smudged interiors, but lack the typical Tanque Verde interior borders. In design there is marked agreement: the plaited band arrangement and opposed and overlapping pendants are frequent. In motif, there is the same preference for the plaited band filler, for interlocking square scrolls, for flagged triangles, for barbed and picoted lines, and for bands filled with longitudinal hatch.

These precise resemblances bespeak a common origin, reverberations of which reached the Gila Basin. In fact, in Tanque Verde Red-on-brown, in San Carlos Red-on-brown, and in Casa Grande Red-on-buff, there is evidently a tripartite manifestation of essentially the same decorative complex. The resemblances are so marked that the relationship must have been direct. However, definitive antecedents are difficult to locate. When a transition between the San Simon and San Carlos phases is known, it may provide a background from which the style could have crystallized. Consistently smudged interiors and preoccupation with the geometric, which characterize both San Carlos and Tanque Verde Red-on-brown, suggest Mogollon ancestry. So also does the polish and absence of buff slip. But Casa Grande Red-on-buff conforms only in jar shape and design; it has the characteristic Gila Basin slip and matte color and is not smudged.

Further evidence of Mogollon persuasion is provided by Salado redware (Gladwin and Gladwin 1930: Plate 7), whose smudged interiors affiliate as does its design treatment. In the latter, however, resemblances are somewhat restricted. Pendant arrangement is common, but the pendants seldom are opposed and are not offset; barbed and picoted lines are plentiful, as is longitudinal hatch; but the diagnostic interlocking square scroll is entirely wanting. Nevertheless, it may be significant that some of the non-Tanque Verde jar shapes that occur in San Carlos Red-on-brown have parallels in Salado redware.

Tanque Verde Red-on-brown, Casa Grande Red-on-buff, and the painted variant of Salado redware appear at about the same time, but San Carlos Red-on-brown is effectively later, nearly always occurring in association with polychrome. Because of the time element, San Carlos Red-on-brown cannot be considered a potential source of the complex. If material intervening between the San Simon and San Carlos phases proves negative, perhaps San Carlos might be regarded as a convergence of influence from both Salado redware and Tanque Verde Red-on-brown.

Geographically Tanque Verde Red-on-brown is peripheral to Mogollon as it is to Hohokam. It would be singular if, after having adhered to Gila Basin decorative patterns for close to a thousand years, the Tucson area suddenly developed a distinctive geometric style which thereupon left its imprint upon a collateral Mogollon type. The fact that the decorated type of the Gila Basin Classic period also adheres, at least in jar shape and in design, must not be overlooked. Although both Tanque Verde Red-on-brown and Casa Grande Red-on-buff have certain antecedents in their respective Sedentary periods, the shift to the Classic pottery is, nevertheless, abrupt and without real transition. Internal evidence implies that the basic complex was developed neither at the Hodges site nor at any known site in the Gila Basin. Thus attention is again focused upon the gap between the San Simon and San Carlos phases.

Comparison with Hohokam and Mogollon Decorated Ceramics

This concludes the descriptive sections on decorated pottery. The following figures give a perspective of the local development in vessel form, in design layout, in motif, and in subsidiary decorative treatment. These charts speak for themselves and little discussion is necessary. [*Ed. note:* Figure 4.40 illustrates vessel form, and Figure 4.41 shows motifs. The other illustrations could not be completed because of missing specimens.]

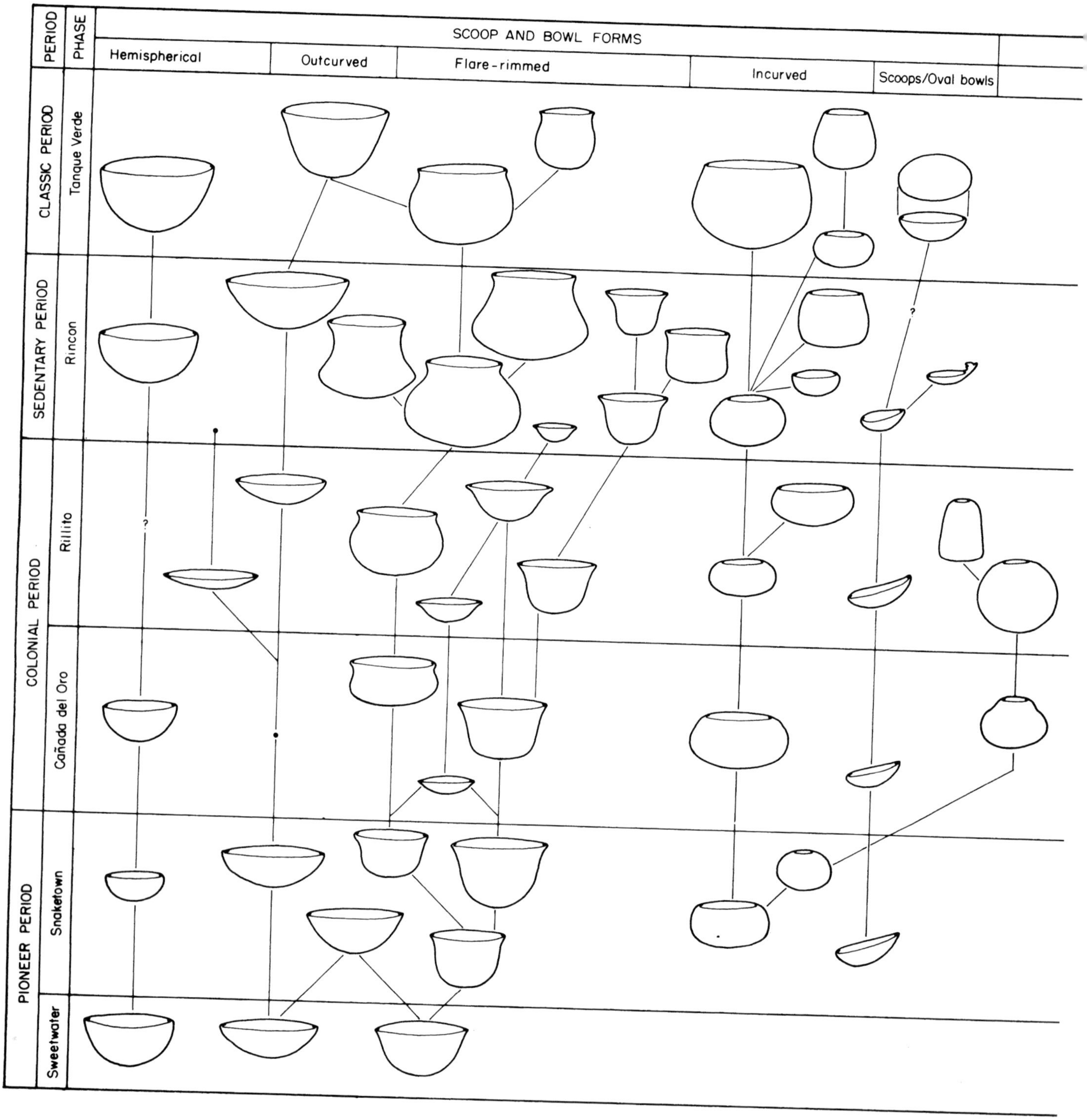

Fig. 4.40 Developmental chart of decorated vessel forms

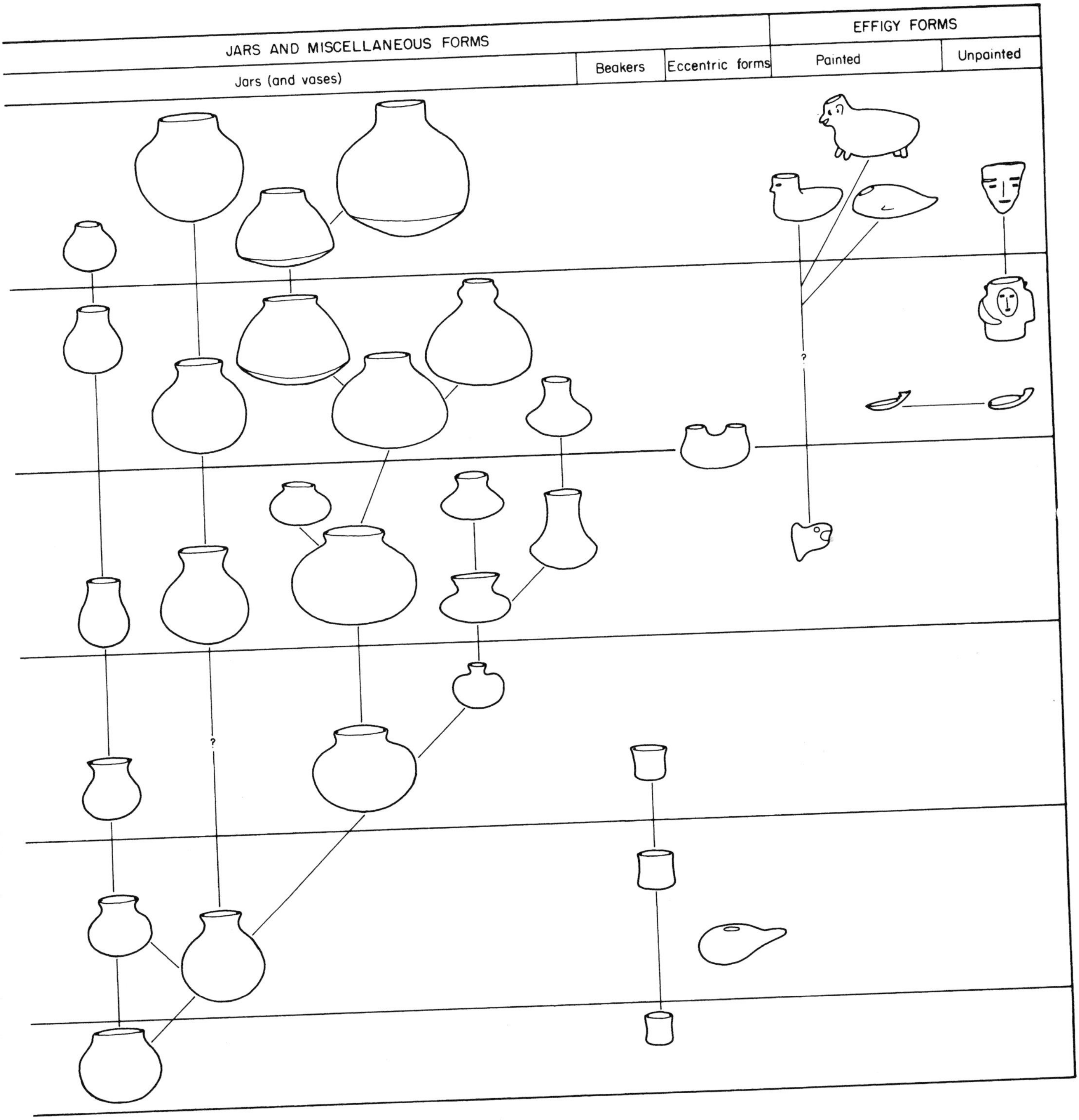

Fig. 4.40 Developmental chart of decorated vessel forms (cont'd)

Concerning form, prototypes of all the major bowl shapes occur in the Pioneer period. Jars also can be traced to the Pioneer period, although the material is scanty and inadequate. With each succeeding phase come specialization and variation; it will be noted that the Rillito phase is particularly rich in jar forms and the Rincon phase in bowl forms.

A comparison of Figure 4.40 with Figure 110 of the Snaketown report (Gladwin and others 1937) indicates a close agreement in major vessel forms as well as in their chronological succession. Some of the outstanding resemblances and contrasts have been summarized in Table 4.11, in which the solid column represents the Gila Basin occurrence, the hatched column the Hodges occurrence.

Several conclusions can be drawn from this comparison. Although in general there is close agreement, ceramics at the Hodges site are somewhat more restricted in shape, lacking the rectangular bowl, the handled scoop, legged vessels, heavy-walled, and multiple vessels. These presumably are Hohokam products that did not penetrate southward. Heavy-walled vessels occur at Tucson, but seem always to be Sacaton Red-on-buff. One fragment only, which from its hatched ornament evidently is of the Snaketown phase, might conceivably be of local manufacture. Inasmuch as the Gila Basin and Hodges aspects of the Snaketown phase are indistinguishable, it seems unwarranted to attribute heavy-walled vessels to the Hodges site on the strength of this single occurrence. One form only, the bottle-necked jar, occurs at Tucson and is without counterpart in the Gila Basin. Represented by a lone specimen, it is probably best regarded as a sport. To be sure, certain Rincon phase bowl shapes are peculiar to the Hodges site, but these are minor variations of major bowl forms common to both areas.

From Figure 4.40 it will be seen that the various vessel forms either are coincident as to phase or that the Hodges appearance shows a slight but consistent time lag. This and the more restricted range in vessel form at Hodges, reinforce the suspicion that the Tucson series as a whole is essentially dependent upon Gila Basin inspiration, and not vice versa.

A close relationship holds for design layout as well as for shape (see Gladwin and others 1937: Fig. 111 for design layout in the Gila Basin; Hodges design layout is not illustrated). By and large the two series are strictly comparable. Perhaps the most noteworthy difference is the weakness of sectioning at Hodges. There is no recognizable occurrence prior to the Cañada del Oro phase, and even then, only one example. Interesting and inexplicable is the absence at Hodges of centered, figured patterns and of vertically paneled jars.

In individual motif the same relationship obtains (compare Figure 4.41 with Gladwin and others 1937: Fig. 112). The weakness of life forms at Hodges, in particular the virtual absence of human representation, already has been mentioned. In this regard Hodges is intermediate between the Gila Basin, where such motifs are highly developed, and the Mogollon area, where they are completely lacking. Otherwise the assemblage of design elements is very much the same at Hodges and in the Gila Basin, and an intimate relationship between the two areas cannot be doubted. Although not evident in Figure 112 of the Snaketown report, the abrupt change in design that comes with the Classic period holds equally for the Gila Basin and the Hodges site. These Classic resemblances have been mentioned previously, in discussing the decorated types of the Tanque Verde phase.

Likewise parallel is the exterior treatment of bowls (see Gladwin and others 1937: Fig. 111, far right column). In both areas there is a gradual decline, with a reduction of ornament from hatched triangles, through trailing lines, to undecorated surface. And, although not indicated in the figure, exterior scoring in both areas is strong until the Colonial period, when it declines, and by late Colonial times it has disappeared entirely. Further parallels are to be seen in the ornamentation of interior rims of jars and of other exterior decorated vessels (Gladwin and others 1937: Fig. 112, far right column). This consists essentially of a progression from hatched triangles, to fringing, to solid triangles. In the Tanque Verde phase, for which we have no comparable Gila Basin material, interior borders become increasingly prominent, and frequently they perpetuate motifs substantially of earlier occurrence and otherwise little utilized in Tanque Verde times.

To summarize, an exceedingly intimate relationship exists between the decorated types at the Hodges site and in the Gila Basin and is manifested in form, in design arrangement, in motif, and in subsidiary ornament. On the whole, analogous traits appear to be contemporaneous in both areas; Hodges may exhibit a slight lag in vessel form, although this lag is less apparent in other regards. All things considered, it is inescapable that the Tucson manifestation was inspired by the Gila Basin and not the reverse.

Nevertheless, the very pronounced Gila Basin influence does not obscure the fundamental Mogollon affinities of the Hodges red-on-brown types. The Mogollon relationship is less easily demonstrable, for it consists of such traits as close-grained rather than porous paste; polished surfaces, with an absence of matte slip; permanent rather than fugitive red pigment; smudging as a deliberate device; and, despite Gila Basin influence, a certain preference for geometric ornament.

In the phases of the Pioneer period, Hodges and Hohokam types are indistinguishable, and, typologically at least, Mogollon types are not far removed. Beginning with the Colonial period, Hodges and the Gila Basin diverge, and Hodges follows a line of development intermediate between Mogollon and Hohokam. During the Colonial and Sedentary periods, the Gila Basin obviously impresses vessel shape and decoration on Hodges. Curiously

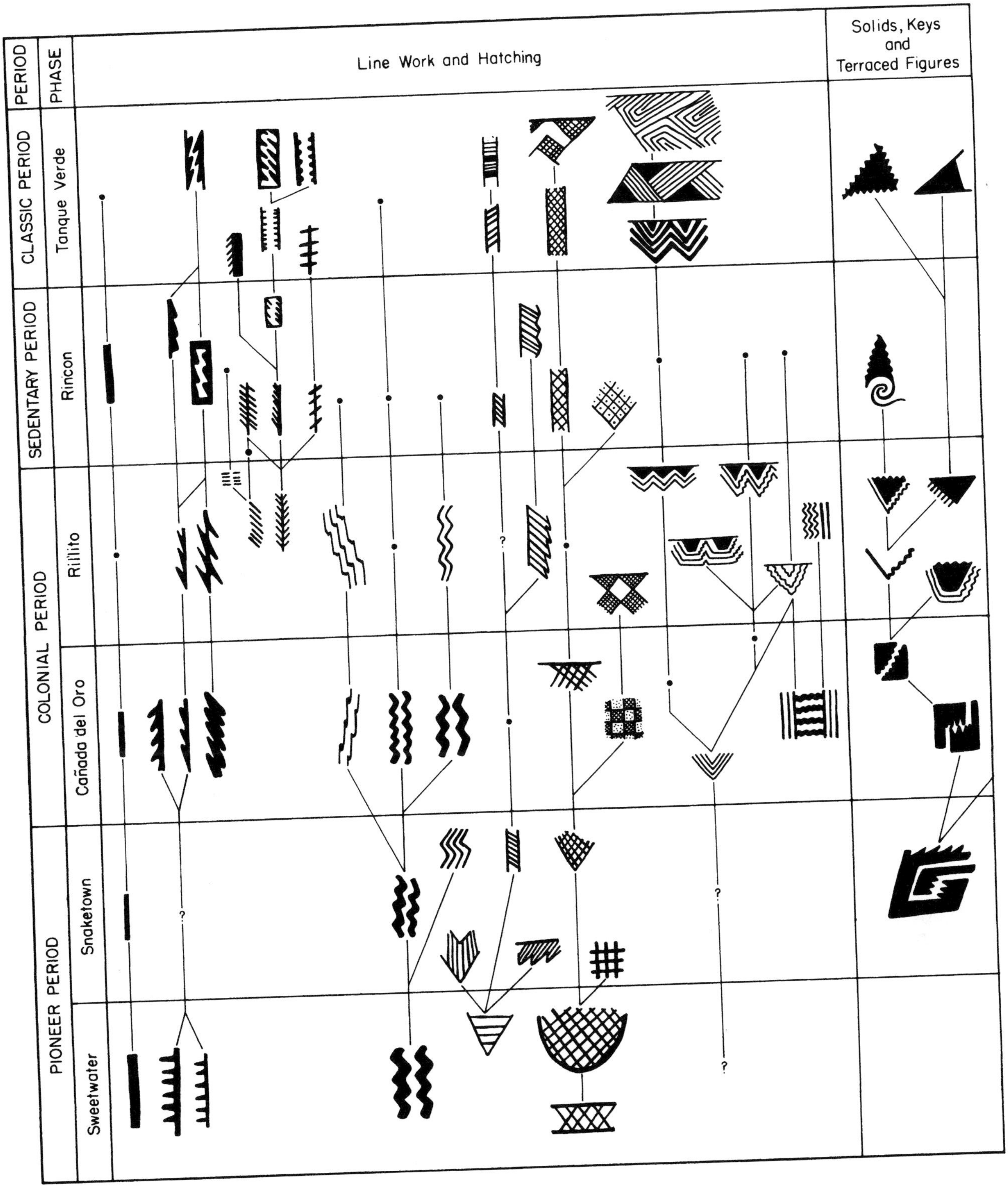

Fig. 4.41 Developmental chart of motifs (cont'd)

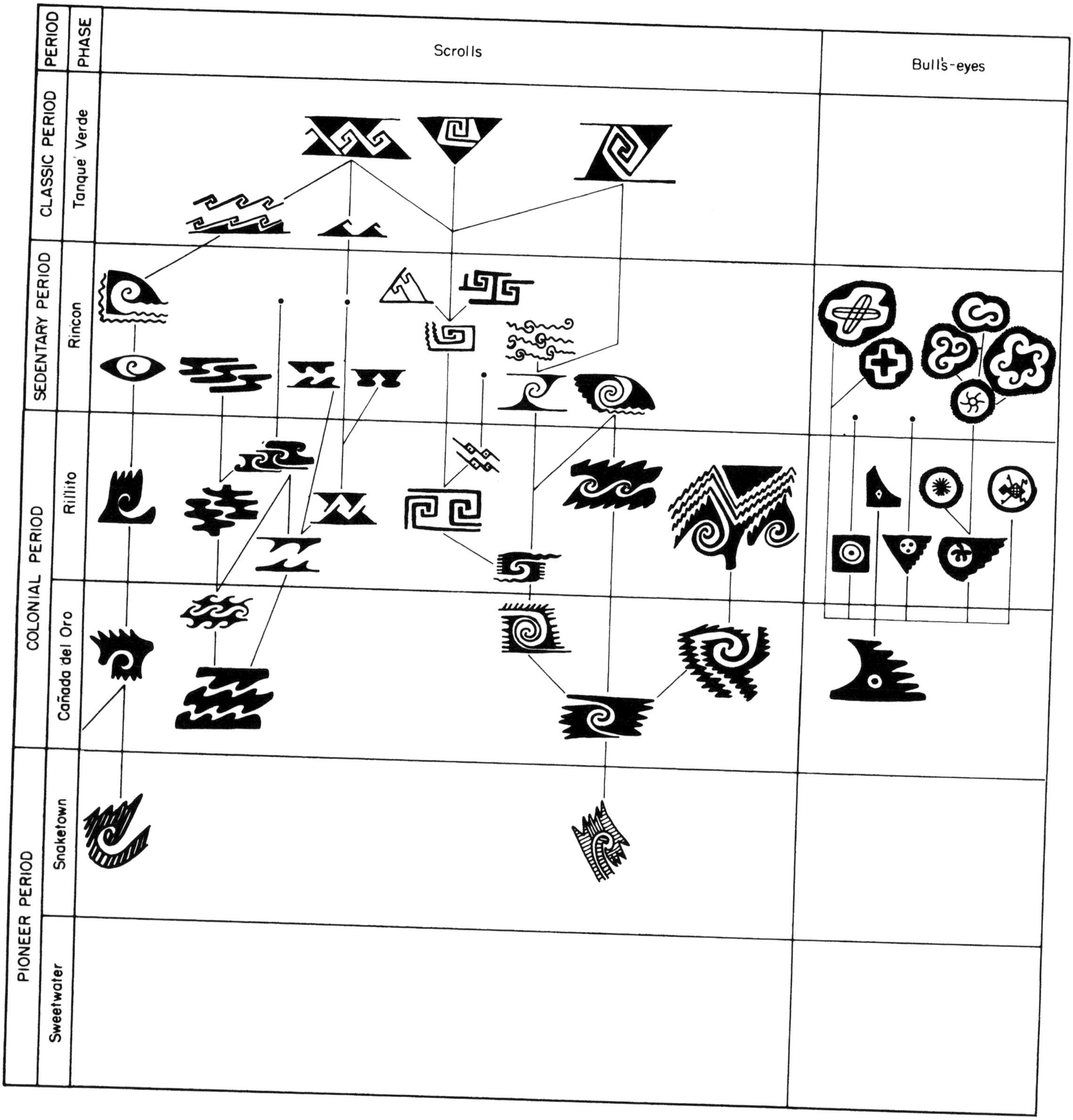

Fig. 4.41 Developmental chart of motifs

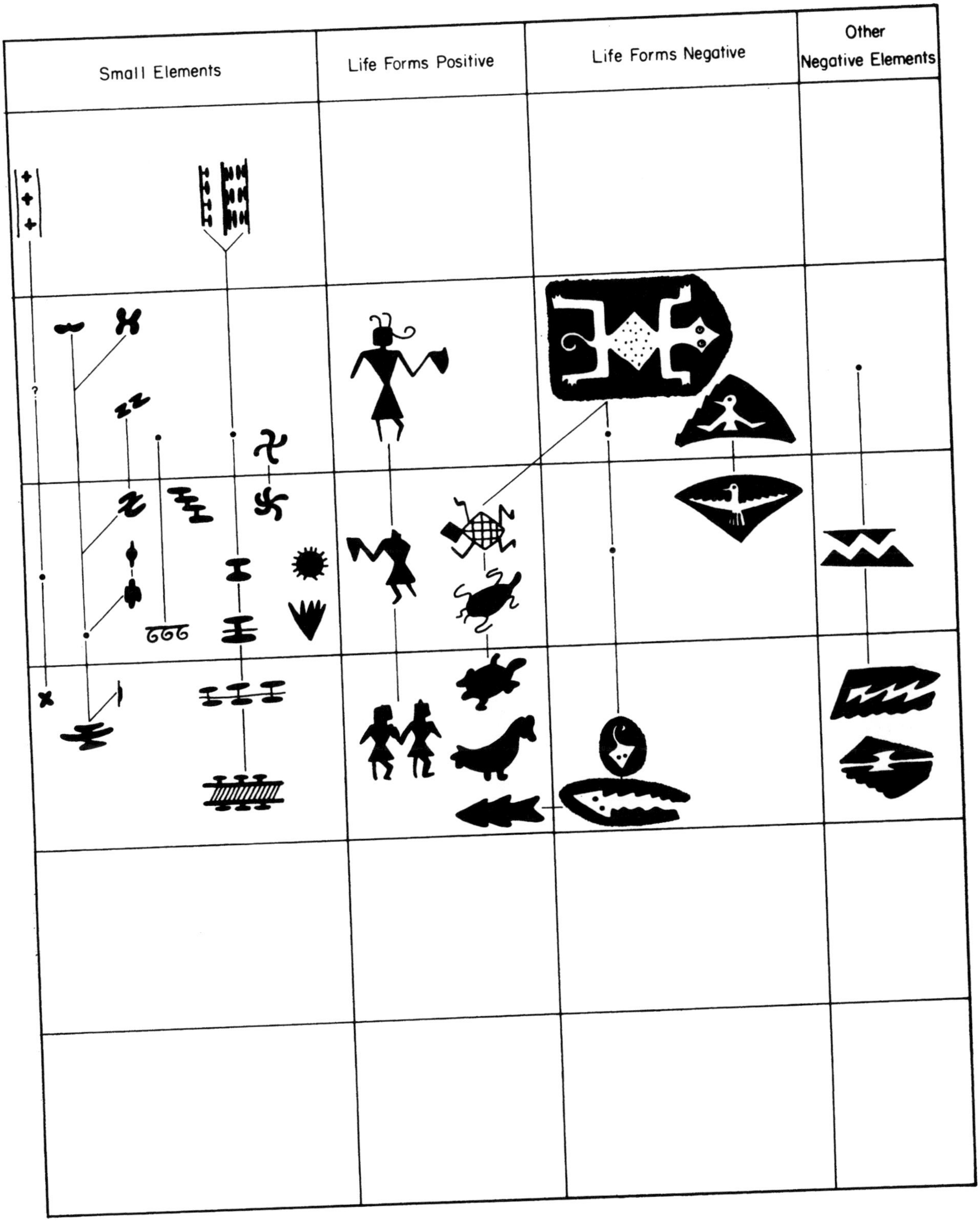

Fig. 4.41 Developmental chart of motifs

TABLE 4.11

Phase Distribution of Certain Decorated Vessel Forms in the Gila Basin and at the Hodges Site

(Dark gray column, Gila Basin occurrence; light gray column, Hodges occurrence)

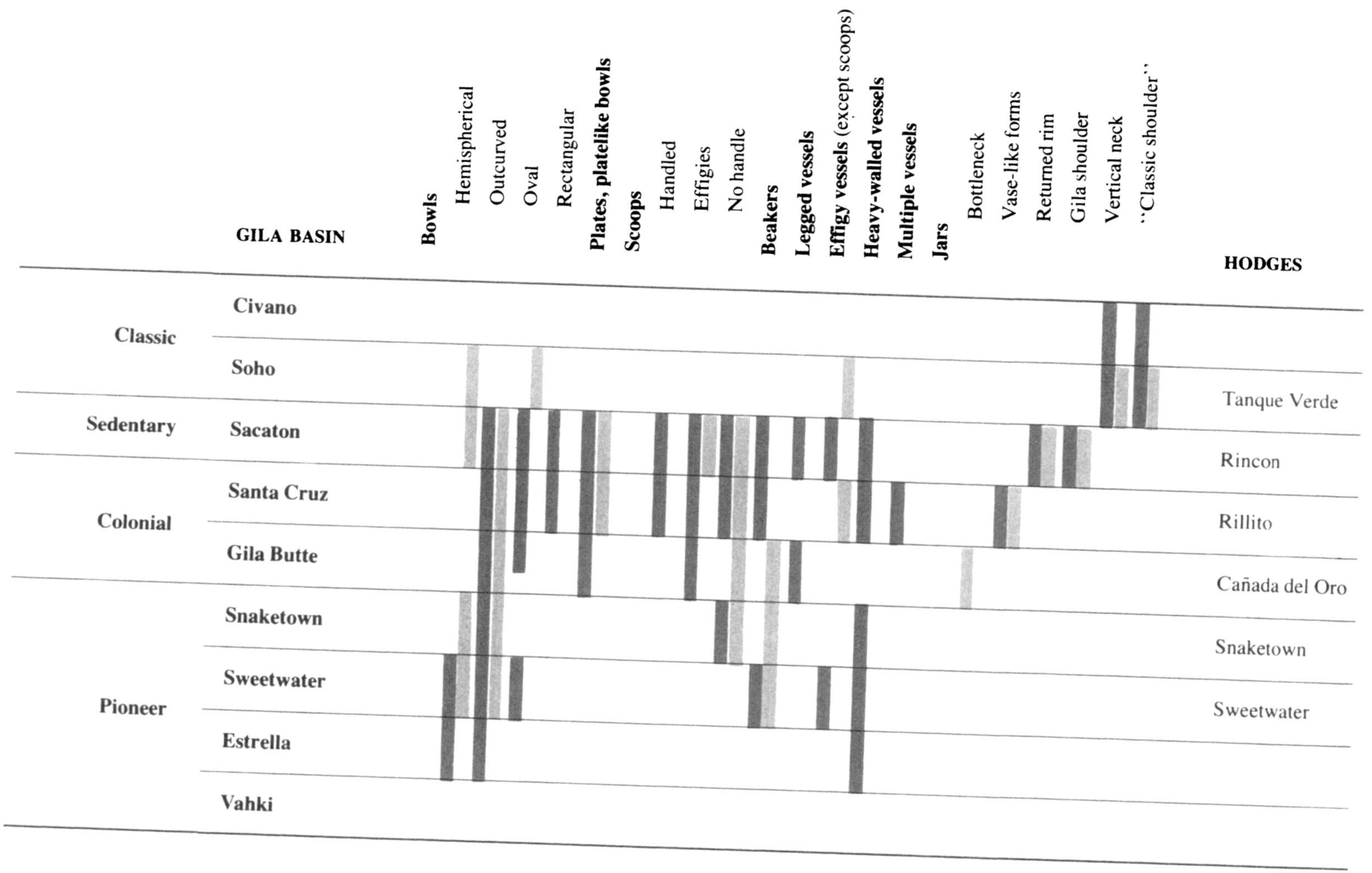

enough, however, life forms and small elements diffuse only moderately, perhaps because of a fundamentally Mogollon preference for the geometric. At any rate, Mogollon resemblances become more pronounced, with the progressive increase of smudging during the Sedentary and Classic periods, and, during the Classic period, in the abandonment of all but geometric, non-curvilinear ornament.

All told, in ceramics as in many other regards, Hodges holds the middle ground between Hohokam and Mogollon, having obvious ties with both, but being neither one nor the other.

REDWARE

Pioneer Period, Snaketown Phase

Five sherds and two restorable redware vessels occur in association with Snaketown phase ceramics. One of the vessels (not illustrated) is a hemispherical bowl, the exterior lightly washed in red, the interior an unsmoothed cream. This redware specimen is from a cremation whose only decorated specimen was the gourd-shaped dipper shown in Figure 4.6*a*. The somewhat dubious allocation of this dipper to the Snaketown phase has been discussed in the section on Snaketown Red-on-brown. We suspect the redware bowl to be intrusive; it appears to have undergone second firing and cannot be recognized as to type.

Of the remaining redware of Snaketown phase association, only two pieces are of discernible shape: a low, apparently outcurved bowl (Fig. 4.42*l*) and a deep bowl with what may be called a semi-flaring rim (Fig. 4.42*m*). None of the material shows any noticeable resemblance to either Vahki Red or San Francisco Red, but the series is too small for valid comparison. We have not attempted to name the redware of this phase, for several types may be represented; at least, each sherd differs slightly from the others. The restorable bowl shown in Figure 4.42*m* has a gray to black exterior and a decidedly maroon interior; the exterior is horizontally wiped, and the interior has at least a suggestion of dimpling. Incidence of vessel form for Snaketown and later phases are shown in Table 4.12.

Colonial Period, Rillito Phase

Evidence of redware during the Colonial period is confined to two sherds found in Rillito phase association. One, the base sherd of a heavy bowl, is not unlike the type defined below as Rincon Red, although less polished. The other fragment is from a jar apparently with a tall, flaring collar; this form is completely anomalous.

These two sherds are scarcely sufficient evidence for regarding redware as a Colonial characteristic. An absence of redware during the Colonial period is in accord with findings in the Gila Basin.

Sedentary Period, Rincon Phase

RINCON REDWARE

In the Rincon phase, a well-defined redware style appears. From cremations definitely identifiable as Rincon come seven entire or restorable redware vessels; and from Rincon trash, three large sherds. Similar fragments occur frequently, but in mixed association. However, they accord well with the Rincon series both in surface finish and in shape.

Rincon Red is of coarse, granular paste, usually sand in color and generally non-micaceous. The surface finish is good to excellent; exterior, interior, or both may be highly polished. What, with further data, might prove to be a separate redware type tends to be less highly polished and more micaceous. The red of Rincon is clear and deep, but sometimes through weathering it becomes powdery and fugitive; the surface tends to pit and flake in weathering.

The range in shape is shown in Figure 4.42*d–i*. There are no jars. Specimen *h* is a deep incurved bowl, with a shoulder; interior finish indicates that the orifice was relatively open. Another bowl, *i*, has a true flare rim.

On the whole, the characteristic form of Rincon Red is a simple bowl, either outcurved or hemispherical. The interiors of such bowls generally are a uniform red, without firing clouds; exteriors vary from tan to red and almost always are clouded. Horizontal stroking marks are prominent on exteriors and are generally less noticeable on interiors.

A flare-rim bowl of redware, but unplaced, may be mentioned here. The interior is polished red, the exterior predominantly tan, with heavy black firing clouds. Both surfaces, but especially the exterior, are dimpled. This device at once suggests Mogollon affinities, and the piece may well be intrusive. Although it cannot be placed definitely in the local chronology, it accompanied a burial which in turn lay beneath a heavy cache of Rincon phase pottery. It cannot therefore be later than Rincon, and it may be earlier. A sherd, not in pure Rincon phase association but probably Rincon Red, suggests that scoops also were manufactured.

Classic Period, Tanque Verde Phase

Such redware as appears in association with the Tanque Verde phase shows no evidence of a Rincon heritage. It is highly probable that the two redwares described below were developed elsewhere.

SAN CARLOS REDWARE

The redware most frequent during the Tanque Verde phase is what Haury is designating as San Carlos Redware. [*Ed. Note:* For a more recent description of this ware see Steen and others 1962:19.] This ware evidently appears at Tucson first during the Tanque Verde phase but survives

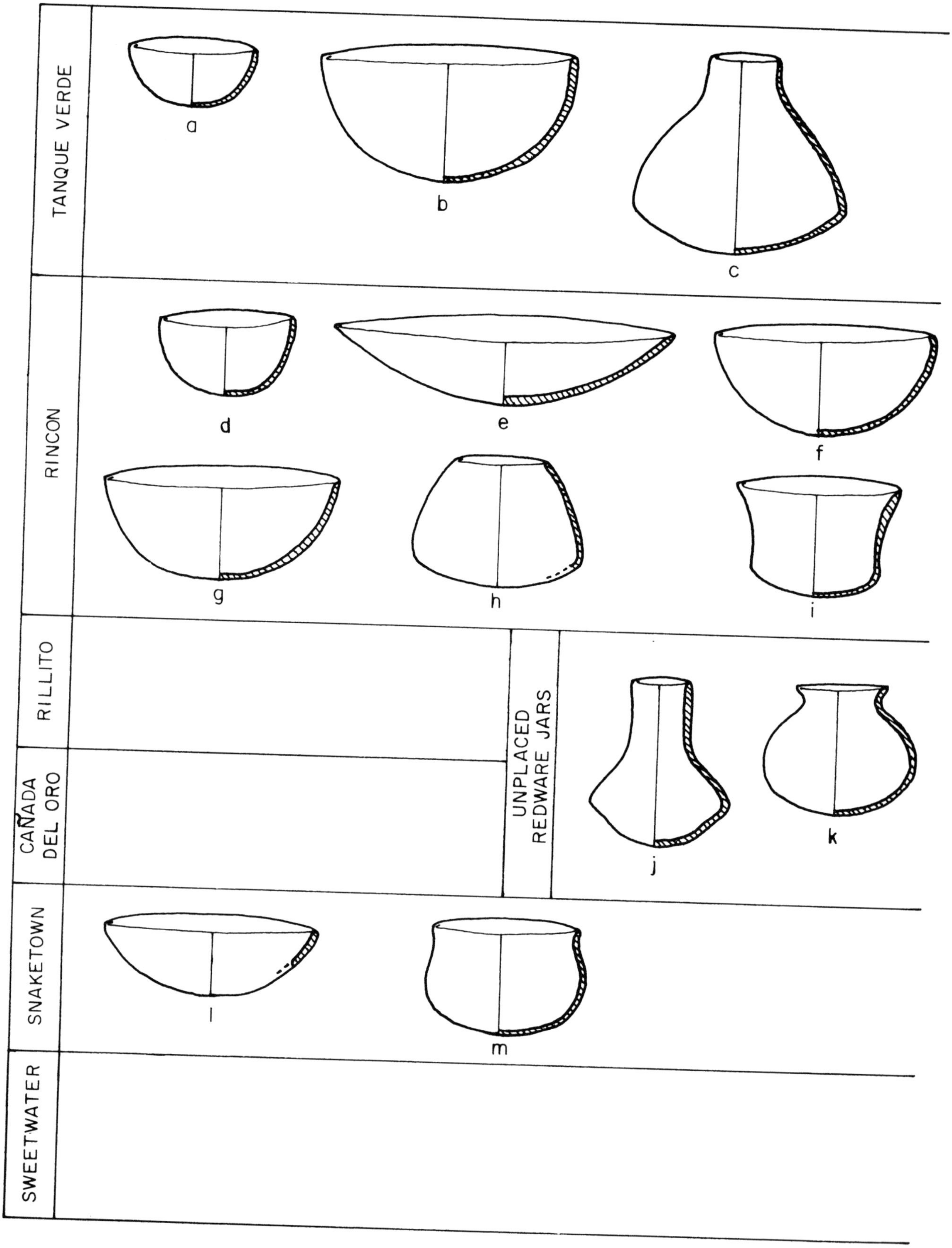

Fig. 4.42 Redware shapes. *Tanque Verde phase: a, b,* hemispherical bowls; *c,* shouldered jar. *Rincon phase: d, f, g,* hemispherical bowls; *e,* outcurved bowl; *h,* deep, incurved, shouldered bowl; *i,* flare-rim bowl. *Unplaced: j, k,* unplaced jars. *Snaketown phase: l,* outcurved bowl; *m,* semi-flare rim bowl.

into the succeeding phase, which is represented at the University Ruin. Forms are confined to hemispherical bowls, varying from 16- to 20-cm diameter at the rim (Fig. 4.42*a*). Vessel walls are excessively thin and uniformly so, except for frequent thickening at the base. The rim usually is squared. The exterior is mottled, from tan to rose red, frequently with black firing clouds. The interior is mostly black, and so consistently so that interior smoking must have been deliberate. Both surfaces are highly polished and sometimes are inconspicuously wiped. The type has a definite thin and satiny feel; it flakes somewhat with weathering.

GILA REDWARE

Also in association with the Tanque Verde phase are several vessels which strongly suggest Gila Redware (Gladwin and Gladwin 1930: 12-15, Plates IX–XI). These consist of three large hemispherical bowls and one jar (Fig. 4.42 *b*, *c*). Bowl diameters range from 25 to 45 cm; rims are squared. The exteriors are tan to red, with firing clouds; interiors are black. The one jar is rather squat, with a low, not very marked shoulder and a tall, straight collar. Both the bowls and jar contain a certain amount of mica and, except for one bowl, are conspicuously wiped.

Unplaced Redware

Above are outlined the instances of redware that can be identified as to phase. On the whole, redware is weak at Hodges and is definitely attributable to three phases only: Snaketown, Rincon, and Tanque Verde. The Snaketown redware is motley; the Rincon and Tanque Verde styles are consistent and well defined as to surface, finish, and shape.

In addition, small sherds of redware crop up from time to time in mixed association. Many indubitably are Rincon Red. But there is a very wide range in surface and in color, although sherds almost invariably are too small for a determination of shape. Two unclassified redware jars are shown in Figure 4.42*j*, *k*. On typological grounds, *j* is almost certainly of the Classic period.

PLAINWARE

A general summary of plainware forms is shown in Figure 4.43; incidence is given in Table 4.13. Included are almost all determinable shapes definitely attributable to phase. While there are few restorable jars from the earliest phases, there is a small series of rims whose range is shown in Figures 4.44, 4.45, and 4.47. Also, the supposed mortuary vessels of the Rillito phase are rather variable in form and are shown in Figure 4.46.

We have preferred not to designate the local plainware by any particular name, comparable to the Gila Plain of the Gila Basin. The series is too diverse to be included under one caption, and differences from phase to phase are not sufficiently marked to justify separate type groupings. For the Tanque Verde phase alone there are certain vessel forms

TABLE 4.12
Redware: Incidence of Vessel Form

Form	Fig. 4.42 (part)	Occurrence	Total
PIONEER PERIOD, Snaketown Phase			7
Outcurved bowl	*l*	1	
Semi-flare-rim bowl	*m*	1	
Rimless sherds, indeterminate shape		4	
Mogollon intrusive bowl (not illustrated)		1	
SEDENTARY PERIOD, Rincon Phase:			10
Rincon Redware			
Hemispherical bowls	*d*, *f*, *g*	5	
Outcurved bowls	*e*	3	
Deep, incurved, shouldered bowl	*h*	1	
Flare-rim bowl	*i*	1	
CLASSIC PERIOD, Tanque Verde Phase			14
San Carlos Redware, hemispherical bowls	*a*	10	
Gila Redware, hemispherical bowls	*b*	3	
Gila Redware, shouldered jar[a]	*c*	1	
UNPLACED Redwares	*j*, *k*	2	2
Total			33

[a] There is one further specimen, from a cremation, with no associated decorated type. [*Ed. note:* The additional specimen is probably from Cremation 90.]

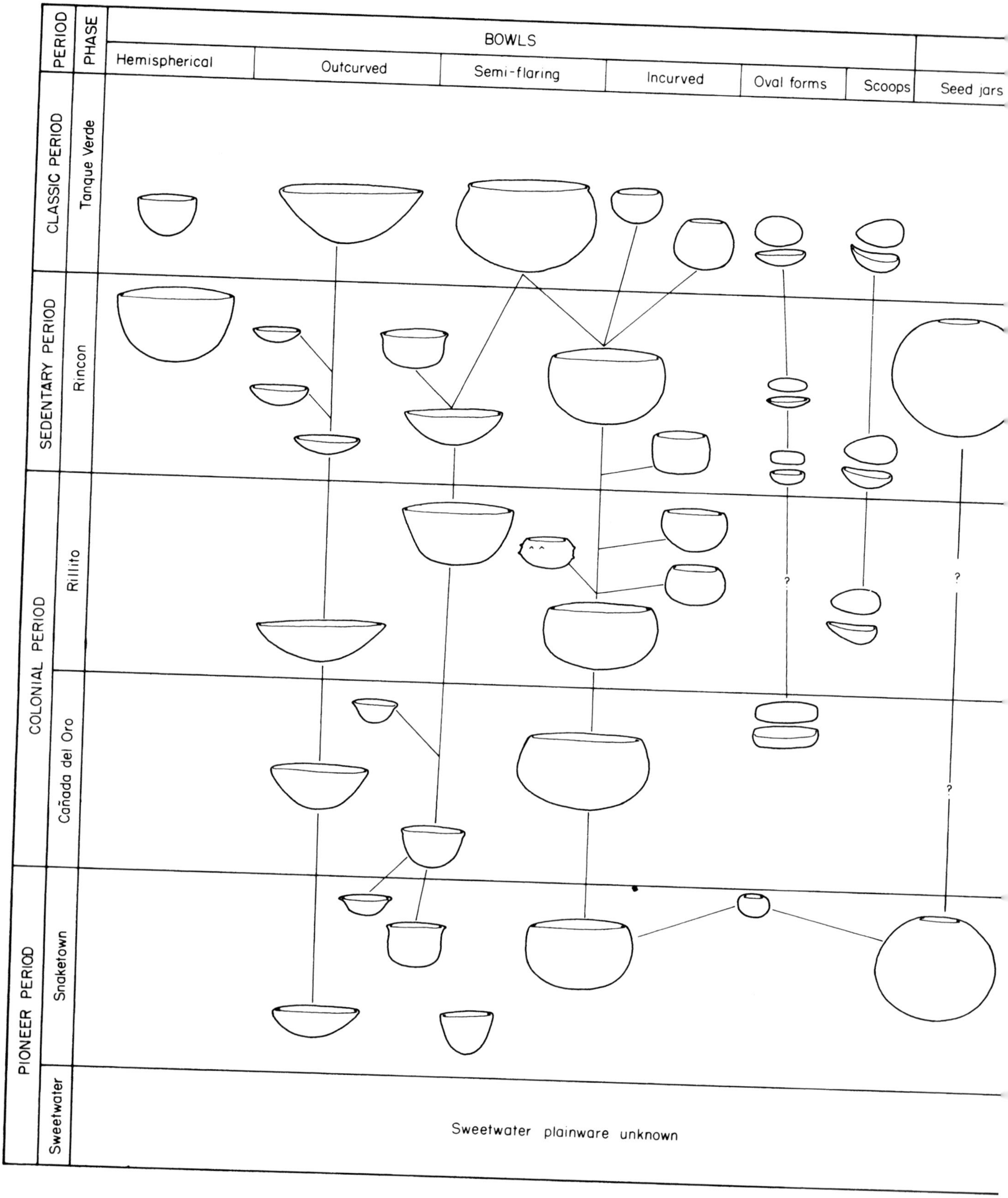

Fig. 4.43 Developmental chart of plainware forms

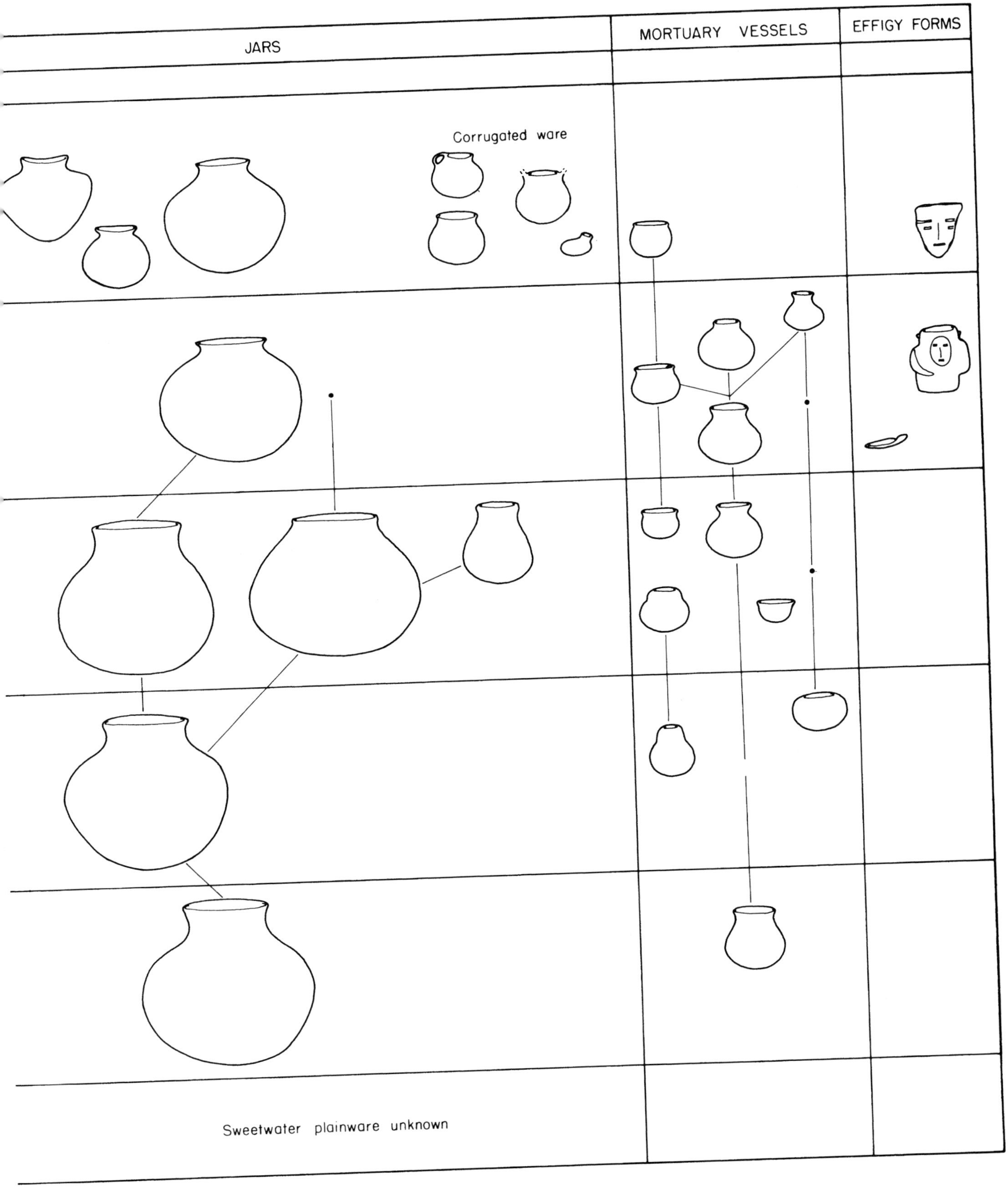

Fig. 4.43 Developmental chart of plainware forms (cont'd)

TABLE 4.13
Plainware: Incidence of Vessel Form
(see also Fig. 4.43)

Form	Incidence	Total	Form	Incidence	Total
Snaketown Phase			*Rincon Phase*		
Bowls			Bowls		
Outcurved	4		Hemispherical	1	
Semi-flaring	5		Outcurved	12	
Sub-conic	1		Semi-flaring	7	
Incurved	4		Incurved	4	
Seed bowl	1		Oval	2	
Jars	16		Scoops	3	
Seed jars	3		Jars	39	
Mortuary vessels	1	35	Seed jars	3	
Cañada del Oro Phase			Mortuary vessels		
Bowls			Incurved bowls	6	
Outcurved	1		Jars	10	
Semi-flaring	1		Effigy forms	2	
Beveled lip	1		Not illustrated		
Incurved	1		Miniature vessels	2	
Boat-shaped	1		Secondary vessel	1	92
Jars	5		*Tanque Verde Phase*		
Mortuary vessels			Bowls		
Incurved bowl	1		Hemispherical	1	
Jar, eccentric	1		Outcurved	1	
Not illustrated			Semi-flaring	2	
Miniature vessels	3		Incurved	2	
Secondary vessel	1	16	Oval (handled?)	1	
Rillito Phase			Scoops	2	
Bowls			Jars		
Outcurved	4		Lipped	3	
Semi-flaring	3		Handled (?)	1	
Incurved	8		Open-mouthed	1	
Incurved, hobnail	1		Handled jugs	2	
Scoops	2		Boot-shaped	1	
Jars	14		Mortuary vessel (?)	1	
Mortuary vessels (Fig. 4.46)	22		Effigy form	1	
Not illustrated			Not illustrated		
Miniature vessels	2		Jar sherd, indeterminate form	1	
Secondary vessels	4	60	Small dish	1	
			Miniature jar	1	22
			Total		225

so distinctive that one might be justified in recognizing a "Tanque Verde Plainware." But this applies to a small number of vessels, and the general run of Tanque Verde intergrades with the plainware of previous phases.

Pioneer Period, Snaketown Phase

From time to time sherds appear which closely resemble Vahki Plain of the Gila Basin. But these do not occur pure and cannot be allocated to any phase. Nor does any plainware occur in clear relationship to Sweetwater material, although from one cremation come sherds of a plain vessel in association with Sweetwater Red-on-gray. Unfortunately the piece is so warped and burned that it is impossible to tell if originally it was a scoop or an incurved bowl. This is our lone instance of a plainware vessel definitely earlier than the Snaketown phase.

The Pioneer period therefore is represented in plainware solely by the Snaketown phase. Snaketown plainware consists of four restorable bowls from cremations and 35 sherds from a deposit of pure Snaketown trash in Block 3B. The series is small and cannot be expected to be fully representative. It is surprising, therefore, that the plainware is so varied that it is difficult to find a common denominator. The paste is consistently grainy. Surface finish varies considerably; most is fine-pored and definitely nonmicaceous. There is little polish, indifferently applied. On the whole, the lot is of medium thickness. Color varies from gray and brown to black, invariably with firing clouds. But most characteristic of all is a reddish cast, ranging from pink to maroon, which seems to be the one constant feature throughout. Jars in particular may have a gray-to-brown-to-black exterior, but often the interior is rose or reddish brown. Occasionally decorated sherds of the Snaketown phase show this same rose interior. Jar interiors have inconspicuous anvil depressions.

Major shapes are shown in Figure 4.43, incidence in Table 4.13. Jar rims are illustrated in Figure 4.44. The early appearance of seed bowls and seed jars should be mentioned. Scoops do not occur, perhaps because the series is too small. It may be noted that decorated scoops were manufactured during the Snaketown phase. A peculiar sub-conical bowl form is unique, being represented by one vessel and, doubtfully, by one sherd. This shape does not occur later. Perforations indicate that crack lacing was known; it occurs as well throughout the succeeding phases.

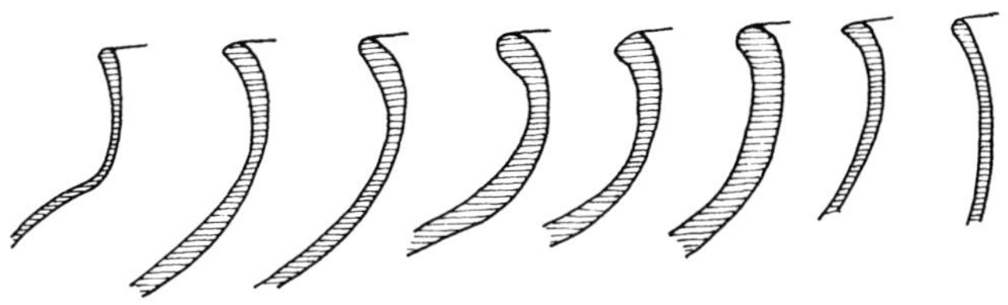

Fig. 4.44 Snaketown plainware: Jar rims

Colonial Period, Cañada del Oro Phase

Even less plainware is definitely attributable to the Cañada del Oro phase than to the Snaketown phase. For Cañada del Oro, the small series of vessels from placed cremations and houses cannot be supplemented by sherd material, for we have no pure Cañada del Oro trash. Although the large rubbish mound in Block 2X–3X is predominantly of this phase, there is sufficient admixture to make plainware affiliation uncertain. Knowledge of Cañada del Oro plainware is therefore confined to 16 restorable and near-restorable vessels.

While the series is unfortunately small, comparison to the plainware of the Snaketown phase is possible. On the whole, there is a noticeable Snaketown heritage in shape and in the rose-colored cast, which persists although it is not characteristic. The most pronounced variance is the vast increase in mica content. Unlike Snaketown plainwares, Cañada del Oro phase vessels, particularly micaceous jars, show signs of light, vertical wiping. A concomitant of the increased mica content is a surface sheen and a grainy, rather than a closed-pore surface. In thickness there is greater range than in the Snaketown phase, with cross sections varying from excessively thin to definitely thick.

The prevalence of mica and of occasional thin-walled vessels bring to mind Vahki Plain. It is most unlikely that the presence at Hodges of these two traits is to be regarded as the result of Gila Basin influence. If so, it must be remarkably retarded, and any direct influence should have manifested itself earlier, instead of in the Cañada del Oro phase, when the decorated types first begin to diverge and centuries after the discontinuance of Vahki Plain in the Gila Basin. Provided the projected dating is correct, a Gila Basin derivative for these two traits is practically out of the question.

Paste, as in the Snaketown phase, is gritty and granular. Surface color generally is mottled, with marked firing clouds. Anvil marks on jar interiors are more prominent. In one or two instances jar interiors seem to be uniformly smoked.

Major bowl shapes continue much the same. Seed bowls and jars are lacking, as are scoops. A new form is the boat-shaped dish. Jars also show relatively little change in shape; necks are open and gently flaring; rims are rounded or flattened (Fig. 4.45a–c) but not definitely squared, as are occasional Snaketown sherds.

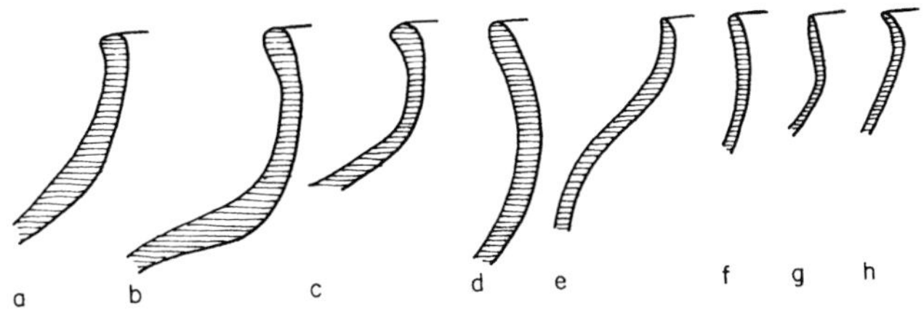

Fig. 4.45 Plainware of the Cañada del Oro and Rillito phases: Jar rims. *a–c*, Cañada del Oro; *d–h*, Rillito.

Two vessels—one a curious cinctured jar, the other an incurved bowl—have been segregated as possible mortuary vessels. Evidence of the manufacture of pottery expressly to serve as burial furniture is not strong until Rillito times, but on typological grounds, two Cañada del Oro and one Snaketown phase vessel from cremations seem sufficiently close to the Rillito series to be considered mortuary specimens. Characteristically these pieces are excessively thin, micaceous, and wiped.

In the Cañada del Oro phase comes the first instance of a secondary vessel, a jar sherd reworked to form a shallow plate.

Colonial Period, Rillito Phase

Thanks to cremations, 60 plainware restorable and near-restorable vessels are identifiable as belonging to the Rillito phase; on these the following comments are based.

In general features there is no very marked change from Cañada del Oro. The majority of plainware is heavily micaceous. Wiped surfaces, however, are less frequent, except in a special category of Rillito plainware described below as mortuary vessels. Thickness of vessel walls is too variable for a generalized statement. Color, as in Cañada del Oro, is mottled; gray is predominant, but there are traces of rose or of rosy tan on nearly every specimen. Firing clouds are universal. Several specimens, both bowls and jars, have black interiors so uniform as to suggest deliberate smudging.

In form there is no major break in the shift from Cañada del Oro to Rillito. A plainware scoop appears for the first time in the Rillito phase, as may a small incurved bowl with hobnail ornament; several small sherds of such hobnail vessels were found. However, a hobnail sherd was found in Cremation 27, dated as Snaketown phase. At the site of Snaketown such knobbed ornament appears to be prevalent on painted ware (Gladwin and others 1937: Plate CXXXVII). The boat-shaped Cañada del Oro vessel is without Rillito counterpart. A complete absence of seed bowls and seed jars in a series as large as the Rillito suggests that such constricted-orifice forms may be genuinely absent from the Colonial period at Hodges, although present in the immediately preceding and succeeding periods.

Noticeably distinct from the general run of Rillito plainware is a group of small jars and bowls which, from their concentration in cremations, seem to have been made primarily for mortuary use. The series comprises 22 vessels, the range of which is shown in Figure 4.46. Incidence is listed in the caption to that figure. Jars are thin and micaceous; characteristically the exterior is vertically wiped. Surface color is mottled, from rose or rosy tan to gray and black; firing clouds are pronounced. Jar bodies are

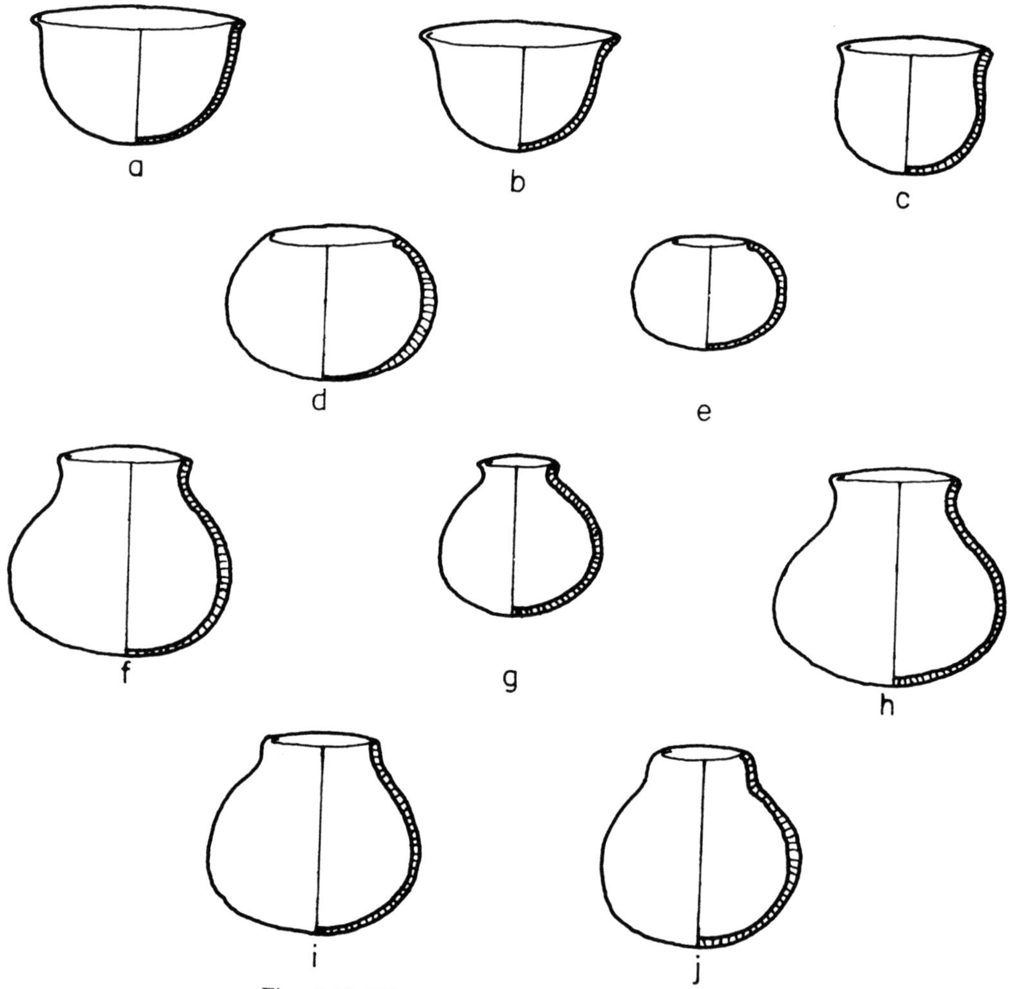

Fig. 4.46 Rillito plainware: Mortuary vessels.
Incidence: a–c, 3; *d, e,* 5; *f,* 5; *g,* 3; *h,* 2; *i,* 3; *j,* 1.

globular, but there is considerable range in mouth treatment. Jar rims are illustrated in Figure 4.45*d–h*. Most bowls are incurved, with sharply beveled rim. They share the same surface characteristics as jars, but wiping is less noticeable. In thinness, in wiping, and in general rose cast, there is a suggestion of conservatism that might be expected of mortuary artifacts. Functionally these small vessels may be regarded as the Tucson equivalent of Santa Cruz Buff (Gladwin and others 1937:185), but there the resemblance ceases save for a generic similarity in thinness and in micaceous paste. The handled jar and slipped surface of the Santa Cruz vessels are not found in the Rillito phase.

Sedentary Period, Rincon Phase

From the number of Rincon cremations it might be expected that a large series of plainware would be attributable to this phase. However, sherd cremations were in vogue during Rincon times, and often the accompanying pottery consisted merely of large rimless sherds, without clue to exact shape. The description below is based upon 45 restorable and near-restorable vessels, amplified by 47 rim sherds from two large cremations.

The plainware is extremely varied. On the whole it is thicker and is markedly less micaceous than that of the Rillito phase. Often it is heavy and "wooden." The surface is smoothed and close-pored rather than grainy; the latter characteristic seems to be a concomitant of heavy micaceous content. Some areas appear puddled, as though water had been slapped on during the finishing process and the vessels allowed to dry without being smoothed. Wiped surfaces are infrequent and seem to be confined to a series of small bowls and jars that probably are a survival of Rillito phase funeral vessels.

In color there is a wide range. Many vessels vary from brown to black but are definitely dark; at the same time others cluster about a light tan. Compared with Rillito, there seems to be a general darkening on the one hand, and a general lightening on the other; middle tones are less frequent. Among funeral vessels, however, gray to tan to rose still obtains. Firing clouds are prominent on almost every specimen; a jar may be almost black save for occasionally large splotches of red-yellow and gray. Interiors sometimes are a fairly even black, but this is not sufficiently consistent to be regarded as a conscious stylistic device, although in Rincon Red-on-brown smudging seems to be deliberate.

Major shapes and their incidence are shown in Figure 4.43 and Table 4.13. The hemispherical bowl is new; otherwise bowl shapes are much as before, although there are differences in frequency. The incurved bowl, for example, is relatively weak in the Rincon phase. Large jars generally are globular bodied, but some tend to have the point of greatest diameter rather low. Jar rims (Fig. 4.47) are not characterized by thickening on the inner side as in the Gila Basin.

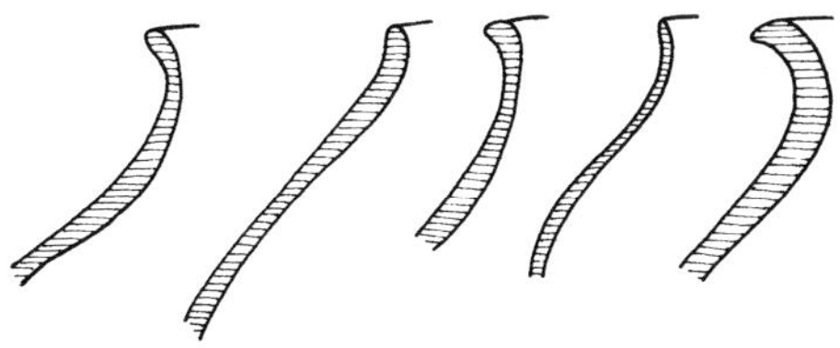

Fig. 4.47 Rincon plainware: Jar rims

As mentioned above, a number of pieces of Rincon plainware, both bowls and jars, are reminiscent of the Rillito funeral vessels. Compared with the remainder of the plainware from the Rincon phase, they are relatively thin and micaceous and show an appreciable percentage of wiped surfaces.

Included in the unpainted ware of the Rincon phase are two effigy vessels, one a scoop, the other of indeterminate shape, but probably a jar fragment (Fig. 4.43).

Classic Period, Tanque Verde Phase

Evidence of Tanque Verde plainware comes exclusively from cremations and house floors. We have virtually no trash of this phase; presumably most of it was cut away by the gravel pit that impinges on the west, adjoining the most concentrated Tanque Verde occupation.

The description below is based upon 22 specimens of plainware in undoubted Tanque Verde association. Several innovations in form are apparent, in particular, a lipped jar, a handled jug, and a boot-shaped vessel. These forms consistently are heavy, non-micaceous, and slightly puddled in spots; smoothed, but with little polish. Surface color is dark, generally brown to black, but with occasional patches of tan and red. It seems likely that this heavy ware and the new shapes described above are truly diagnostic.

The remainder of the plainware is, however, extremely variable. A new form is the large, more or less hemispherical bowl, with a semi-lip. Several vessels, in micaceous content and wiped surface, suggest a survival of earlier plainware styles. One specimen, in its thinness, heavy mica content, and tan color, is so reminiscent of Colonial and Sedentary period funeral vessels that it has been considered a mortuary piece.

Also unpainted, but a thing apart from standard plainware, is corrugated ware (not illustrated). This occurs sparingly, amounting to perhaps 50 sherds in all. These are, so far as determinable, always in association with Tanque Verde. The corrugations are variable, but the lot as a whole is excessively coarse and gritty. There is little clue as to shape, although one rim sherd suggests a bowl; the remainder doubtless are jar fragments. It seems likely that the corrugated ware is not of local manufacture. Its presence in the Tanque Verde phase, together with the one boot-shaped vessel, suggests Puebloan influence.

A fragment of an unpainted human effigy has been allocated dubiously to the Tanque Verde phase (Fig. 4.32).

It comes from the floor of House 42, a Tanque Verde phase house, but the associated floor sherds are Rillito to Tanque Verde.

Remarks

This completes the descriptive section concerning plainwares. By comparing Figure 4.43 with Gladwin and others (1937: Fig. 108) and with Haury (1936: Fig. 8), comparisons and contrasts with the Hohokam and Mogollon complexes are at once evident.

The Tucson-Hohokam resemblances and differences are summarized graphically in Table 4.14. The hemispherical bowl is weak at Hodges and, as the chart shows, comparatively late. Beakers, heavy-walled vessels, and legged vessels are lacking and evidently are to be regarded as Hohokam specializations that did not spread to the Tucson area.

Little is known of the Gila Basin Classic period, but several plainware vessels in the Gila Pueblo collection indicate that scoops and bowls, both hemispherical, outcurved, and incurved, may be attributed to it. These have been entered on the chart in dotted lines. In all likelihood boot-shaped vessels and lipped vessels are genuinely absent from the Gila Basin Classic period; their presence in the Tanque Verde phase at Hodges, therefore, cannot be explained as borrowing from the Hohokam. Nor can they be attributed to Mogollon influence. The boot-shaped vessel suggests Puebloan contact, but the lipped jar, sometimes with pointed base, has no obvious source.

One of the outstanding differences between the Hohokam and Tucson plainware series is the continuous occurrence at Hodges of a bowl with semi-flaring rim. This contrasts sharply with the complete absence of such a form in the Gila Basin. The Tucson occurrence cannot be attributed outright to Mogollon influence, but a flare-rimmed bowl occurs in the plainware of the Georgetown phase, and in San Francisco Redware of both Georgetown and Three Circle phases (Haury 1936: Figs. 8:1, 7:1, 7:13). Moreover, the presence of seed bowls and seed jars in the Pioneer period at Hodges contrasts to the relatively late occurrence of these forms in the Gila Basin. The early appearance of constricted orifice vessels also parallels an early occurrence in the Mogollon area (Haury 1936: Figs. 8:4, 8:5).

In summary, Hodges materials show discernible Hohokam and Mogollon features in the plainware as well as the decorated ware. When one compares the Tucson plainware as a whole with that of the Mogollon complex, a generic similarity is evident, although the Hodges inventory appears more specialized, particularly in its variety of bowl forms.

TABLE 4.14

Phase Distribution of Certain Plainware Vessel Forms in the Gila Basin and at the Hodges Site

(Dark gray column, Gila Basin occurrence; light gray column, Hodges occurrence)

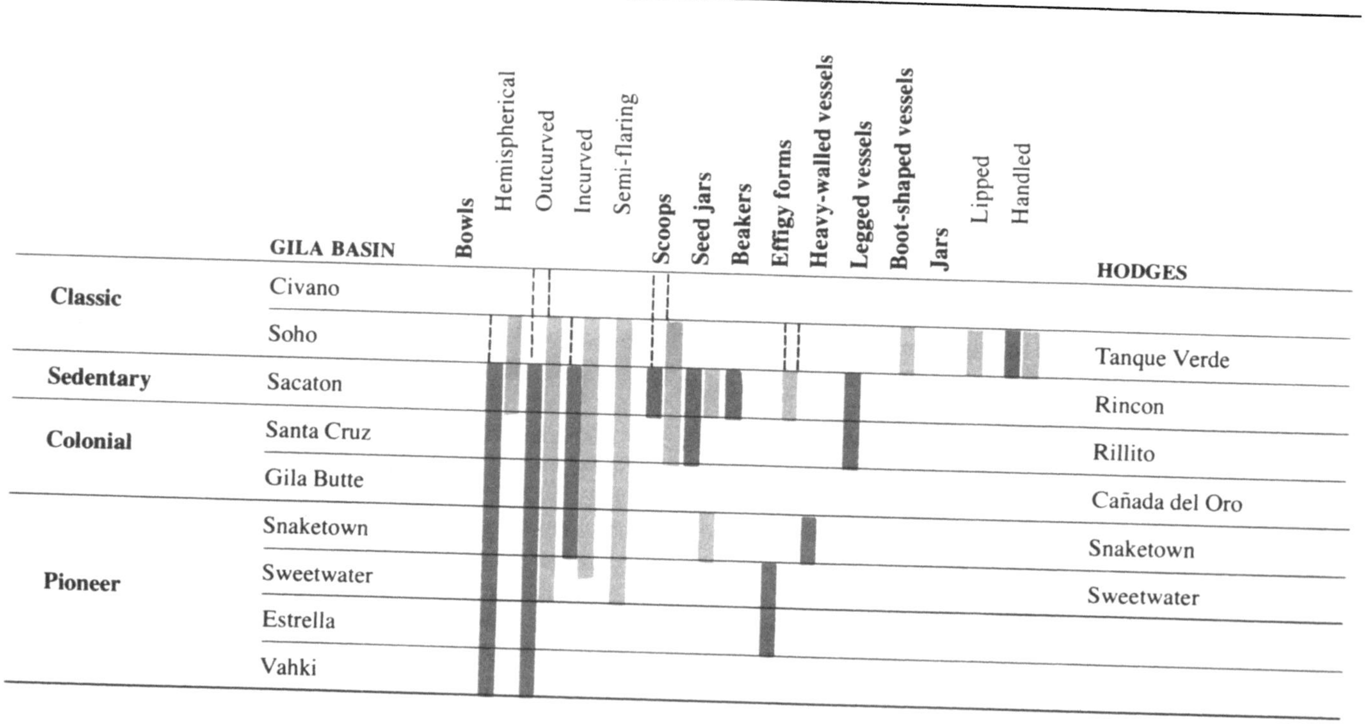

INTRUSIVE POTTERY

Intrusive specimens consist overwhelmingly of red-on-buff, both sherds and whole vessels. Such material is preponderantly of the Santa Cruz and Sacaton phases, but the Gila Butte phase is moderately represented, and the Soho phase, sparsely. The latter, in fact, consists of one entire jar and no sherds. Red-on-buff sherds are plentiful in trash and in house fill; in certain cuts they amount to as much as 40 percent of the decorated specimens. But such occurrences are of no chronological significance because of the mixed character of our debris; they have not been included in Table 4.15. However, from cremations comes strong evidence of the Tucson–Gila Basin temporal relationship. All told, 49 Hohokam vessels occur in cremations; over half of these are without associated local types, but the ample cross-ties indicated in Table 4.15 are definitive. The association is precisely what is expectable on typological grounds, and it corroborates the local chronology which, it will be remembered, is in part dependent upon typological analogies with the Gila Basin.

Other intrusive types occur sparingly. They consist almost exclusively of small sherds and with few exceptions come from mixed trash—hence cannot be placed in the local series. The entries on Table 4.15 are significant chiefly in that they indicate range of contact rather than evidence of cross-dating. Except for the strong and obvious Hohokam relationship, intercourse seems to have been confined largely to the Mogollon complex, with little evidence of Puebloan contact. The virtual absence of the various Salado polychromes is expectable, inasmuch as these post-date, for the most part, the occupation at the Hodges site.

TABLE 4.15

Intrusive Pottery

	CERAMIC TYPE															
PHASE	Gila Butte Red-on-buff	Santa Cruz Red-on-buff	Sacaton Red-on-buff	Casa Grande Red-on-buff	Pinto Polychrome	Gila Polychrome	San Lorenzo Red-on-brown	Mogollon Red-on-brown	Mimbres Classic	San Francisco Red	Alma Plain	Dragoon Red-on-brown	Sonora Red-on-brown[b]	Trincheras (Nogales) Polychrome[c]	Tularosa Black-on-white	Unidentified Polychrome[d]
Tanque Verde											1[a]					
Rincon			10[a]								1[a]		2	2		3
Rillito		7[a]														
Cañada del Oro	1[a]															
Snaketown																
Sweetwater																
Unplaced	2[a]	18[a]	10[a]	1[a]	2	1	1	2	1	4 1[a]		2		3	3	
Total	3	25	20	1	2	1	1	2	1	5	2	2	2	5	3	3

[a] Restorable or near-restorable vessels.

[b] Save for the lack of hematite paint, these two sherds answer the description of the type designated by Sauer and Brand (1931: 108–109) as Trincheras Purple-on-red.

[c] This type was illustrated by Sauer and Brand (1931: Plate 18). Of the 5 sherds, 2 are associated with Rillito to Rincon phase material but cannot be placed more precisely.

[d] Black-and-white-on-red fragments, pigment fugitive. Probably two types are represented. One sherd is decorated interior and exterior with large white hatched, the component lines alternately white, black. The other has an exterior interlocking fret, one arm of which is black, the other, white. In addition it has a diagonal white band, overpainted in black with a series of small T-shaped elements. Both the latter sherds have small black triangles pendant from the interior rim. The two others apparently are deep bowls with semi-flaring rim. The exterior of one is chevron motif, apparently a key or fret, edged in black.

5. CERAMIC ARTIFACTS

Miscellaneous pottery manufactures include figurines, both human and animal, spindle whorls, reel-shaped objects, an ear plug (?), pot rests, and pot covers. Most of the material comes from general trash which, because of its mixed nature, does not permit the bulk of these items to be identified by phase. By and large, however, a sufficient number of specimens of each category are placed so that a general idea of the sequential development and, to a lesser extent, of the range within each phase is possible.

HUMAN FIGURINES

Figurines constitute one of the knottiest of the local problems. In many instances the few placed pieces are small body or appendage fragments, without clue to the form as a whole. For the Cañada del Oro phase alone, we have a fair-sized series (Figs. 5.1*a–f* and 5.2*d*, *e*, *g*). Figurines evidently did not constitute a favored article of grave furniture; some come from cremations and some from house floors, but most from mixed trash.

General Characteristics

Sex. All of determinable sex are female, most with prominent breasts (Fig. 5.3*j–m*); a few are markedly pregnant (Figs. 5.4*n*, 5.5*p*).

Body and face features. Characteristically, the body is a flattened cylinder. Position is almost invariably standing, with the legs slightly spread. Seated figures, so far as we can determine, are confined to the Cañada del Oro phase. A few specimens seem to have consisted of a head, terminating in a brief stub (Fig. 5.3*b*, *e*) which perhaps was affixed to a perishable body (cf. Kelly 1945: Fig. 64*j*). One unique specimen (Fig. 5.3*h*) evidently had a hollow

Fig. 5.1 Figurines: Cañada del Oro phase and unplaced. *a–f*, Cañada del Oro; *g*, unplaced. Length of *g*, 8.2 cm.

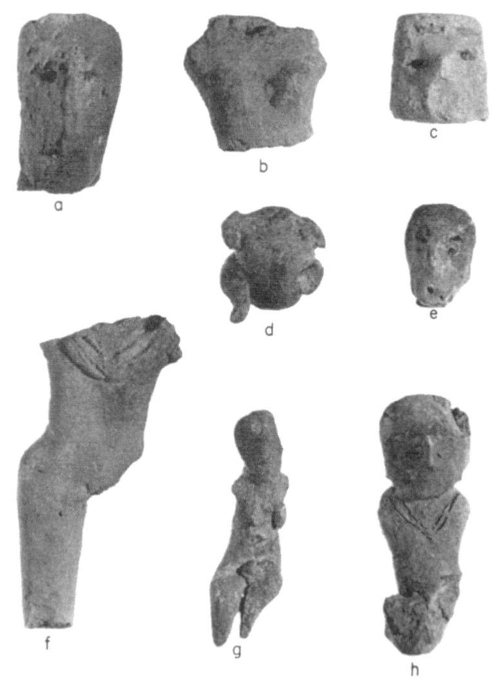

Fig. 5.2 Figurines: Various phases. *a*, Snaketown; *b*, *f*, Rillito; *c*, Unplaced; *d*, *e*, *g*, Cañada del Oro; *h*, Unplaced. Height of *h*, 5.5 cm.

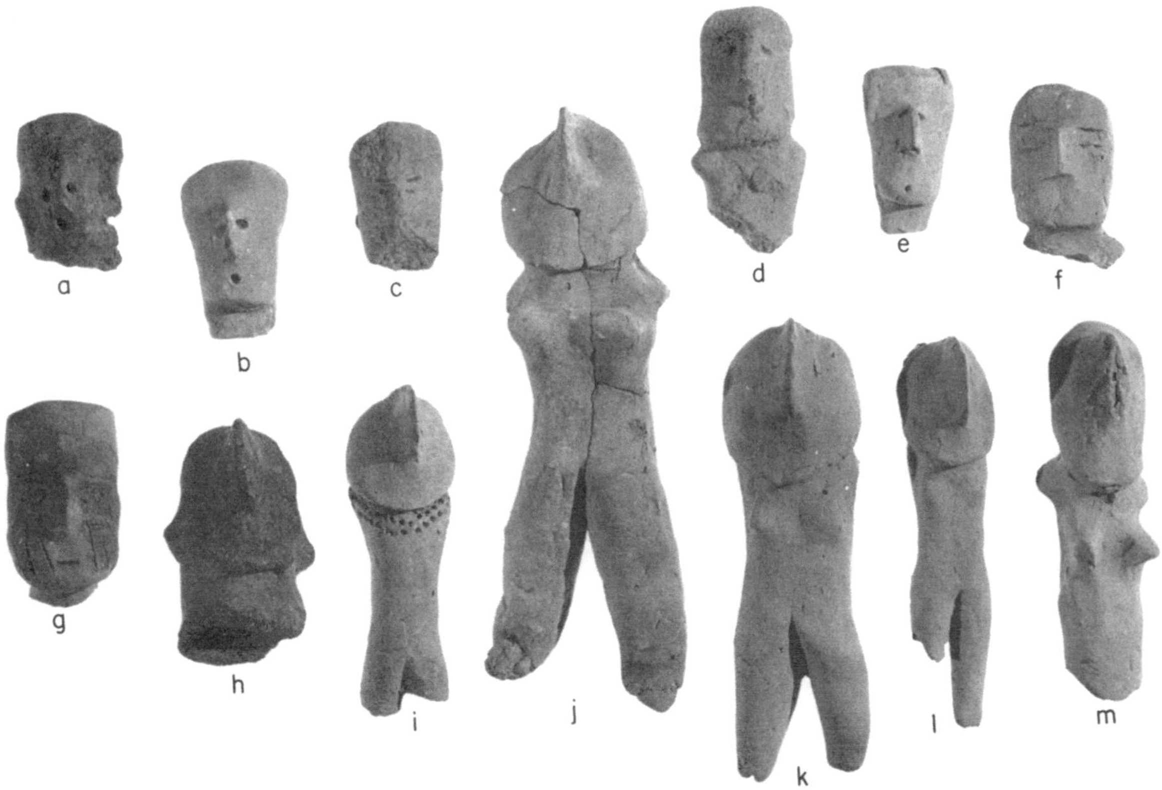

Fig. 5.3 Figurines: Unplaced as to phase. Typologically *a–e*, are Pioneer; *f*, Cañada del Oro; *g*, either Cañada del Oro or Rillito; remainder, Rillito or Rincon. Length of *j*, 12 cm.

body—possibly with a rattle-filled base such as is characteristic of some central Sinaloan figurines (Kelly 1945: Fig. 62*c*).

Arms generally are represented by wing-like nubbins at the shoulder. There are only two instances of arms in-the-round (Figs. 5.1*a*, 5.2*d*), and one of arms in low relief (Fig. 5.5*k*). Limbs generally are straight and rod-like; but occasionally the calf and knee are indicated (Figs. 5.1*f*, 5.2*g*). The tip of the leg is pinched forward to indicate a foot, but feet did not receive detailed treatment; often they are not represented at all.

Facial features vary. The nose generally is prominent, the clay being pinched into a beak-like contour. Eyes, mouth, eyebrows, and occasionally nostrils, are represented by gouges, slits, or delicate incision; the latter seems to be confined to the Colonial period. In some instances the nose is the only facial feature depicted. There is no instance of the "coffee-bean" eye, as described for the Santa Cruz phase in the Gila Basin (Gladwin and others 1937: Plate CXCVII). Ears are not portrayed except in one dubious instance (Fig. 5.3*h*).

Ornament. Ornament is rare. One specimen shows signs of red pigment on the back side of the head (Fig. 5.1*c*), but this is the only instance of painting. Cañada del Oro specimens frequently are turbaned, with hair or other head decoration on either side of the face. The chin ornament common in the Gila Basin occurs in but one case (Fig. 5.1*a*). A strand run through the nasal septum seems to be represented in Figure 5.5*k*. Several specimens (Figs. 5.2*f*, *h*; 5.3*i*) have a necklace or bertha, and two seem to have a neck pendant (Figs. 5.1*a*; 5.3*d*). Other indications of raiment and ornament are confined to an anklet and wristlet (?) (Fig. 5.5*o*). Tattooing may possibly be indicated by the one instance of elaborate leg incision (Fig. 5.5*m*) and one of facial incision (Fig. 5.3*g*).

Manufacture. As in the Gila Basin, figurines are not mold-made. The two-piece method of manufacture, described by Haury (Gladwin and others 1937: 234), occurs in the local series at least as late as the Rillito phase, although in the Gila Basin it had by that time been abandoned in favor of a one-piece technique. Even so, our pre-Rillito figurines were not made exclusively of two pieces. In particular, the Cañada del Oro specimen shown in Figure 5.2*d* consists of a flattened ball of clay, to which appendages have been added. Moreover, several Cañada del Oro specimens appear to have the head modeled separately and then added to the body. Furthermore, one Rillito torso (Fig. 5.4*l*), which has been perforated by two small rods, suggests that the head may have been formed separately and then been affixed to the body by means of small sticks. It is impossible to say anything whatsoever concerning figurine manufacture during Rincon times, for the fragments are too small to provide a clue. It is not unlikely that the two-rod method survived into the Rincon phase.

Many of the figurines are badly burned; this suggests that, in certain cases at least, firing may have been of a secondary nature—either through the burning of a house or through cremation fire. Moreover, several of the specimens are of unbaked clay. We believe, however, that the majority were deliberately fired.

Data concerning figurines are presented graphically in two illustrations (Figs. 5.4 and 5.5). The first shows the placed specimens, segregated according to heads, relatively complete figures, and torsos. This chart includes every specimen allocated to phase, barring virtual duplicates and small unidentifiable fragments. The second chart shows a representative lot of unplaced specimens, a few of which can be placed on typological grounds.

In discussing the sequential order of figurine styles we are severely handicapped. Only one head is attributable to the Pioneer period, but the Cañada del Oro phase of the Colonial period is moderately well represented. Rillito phase figurines consist of two heads and two torsos while the Rincon phase consists of a lone fragment so broken that its major features are indeterminate. In addition, the numerous small leg or body bits are virtually useless for dating purposes. The distribution of figurine styles through time is summarized in Table 5.1.

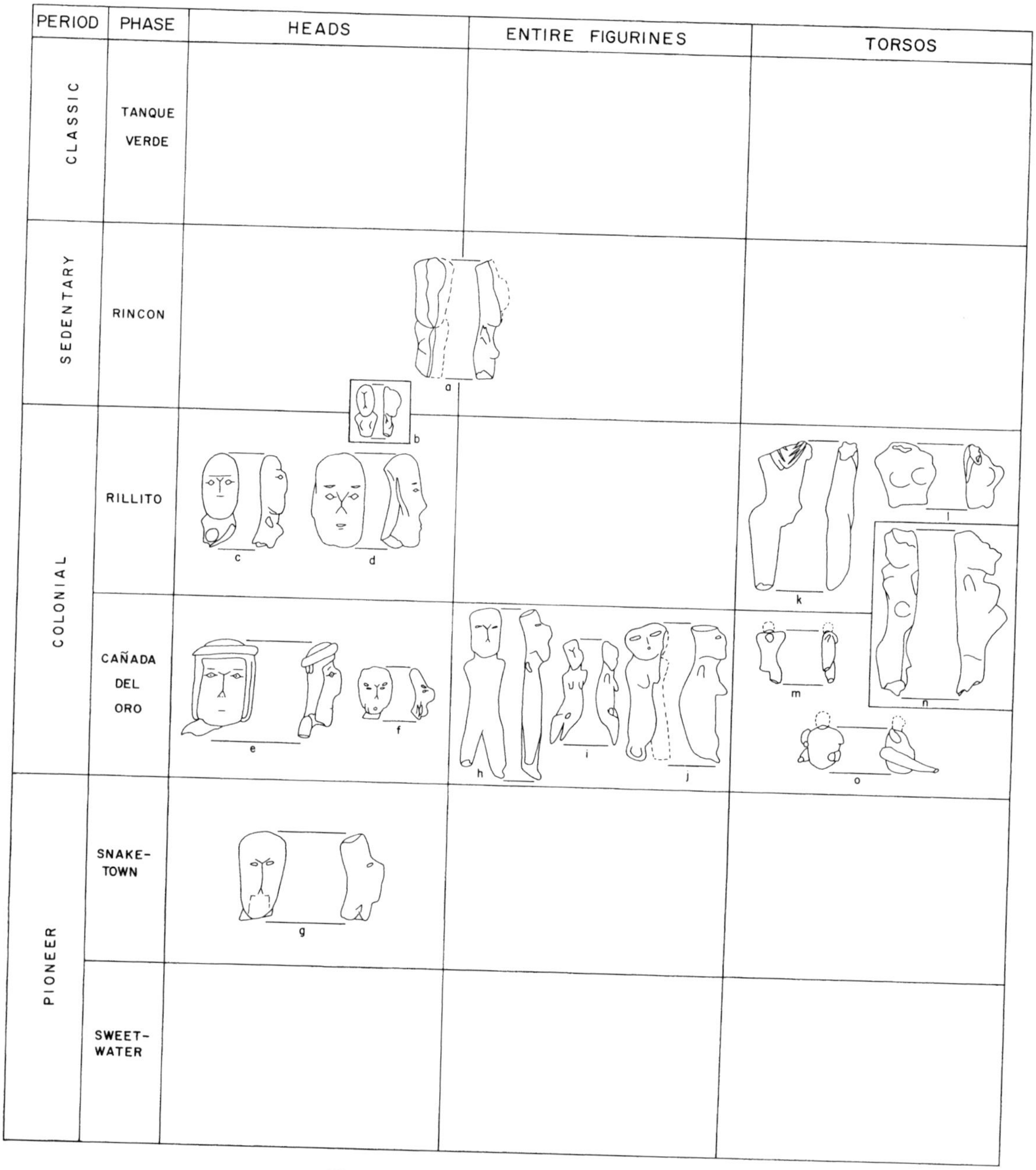

Fig. 5.4 Developmental chart of figurines

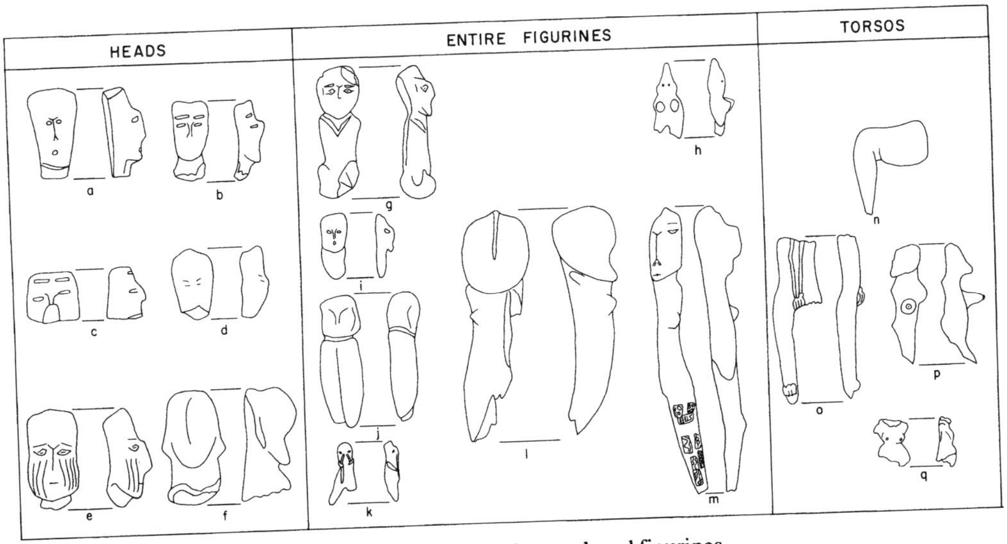

Fig. 5.5 Representative unplaced figurines

All of these are without adequate association for dating; for a number of them, however, phase affiliation can be suggested on the basis of typological resemblance to placed specimens. Length of *l*, 10.4 cm.

a, d Without precise analogies in the dated series; they are similar to Pioneer period specimens, to judge from Gila Basin data.

b Typologically closer to the Cañada del Oro phase than to other phases, by virtue of the "slit" eye. This eye feature occurs also in the equivalent Gila Butte phase (Gladwin and others 1937: Plate CXCIX, *b–d, f*).

c In all likelihood, from the Cañada del Oro phase. There is a generic resemblance to the specimen shown in Figure 5.4*f* (?), and an even more marked relationship to the Gila Butte phase head illustrated in Gladwin and others 1937: Plate CXCIX, *f*.

e Probably from the Colonial period; finely incised features appear to be confined to the Cañada del Oro and Rillito phases.

f Figures with cursive facial treatment probably are Rillito or Rincon. The hollow body is unique and strongly suggests the rattled bodies of figurines from Culiacán, Sinaloa, although otherwise there is no resemblance.

g A seated figurine, with incised eye; typologically this should be from the Cañada del Oro phase.

h, n–q Without analogies.

i Also without analogy, although the Pioneer period may be suggested.

j Likewise without analogy in the dated series and with no apparent resemblance to Gila Basin forms. Made by the two-rod method. The virtual lack of nose is noteworthy, as is the tubular body, without separated legs.

k Again without analogy in the dated series. This specimen appears to have a long strand run through the nasal septum; arms are shown in low relief.

l, m Assignable, with relative assurance, to the Rillito or Rincon phases, probably the latter.

TABLE 5.1

Phase Distribution of Figurine Styles

		Figure 5.4															Figure 5.5																	Indeterminate Body Fragments	Indeterminate Appendages	Total
	Phase	*a*	*b*	*c*	*d*	*e*	*f*	*g*	*h*	*i*	*j*	*k*	*l*	*m*	*n*	*o*	*a*	*b*	*c*	*d*	*e*	*f*	*g*	*h*	*i*	*j*	*k*	*l*	*m*	*n*	*o*	*p*	*q*			
Classic	Tanque Verde																																	1		2
Sedentary	Rincon	1																																	8	9
	Rincon-Rillito		1																																2	7
Colonial	Rillito			1	1							2	1																					1	12	15
	Rillito-Cañada del Oro								1						1																			5	2	19
	Cañada del Oro					3	1		2	2	1			1		2																			4	5
Pioneer	Snaketown							1																												0
	Sweetwater																																			
	Unplaced					1		1								1	5	3	1	1	1	1	1	1	1	1	1	8	2	1	1	1	1	13	34	81
	Total	1	1	1	1	4	1	2	3	2	1	2	1	1	1	3	5	3	1	1	1	1	1	1	1	1	1	8	2	1	1	1	1	20	62	138

Dating of Specimens

Snaketown phase. Barring several small leg fragments, this phase is represented by one head only (Fig. 5.4*g*) of unfired clay. The face is long and narrow, with a more-or-less squared chin. The nose has been pinched into prominence; eyes are represented by two horizontal gouges; other facial features are wanting. The top of the head has been flattened, and the contour at the back is concave.

Cañada del Oro phase. This phase is relatively well represented, thanks to a cache of figurines found in a well-identified house. A rather surprising range in style and in size is indicated. A head similar to that described for the Snaketown phase evidently survived into the Cañada del Oro phase (Fig. 5.4*h*). The associated body has a more-or-less flattened trunk and no breasts; arms are indicated by nubbins at the shoulder. The legs taper and are pinched forward to approximate feet.

Characteristic of the Cañada del Oro phase, as of the equivalent Gila Basin phase, is the figurine type shown in Figure 5.1*c*. The head is turbaned and ribbons of clay flank the face on either side. Eyes, eyebrows, mouth, and sometimes nostrils, are delicately incised. Placed specimens of this style consist of heads only, but a typologically similar specimen (Fig. 5.2*h*) indicates that the body shown in Figure 5.2*f* has this style of head in at least one case.

Two semi-seated specimens are definitely from the Cañada del Oro phase (Figs. 5.1*f*; 5.2*g*). The body is modeled in the round, with considerable realism, in contrast to almost all other types, which are highly conventionalized. Moreover, this type is not rigidly symmetrical. Another, somewhat different Cañada del Oro style figurine, also is seated (Fig. 5.2*d*). The body consists of a flattened ball of clay, to which a narrow roll has been added across the back and brought forward on either side of the body to form outstretched legs. Arms in the round also are indicated.

Of the other Cañada del Oro figurines (Fig. 5.4*f*, *j*, *m*), there is but one instance each; therefore, they may not be standard and generally favored types.

The figurine fragment shown in Figure 5.4*n* occurs in association with Cañada del Oro and Rillito phase ceramics and thus may be placed in the Colonial period, although it cannot be attributed to either one of the component phases. Facial features are obscure; its pregnant state is pronounced.

Rillito phase. Rillito is poorly represented. Except for small indeterminate bits, only two heads and three torso fragments were located. The heads are rounded at the top, and the facial features—eyes, brows, and mouth—are incised. Such incised features appear to be confined to the Colonial period. It is noteworthy that we have not a single instance of the "coffee-bean" eye which characterizes the Santa Cruz phase figurines from the Gila Basin (Gladwin and others 1937: Plate CXCVII).

The torso shown in Figure 5.2*f* has a well-marked waistline; no breasts are indicated, but the upper part of the body is ornamented by an appliqued and incised yoke or necklace. The other torso is noteworthy for its vertical perforations, which suggest that the head may originally have been affixed by means of two slender wooden rods.

The small figurine shown in Figure 5.4*b* is associated with both Rillito and Rincon phase sherds. This specimen is remarkable chiefly for the prominence of the nose, which dominates the entire face; no other facial details are represented. By analogy to this particular specimen, it may be suggested that the unidentified type shown in Figure 5.5*l* may be from either the Rillito or Rincon phase. Typologically, this unplaced specimen (Fig. 5.5*l*) is fundamentally the same as the Santa Cruz figurines (Gladwin and others 1937: Plate CXCVII), although it lacks the "coffee-bean" eye and the chin ornaments. It seems most likely, then, that it belongs to the Rincon phase. It is similar in head treatment to a Rincon phase effigy scoop (not illustrated) and logically, to judge from general pottery trends, one might expect Rincon phase figurines to be somewhat cursive compared with those from the Rillito phase. A further Rincon effigy scoop (Fig. 4.23*g*) shares the same fundamental profile but has incised eyes, with nostrils and mouth indicated by punches. The eye incision is quite different from the delicate delineation which characterizes Cañada del Oro and Rillito figurines. Moreover, seven of the eight specimens of this type (Fig. 5.5*g–m*) come from a single cremation; although accompanied by plainware only, the interment lies in the midst of a concentrated Rincon phase cremation area. It must be noted, however, that all but one of these particular unplaced specimens were made by the two-rod method, which in the Gila Basin is essentially earlier than the Santa Cruz phase. Should our figurines actually prove to be from the Rincon phase, the implication is that this technique of manufacture survived in the Tucson Basin long after its abandonment in the Gila Basin.

Rincon phase. There is but one large fragment attributable with certainty to the Rincon phase (Fig. 5.4*a*). It has the usual nubbin arms and prominent breasts, but facial features unfortunately are indeterminate. There is no suggestion in our collection (either from the Rincon phase or as unplaced specimens) of the hollow-head, realistically modeled faces that occur in the Gila Basin Sedentary period (Gladwin and others 1937: Plate CXCV).

Tanque Verde phase. No figurines and no fragments can be assigned to the local Classic period. The Gila Basin Classic period is so little known that it cannot be said whether or not this apparent absence holds for that area as well.

ANIMAL FIGURINES

Animal figurines are rare; the entire selection is shown in Figure 5.6. [*Ed. note:* Unfortunately, the one whole specimen sketched by Kelly could not be located; hence, it is not illustrated]. There are two more or less entire specimens and one fragment. The fragment alone is placed; it is from the Rincon phase.

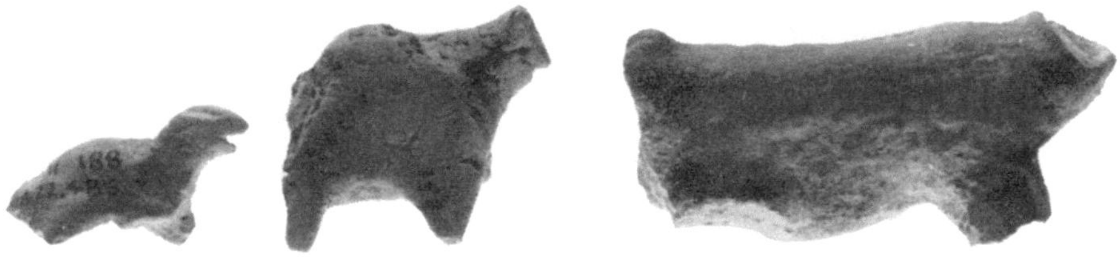

Fig. 5.6 Animal figurines. *d*, Rincon; remainder, unplaced. Length of *d*, 4.5 cm.

WORKED SHERDS

Worked sherds are relatively plentiful. Because of their occurrence in general trash, most are without phase association. Allocated specimens range from the Cañada del Oro to the Tanque Verde phase (Fig. 5.7; Table 5.2). As a whole, they are carelessly shaped and not well finished. Some are imperforate (Fig. 5.7*a, b, d, e, h, i*); these vary from 2 to 9 cm in diameter. About half (11) are made from decorated sherd fragments, none of which seems to be earlier than the Rincon phase. Their provenience also is Rincon phase and later.

Perforated worked discs (Figs. 5.7*g*; 5.8*d*) are more abundant. Diameters are from 3 to 6.5 cm. Proportionately fewer are made from decorated pottery. The decorated fragments range from the Rillito phase to the Tanque Verde

TABLE 5.2
Phase Distribution of Worked Sherds, Spindle Whorls, and Related Worked Ceramics

		Worked sherds					**Spindle whorls**		**Reel-shaped objects**				
	Phase	**Disc, imperforate (Fig. 5.7*a, b, d, e, h, i*)**	**Disc, perforate (Fig. 5.7*g*, 5.8*d*)**	**Rectangular (Fig. 5.7*a, b*)**	**Ring-shaped (Fig. 5.7*f*)**	**Pendants (Fig. 5.7*c*)**	**Stone (Fig. 5.8*b*)**	**Pottery (Fig. 5.8*a, c, d, f, g, h, i*)**	**Convex-end (Fig. 5.8*l*)**	**Concave-end (Fig. 5.8*j, k*)**	**Earplug (?) (Fig. 5.8*e*)**	**Pot rests (not illustrated)**	**Pot covers (not illustrated)**
Classic	Tanque Verde	2	3				2	1					
Sedentary	Rincon	1	3	1						1	1		
Colonial	Rillito		1	1		1							
	Cañada del Oro			1									1
Pioneer	Snaketown												1
	Sweetwater												
	Unplaced	18	40	5	1	1	1	5	1	6	0	2	5
	Total	21	47	8	1	2	3	6	1	7	1	2	7

Fig. 5.7 Worked sherds: Various phases. *a, d,* Rincon; *b,* Cañada del Oro; *c, e, g,* Tanque Verde; *f, h, i,* unplaced. Greatest dimension of *h,* 7.4 cm.

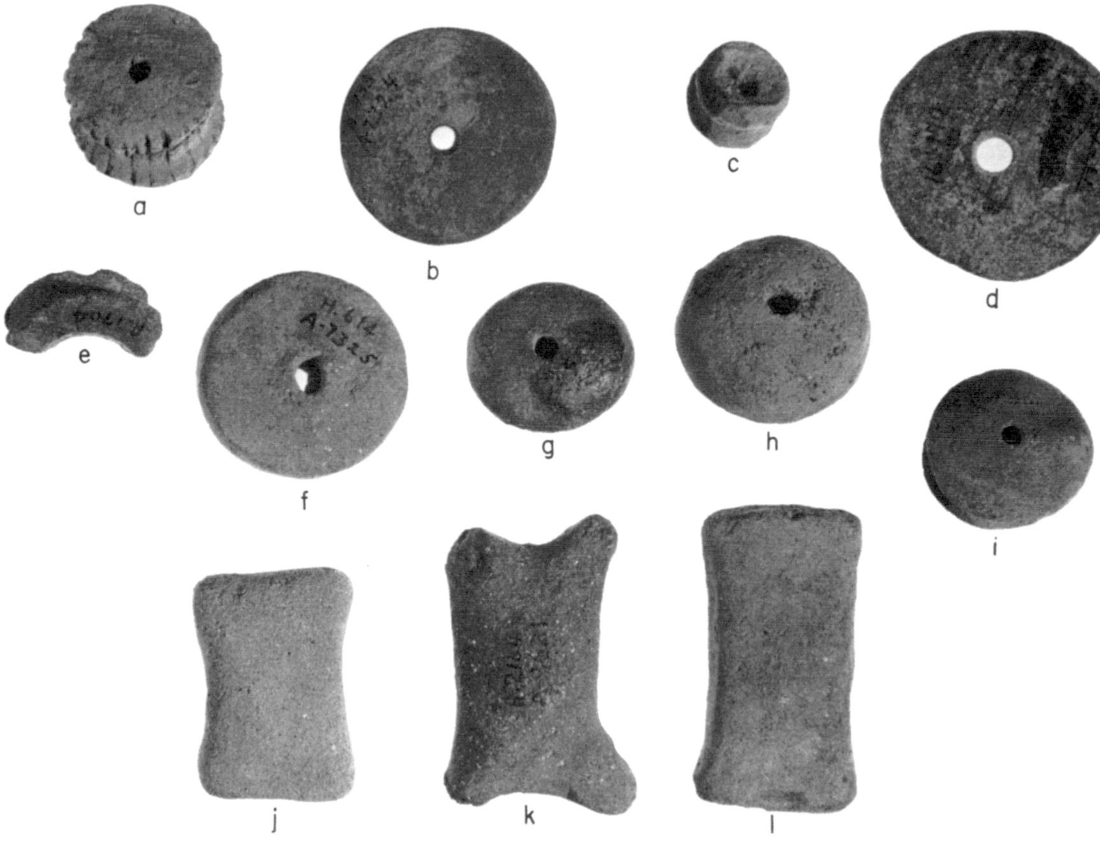

Fig. 5.8 Worked objects: Pottery and stone. *Spindle whorls:* (pottery) *a, c, d, f, h, i,* unplaced; *g,* Tanque Verde; (stone) *b,* unplaced. *Ear plug:* (pottery) *e,* Rincon. *Use undetermined:* (pottery) *i,* Tanque Verde. *Reel-shaped objects* (pottery) *j, k, l,* unplaced. Length of *l,* 5.8 cm.

phase, which again is precisely the known association of such artifacts. Because of their central perforation, use as spindle whorls may be suggested (see below).

Rectangular worked sherds (Fig. 5.7*a*, *b*) are rare; all are imperforate, and no utility suggests itself. On the whole, these are somewhat more carefully manufactured than are the sherd discs. The few placed specimens range from the Cañada del Oro to Rincon phases.

A curious ring-shaped worked sherd (Fig. 5.7*f*) is unique. Evidently it is the fragment of a plainware vessel handle which has been filed to a shape approximating that of a signet ring. This specimen is noteworthy in view of the complete absence at the Hodges site of small loop handles.

Two worked sherds of decorated pottery, perforated at the top, evidently were pendants. Both have been shaped with care; one (Fig. 5.7*c*) is circular; the other, oval. Both are made from Rillito sherds, and one has, moreover, adequate Rillito phase association.

SPINDLE WHORLS

Included here for the sake of convenience are three well-shaped stone discs (Fig. 5.8*b*), their form identical with that of the perforated worked sherd discs. Presumably they were used as spindle whorls. Two are from the Tanque Verde phase; the third is unplaced.

Also identified as spindle whorls is a series of clay objects (Fig. 5.8*a*, *c*, *d*, *f–i*), varying from discoidal, to globular, to spool-shaped. One has simple incised lines as ornamentation. Of this series, the only placed specimen is from the Tanque Verde phase (Fig. 5.8*g*). On the basis of the Cushing collection, Haury (Gladwin and others 1937: 245) has concluded that this type of spindle whorl was not current in the Gila Basin in pre-Classic times; with this our one placed specimen is consonant.

REEL-SHAPED OBJECTS

These clay objects of unknown utility are of coarse, fired pottery, undecorated and mostly unpolished (Fig. 5.8*j–l*). They are not plentiful. One, unplaced, is flat, with convex ends (Fig. 5.8*l*). The Snaketown data (Gladwin and others 1937: 243) indicate that this type was known from the Sweetwater phase until the Santa Cruz phase. The other reel-shaped objects all have concave ends, some being nearly forked; the body is either flat or cylindrical. Of the concave-end group, one is placed in the Rincon phase, which agrees with the Gila Basin occurrence in the Sedentary period.

EAR PLUG

The spool-shaped clay object shown in Figure 5.8*e* appears to be our one instance of an ear ornament. It is from the Rincon phase.

POT RESTS

Two truncated cones of clay were presumably used as pot rests. The whole cone resembles one of the specimens illustrated in the Snaketown report (Gladwin and others 1937: Plate CCXII*b*), except that the top is flat and slopes to one side. This specimen is undated; it was found in the midst of a large cache of stones composed chiefly of metate and mano fragments. The second specimen, a fragment of indeterminate shape, was found on the floor of House 70 and is undated.

POT COVERS

Seven more or less dish-shaped fragments of unbaked clay indicate that mud was placed over the orifice to seal a vessel. The vessel rim is imprinted clearly, and in two instances impressions show that leaves were spread over the mouth before the application of the clay, while a third has the imprint of a simple checkerwork mat. In each case the containers appear to have been filled completely, for the clay did not penetrate the neck, as in the specimens illustrated by Gladwin and others (1937: Fig. 115).

On the whole, our specimens are earlier than those of the Snaketown site; one is from the Snaketown phase, another from the Cañada del Oro phase.

6. STONE

INTRODUCTION

Except for stone vessels and some projectile points, most of the stone covered in the present chapter was found in trash. Because of the lack of unmixed rubbish, few specimens could be allocated to phase. Some, principally manos, came from house floors. When the manos were securely dated, it was assumed that the associated stone artifacts belonged to the same phase as the house. This assumption, made confidently when heavy stone objects were concerned, was felt not applicable to items of lighter weight, such as projectile points, which might have worked in with the fill. Owing to the scarcity of stone objects with secure phase allocation, typological sequences have not been prepared.

In the pages to follow, all abrading tools are lumped together, irrespective of the technique used in their manufacture. Next, chipped artifacts are considered, then ground stone implements, followed by stone bowls and effigies. Because of their special interest, stone palettes, mosaics, and ornaments are treated separately, in Chapter 7.

ABRADING TOOLS

Reamers

These were probably used most extensively in the preparation of shell ornaments. The reamers at the Hodges site were fashioned from granite, diorite, and scoria. Data for a typological series are inadequate since only two reamers could be given phase assignments (Fig. 6.1*a*, *b*). Both are of the Rincon phase.

Knives

Twenty-four stone knives were listed in the field catalogue, with no indication given as to which were flaked and which were ground. I was able to find in the existing Hodges collection only two of the catalogued objects. Both of these are of ground slate. Objects that could be classified as flaked knives were noted during later observations at the site. If Kelly excavated any such artifacts, they apparently were not entered in the field catalogue and are not now in the collection.

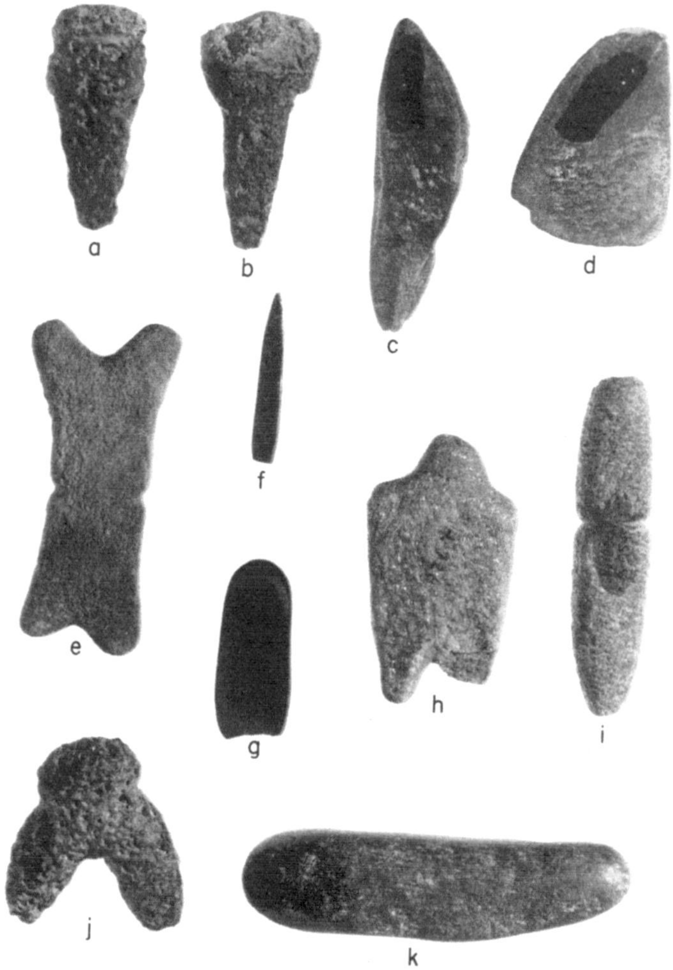

Fig. 6.1 Miscellaneous small stone objects. *Use: a, b,* reamers; *c, d,* knives; *e, h, i, j,* "medicine stones" (?); *f,* awl; *g, k,* polishing stones. *Phase: a, b,* Rincon; others, unplaced. *Materials: a, b, j,* scoria; *c, d, f,* slate; *e,* tuff; *g,* peridotite; *h,* mica schist; *i,* sandstone; *k,* quartzite. Length of *e*, 4.5 cm.

Ed. note: The present chapter is a composite one, prepared in part by Kelly and completed in 1956 by James Officer, who wrote the sections on abrading tools, chipped artifacts, metates, mortars, and pestles. When the first person is used in these sections, the writer is Officer. By 1956, many of the specimens had been lost or discarded, and he was forced to rely heavily on the brief entries in Kelly's field catalogue. According to her notes, the terminology used by Sayles (Gladwin and others 1937: 101–102) is applicable, without significant modification, to the stone from the Hodges site.

Kelly's field catalogue lists 29 artifacts as "blades." Many of these might as properly have been called knives. After examination of three of the so-called "blades," two of them were reclassified as ground slate knives (Fig. 6.1*c*, *d*); the other, as a saw or "grass knife" (Fig. 6.3*d*).

Of the 24 items she catalogued as knives, Kelly indicated that 21 could not be placed as to phase. One each was assigned to the Cañada del Oro, Rincon, and Tanque Verde phases. On the basis of my own observations, I would add to this list two ground slate knives, also unplaced. Knowing nothing of the nature of those artifacts for which phase assignments were made, nothing can be offered in the way of a typological series.

"Medicine Stones"

Four whole specimens classified as "medicine stones" are shown in Figure 6.1*e*, *h*, *i*, *j*. All except *h* are very similar to items found at Snaketown (Gladwin and others 1937: 112, Plate LXXXI). Specimen *h* looks somewhat like a crude human figurine and perhaps did not serve the same function as the others. Specimen *j* is from Cremation 10 listed in the field catalogue as being of Rillito age; the others are not datable. Six other fragments of similar pieces were found at the site.

Awl

This pointed slate implement (Fig. 6.1*f*) is identified in the field catalogue as an awl. It came from beneath the floor of House 45, which is undated. No stone awls are discussed in the Snaketown report (Gladwin and others 1937), although several long, slender rods are illustrated in Plate LXXXIII of that publication. They are also made of slate and are pointed at one end. They are, however, considerably longer than the Hodges specimen. They range from approximately 15 to 45 cm in length, whereas the Hodges specimen is a little over 2 cm long.

Polishing Stones

Kelly listed two categories of abrading stones (rubbing and polishing) in her field catalogue. I was unable to determine what criteria were used in distinguishing between the two. Three examples are illustrated in Figures 6.1*g*, *k*; 6.4*a*. The following table indicates phase frequencies for these items as determined solely from notations in the field catalogue:

Phase	Number
Tanque Verde	3
Rincon	3
Rillito-Rincon	1
Rillito	1
Cañada del Oro	1
Snaketown	0
Unplaced	51
Total	60

Whetstones

Only four whetstones were listed by Kelly in her field catalogue. Two of these were assigned to the Tanque Verde phase; one is illustrated in Figure 6.2*b*. The other illustrated specimen (Fig. 6.2*a*) was not assigned to a phase. The four

Fig. 6.2 Whetstones, grooved stone. *Phase: b*, Tanque Verde; others, unplaced. *Material: a*, quartzite; *b*, quartz diorite gneiss; *c*, mica schist. Length of *b*, 14.5 cm.

excavated specimens are of different materials—felsite, tuff, muscovite, and sandstone.

Grooved Stone

This artifact (Fig. 6.2*c*) is listed in the field catalogue as a "grooved stone" and may have been used as a shaft straightener. It was found near several cremations and cannot be dated. There are no entries in the catalogue for arrowshaft straighteners, and none is currently with the Hodges collection.

Saws (sickles or grass knives)

Only one such implement is entered in the field catalogue. However, later examination of artifacts classified as "hoes" suggests that most of these tools were used with a sawing, rather than a chopping, motion (Fig. 6.3). The field catalogue shows 54 stone hoes, of which 13 could be located. Twelve definitely were not used for chopping. All have saw teeth and striations parallel to the long axis, indicating a sawing motion. Only one of the 13 might have been a hoe. DiPeso (1956: 215) discusses implements of this sort and concludes that they "could have been used in the excavation of house pits, digging post holes, making cooking pots, digging graves and for any chore which called for removal of earth."

Fig. 6.3 Stone saws. *Phase: a*, Rillito; *b*, Tanque Verde; *c, e*, unplaced; *d, f, g*, Rincon. *Material: d*, siltstone; others, sandstone. Blade of *e*, 30.3 cm.

Kelly's catalogue lists one saw which I examined and found generally indistinguishable from the 12 items referred to above. In addition, I classified as a saw one object Kelly had listed in her catalogue as a "blade." A total of 14 tools probably were used as saws, and only one was conceivably a hoe. Assuming that most of the other artifacts classified by Kelly as hoes were actually saws, I would guess that the Hodges collection originally contained around 50 such items.

The large number of saws at the Hodges site indicates economic similarities between this site and Paloparado (DiPeso 1956: 215). Haury, in a personal communication, indicated that these artifacts were common as well at the Tanque Verde site east of Tucson; no such artifacts were listed by Sayles (Gladwin and others 1937) for Snaketown.

The exact function of these sawlike objects is difficult to ascertain. Some were probably harvesting tools used as sickles. The teeth on most of the Hodges specimens are sharp and well defined; employed with a sawing motion, they would have been highly effective tools (Fig. 6.3). Only one of the surviving saws from the Hodges site seems to have been provided with a handle (Fig. 6.3*f*).

The following frequencies are indicated for the items I have chosen to call saws:

Phase	Number
Tanque Verde	2
Rincon	2
Rillito	2
Cañada del Oro	0
Snaketown	0
Unplaced	8
Total	14

So far as could be determined from the few specimens assignable to phases, no typological developments or significant phase differences are indicated. Sandstone apparently was the most popular material from which saws were manufactured. Phyllite (serpentinite), slate, muscovite, schist, and basalt were also represented.

Hoe

The one tool categorized as a hoe is of siltstone and was associated with materials of the Rincon phase (Fig. 6.3*d*). The working edge has been thinned but is not serrated as is the case with the saws.

Anvil

No anvil is listed in the field catalogue. However, one object (catalogued as a mano) has deep "pecking marks" on both surfaces and must have been employed, at least secondarily, as an anvil (Fig. 6.4*b*). It is of basalt and apparently belonged to either the Rillito or Rincon phase.

CHIPPED IMPLEMENTS

Drills

Five drills appear in the field catalogue with no notation as to size or shape. Two were assigned to the Tanque Verde phase, one to the Rillito, and two were unplaced.

Projectiles

[*Ed. note*: According to the field catalogue, the original inventory included 158 points. More than half this number (85) were in the surviving collection examined by Officer. After consultation with Bruce Huckell several of the following projectile point identifications have been modified from Officer's original text.] Although no Pioneer period projectiles were found, the three points shown in Figure 6.5*c*, *d*, *g* could be preceramic in age. Specimen *d* is from a Rillito-Rincon phase house (House 65), and *g* is from a test trench designated in the field catalogue as Cañada del Oro to Rillito in age. However, the points are not characteristic of those phases and may have been retrieved in aboriginal times from preceramic sites.

The other points illustrated (Fig. 6.5*a*, *b*, *e*, *f*) are of less obvious affinity but bear some relationships to ceramic age points from the San Pedro Valley.

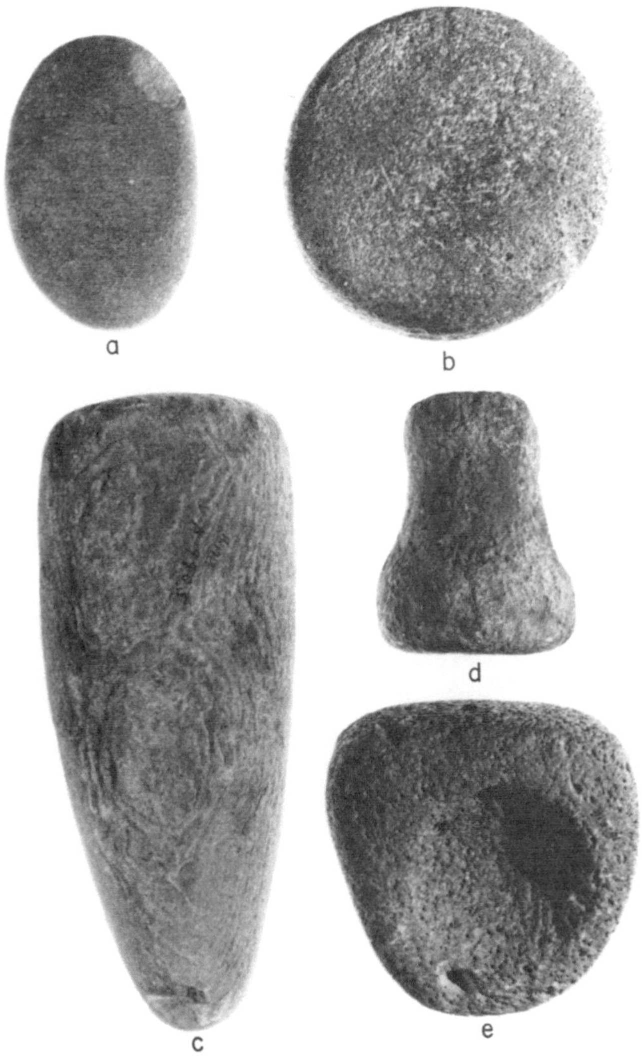

Fig. 6.4 Anvil, mortar, pestles, polishing stone. *Use: a*, polishing stone; *b*, anvil; *c*, *d*, pestles; *e*, small mortar. *Phase: b*, Rillito or Rincon; *e*, Tanque Verde; others, unplaced. *Material: a*, diorite; *b*, basalt; *c*, gneiss; *d*, *e*, scoria. Length of *c*, 23.5 cm.

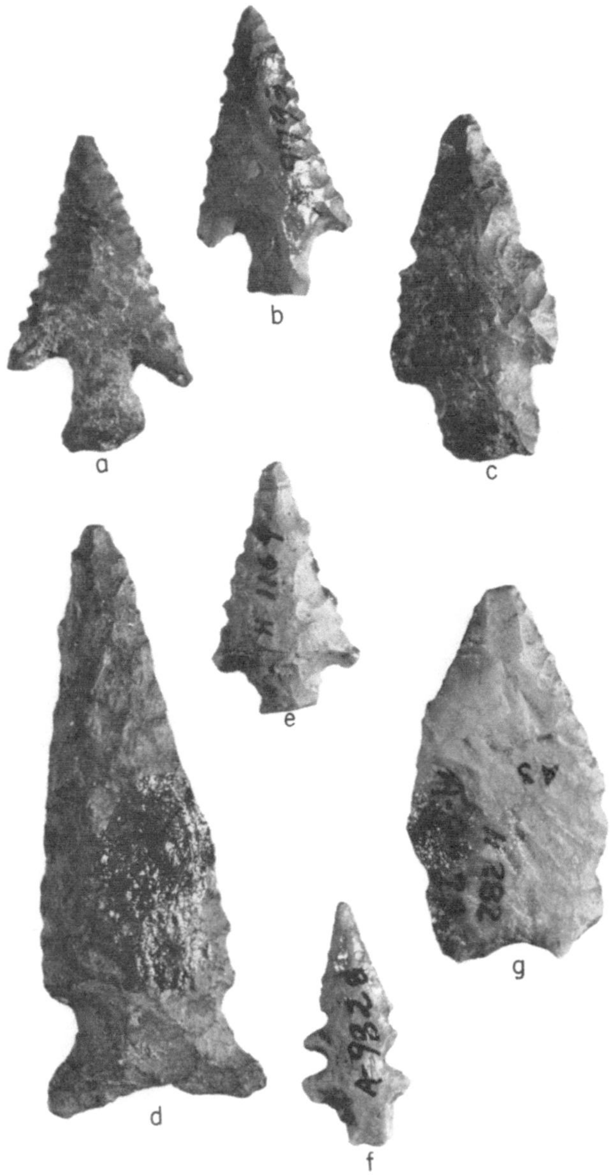

Fig. 6.5 Miscellaneous projectiles. *a*, *b*, *e*, *f*, unplaced; *c*, *d*, *g*, possibly preceramic. Length of *g*, 3.8 cm.

Specimens from the Cañada del Oro phase are barbed and serrated (Fig. 6.6*i–l*) with either concave or short stem bases. These were apparently the most common point types at the Hodges site prior to Tanque Verde times, when a distinct new type became dominant. [*Ed. note*: None of the points illustrated in Figure 6.6*i–l* comes from associations that are definitely Cañada del Oro. Specimen *j* is from a cremation identified in the field catalogue as Cañada del Oro to Santa Cruz. The others are not datable.]

Nearly half the projectiles assignable to phase are Rillito. If we include those found in mixed Cañada del Oro–Rillito and Rillito–Rincon contests, the number is well over half. Almost without exception, Rillito projectiles (Fig. 6.7) are like those indicated for the Cañada del Oro phase.

Only three points definitely belong to the Rincon phase. Two are of the barbed and serrated types previously mentioned (Fig. 6.6*f*, *h*). The third type is a new one that apparently became dominant during the succeeding Tanque

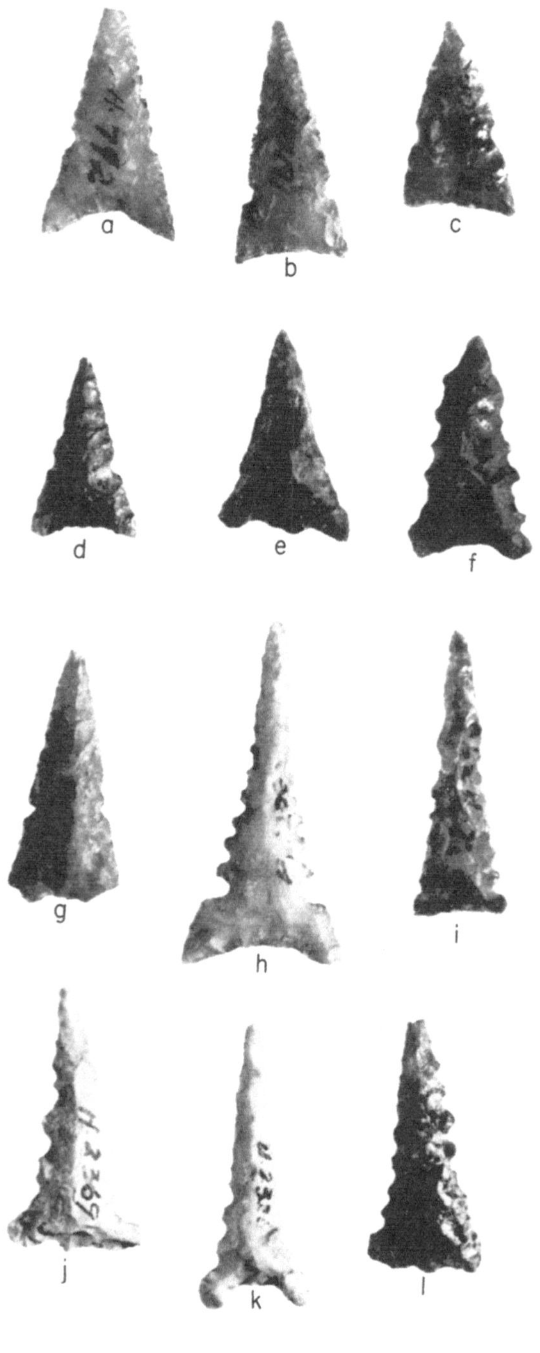

Fig. 6.6 Miscellaneous projectiles. *Phase: a–d,* Tanque Verde; *e–h,* Rincon; *i–l,* Cañada del Oro (?). *Material: a–c, g, i;* chalcedony; *d–f, l;* chert; *h, j, k,* flint. Length of *l*, 2.8 cm.

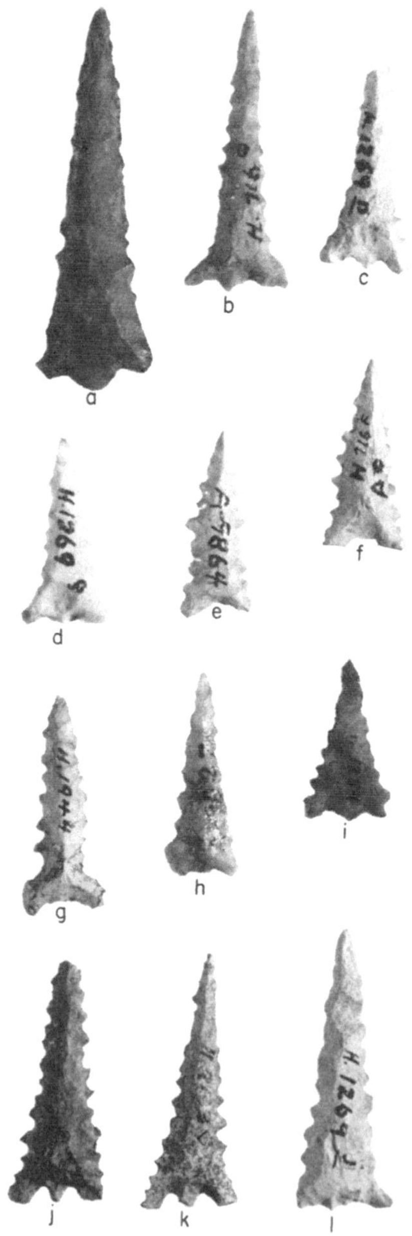

Fig. 6.7 Barbed and serrated projectiles: Rillito phase. Length of *l*, 3.4 cm.

Verde phase. It is relatively small, concave-based, and side-notched (Fig. 6.6*a–d*).

A summary of the more diagnostic point types from the Hodges site follows:

Phase	Principal Point Type
Tanque Verde	Concave-based, side-notched
Rincon	None diagnostic; first appearance of concave-based, side-notched
Rillito	Barbed, serrated with either concave or short-stem base
Probable Cañada del Oro	Similar to Rillito
Snaketown	None indicated

Knives

Kelly's notes did not indicate the presence of flaked stone knives at the Hodges site, although objects that could be classified as knives were noted during later observations at the site. If Kelly excavated any such artifacts, they were not entered in the field catalogue and are not now in the collection.

Scrapers

These were apparently scattered throughout the site, generally in contexts that could not be dated. Two are listed in the field catalogue and are still in the collection. One is from a Rincon phase cremation and one is from the floor of House 69 (unplaced).

GROUND IMPLEMENTS

Axes and Hammerstones

With two exceptions, all axes identifiable as to phase are sketched in Figure 6.8. All are well shaped and most are

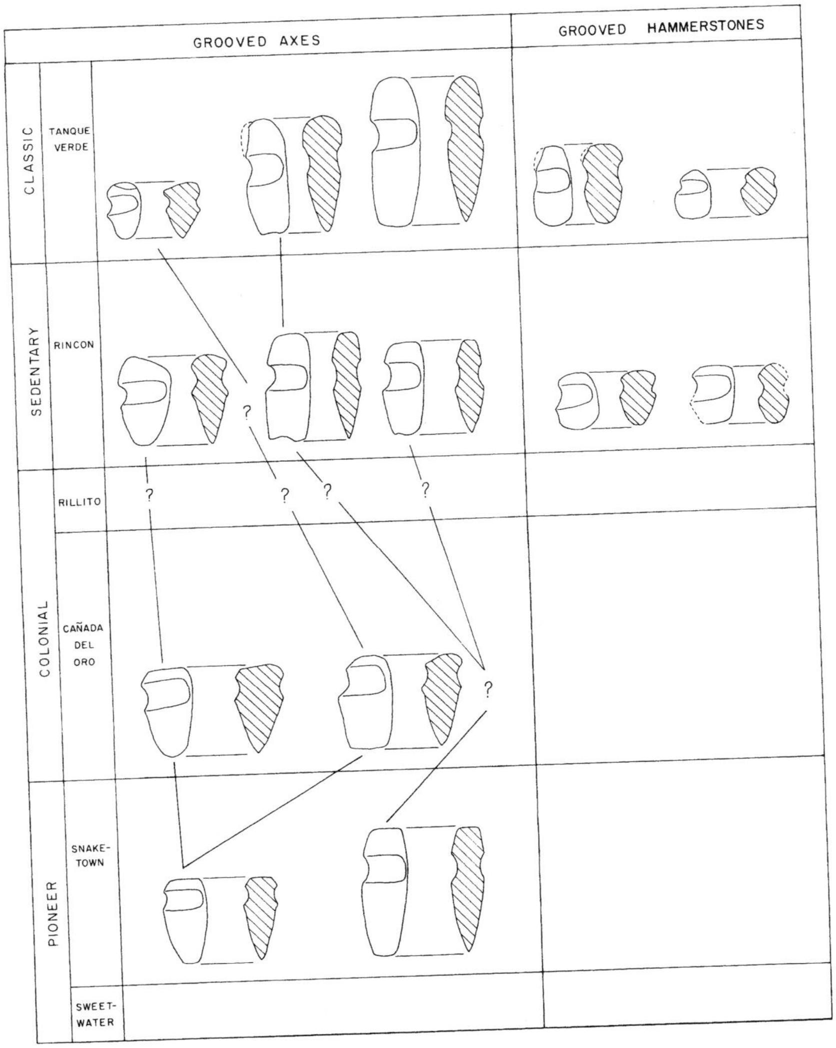

Fig. 6.8 Developmental chart of axes and hammerstones

polished. The two specimens not illustrated are both fragments from the Rincon phase; one is ridged at the juncture between the poll and the groove; the other is unridged.

Some general statements can be made concerning sequential change in form, but there is no clear-cut cleavage between the various phases, nor indeed between the several periods. Terminology used here is that suggested by Cosgrove and Cosgrove (1932:41) and reproduced by Sayles (Gladwin and others 1937: Fig. 40). Axes are discussed according to morphological characteristics.

General Features. All axes, from the Pioneer to Classic periods, are three-quarter grooved. Through time, there appears to be a progressive shortening of the bit in relation to the ax as a whole. Moreover, in the Pioneer and early Colonial periods the greatest diameter occurs generally at the ridge below the groove (Fig. 6.9*a*), whereas in later phases the maximum diameter frequently is at the poll. In absolute size, the greatest range is found in the Tanque Verde phase, which includes both a miniature and an oversized form (Fig. 6.10*a*, *b*).

Fig. 6.9 Grooved axes: Pioneer to early Colonial periods

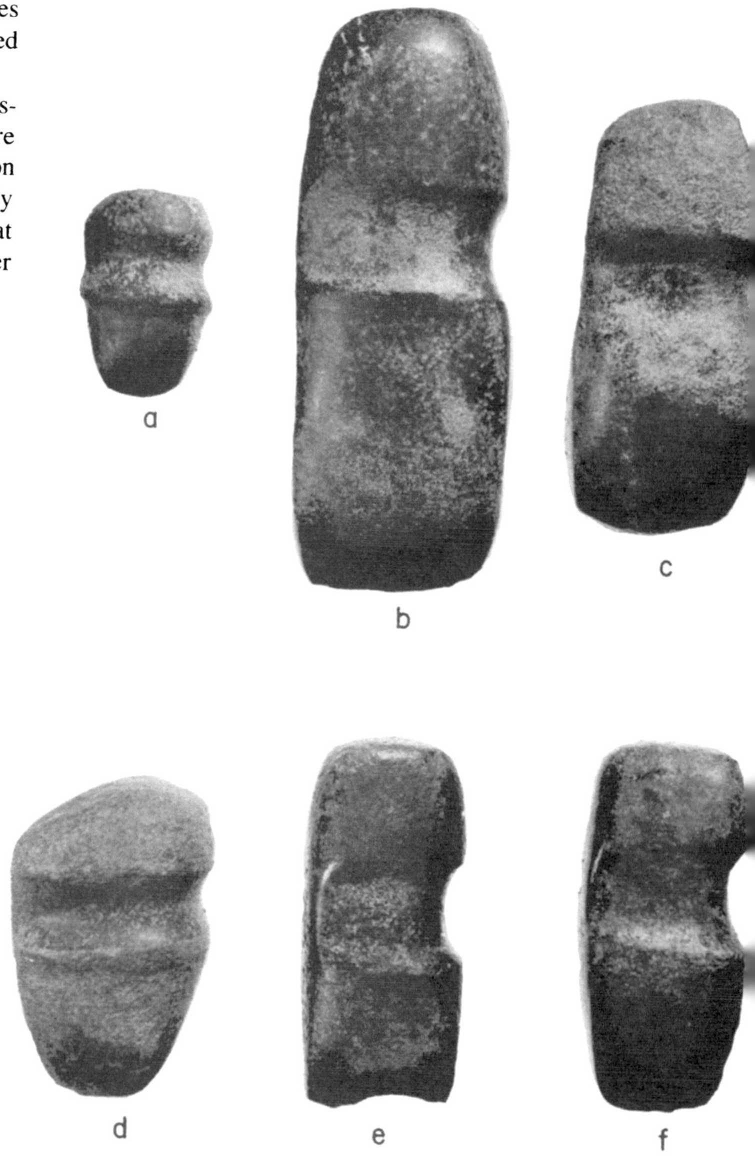

Fig. 6.10 Grooved axes: Classic period, Tanque Verde phase. Length of *a*, 7.2 cm.

Ridging. Heavy ridging above and below the groove is marked in Pioneer and early Colonial specimens (Fig. 6.9*a*, *b*). This is also the case in the Gila Basin (Gladwin and others 1937: 114). A single ridge below the groove continues through the Rincon phase into the Tanque Verde phase. The single ridge also survives into the Sedentary and

Classic periods in the closely related hammerstone (Fig. 6.11*a–d*). But it must be noted that one of the two axes of the Snaketown phase is weakly ridged, if at all (Fig. 6.9*d*?). Moreover, the one Rincon fragment not figured is heavily

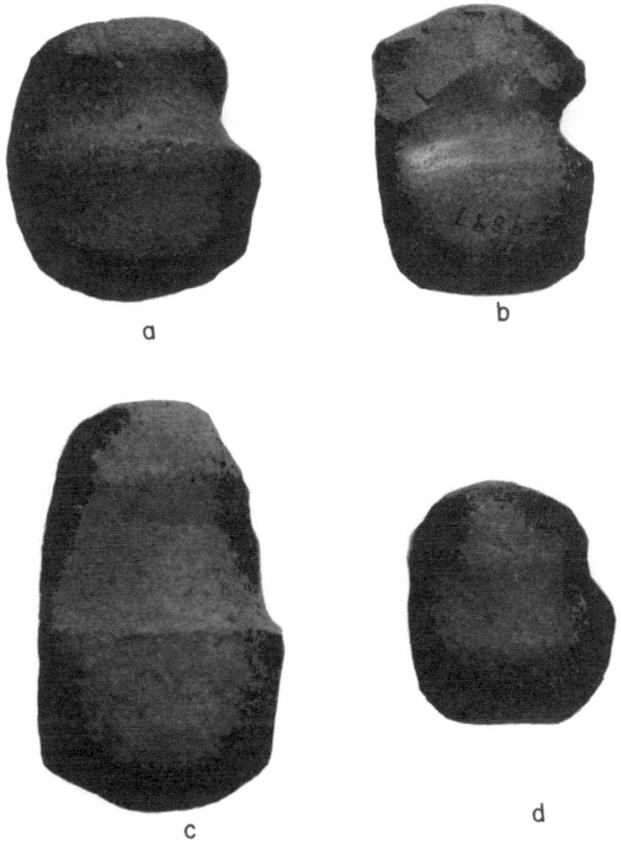

Fig. 6.11 Hammerstones. Length of *b*, 13.7 cm.

ridged. Ridging, therefore, may be a trait that continues through the entire series but which is more pronounced in pre-Sedentary times, as is also the case at Snaketown (Gladwin and others 1937: Fig. 44).

Poll Form. The flattened poll seems also to be early (Fig. 6.9*c*), although the miniature ax of the Tanque Verde phase (Fig. 6.10*a*) may originally have had this form. A rounded poll—convex in profile and circular or oval when viewed from above—is rather rare. Figure 6.9*a* is the best example, but all the grooved hammerstones have polls rounded to a greater or lesser degree (Fig. 6.11). On the basis of this material, the rounded poll appears to be Colonial period and later. The most common poll form may be described as semi-squared. Its top is convex or slightly flattened and, viewed from above, it is a quadrilateral with rounded corners. It occurs as early as the Snaketown phase (Fig. 6.9 *a, b*) and is still present in Rincon and Tanque Verde times.

Inner Edge. Flattening of the inner edge of the ax is a trait that occurs from the Snaketown to Tanque Verde phases. A rounded inner edge is somewhat later, confined to the Rincon and Tanque Verde phases. Strangely enough, a grooved inner edge, with the depression extending from the head to at least half the length of the bit, is late. In axes, it is confined to the Tanque Verde phase; in hammerstones, to the Rincon and Tanque Verde phases. In the Gila Basin, on the contrary, this grooving is characteristic of the Pioneer period. Also characteristic of early axes in the Gila Basin is a raised area on the inner edge opposite the groove. None of our specimens has even a suggestion of this form.

Metates

To judge from the field catalogue, 21 metates were excavated. This is not a large representation, considering the number of houses uncovered. Only three of these—all of the open-end trough variety—were examined.

In her section on manos, Kelly implies the open-end trough metate was dominant in all phases at the Hodges site. The field catalogue does not list metate types, but in one case, a parenthetical notation "not troughed" tells us that such a specimen was unusual enough to provoke comment.

Kelly identified one Snaketown phase metate and noted that it was concave-troughed to accommodate a convex-faced mano found nearby. Other manos suggest that metates with narrow troughs may have been characteristic of the early Sedentary period. However, one narrow-troughed type, associated with Tanque Verde phase materials, indicates these metates survived into Classic period times.

The following phase identification of metates was compiled entirely from information in the field catalogue.

Phase	Number
Tanque Verde	3
Rincon	1
Rillito-Rincon	1
Rillito	2
Cañada del Oro	0
Snaketown	1
Unplaced	12
Total	20

The one "non-troughed" metate shown in the field catalogue came from the floor of a Rillito house. Metates were made from diorite, latite, and scoria.

Manos

Manos are predominantly of lava; other volcanic stones, granite, and granitic materials are scarce. Typologically, manos are mostly quadrilateral and unifacial with a convex grinding surface along the long axis. The short axis

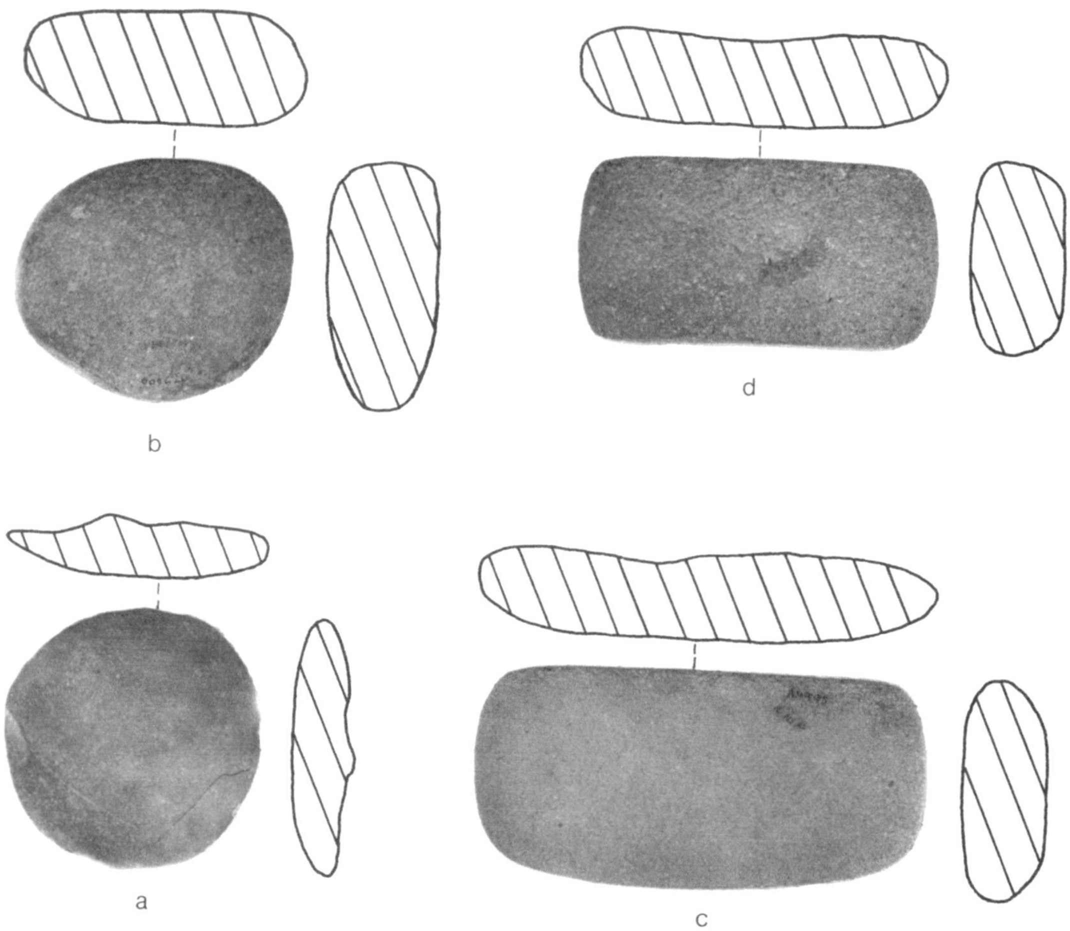

Fig. 6.12 Manos: Short and long types. Length of *c*, 20.5 cm.

is more nearly flat. The form, in particular the convexity, suggests use with a trough metate.

The chief difference within the series lies in length. Short manos average about 15 cm in length, while long ones are 20 cm and greater. Length varies directly with the width of the metate trough. Examples of both short and long manos are shown in Figure 6.12.

Although not provable, it seems from general excavation that the short mano is somewhat earlier than the long. On the whole, the few placed metates would tend to substantiate this belief, but in one case, at least, a short, narrow-troughed metate is attributable to the Tanque Verde phase. It is not possible, therefore, to demonstrate any time differences for the specimens.

Mano width is consistently between 8 and 11 cm and probably is determined by the grasping capacity of the hand. Thickness is another matter. Typologically it seems to be of no significance, as it varies directly with the amount of wear. The extremes in thickness range from 2 to 9 cm. Those near the maximum have been freshly shaped and little used, while those near the lower extreme are well worn.

Unclassified and aberrant manos include a variety of forms and the full range in dimensions and materials:

Unclassified—9 specimens: One is very convex and suggests use with the type of metate that is apparently from the Pioneer phase. The wear is approximately what might be expected from such use. Moreover, the mano is dated as Snaketown phase or earlier and comes from the same house floor as the one Snaketown phase metate.

Asymmetrical—18 specimens: The sides of some are unworked. Most are unifacial, although some are bifacial.

Keeled—5 specimens.

Miscellaneous handstones with rubbed surface or surfaces—20 specimens: Most are bifacial, either convex or plano-convex. They may be unshaped, pecked on the edges, or worked into ovoid, circular, or nearly quadrilateral forms. One of these, placed as Tanque Verde phase, has evidence of red paint on the grinding surface.

Unfinished, in various stages of manufacture—12 specimens.

The following chart presents information concerning phase identification of the various mano types:

Phase	Quadrilateral Convex, Uniface		Unclassified and Aberrant
	Long	Short	
Tanque Verde	6	1	1
Rincon	21	2	11
Rillito-Rincon	6	2	4
Rillito	1	1	2
Cañada del Oro	1	0	1
Snaketown (or earlier)	0	1	1
Unplaced	60	5	44
Total	95	12	64

Mortars

Only three are listed in the field catalogue. The two specimens still in the collection are both of the type illustrated in Figure 6.4*e*. The illustrated specimen is of sandstone; the other is of scoria. The third specimen is listed in the field catalogue as being of latite porphyry; nothing of its size or shape is indicated. The illustrated specimen and the one of latite porphyry were associated with Tanque Verde phase materials. The other was found in a mixed Rillito–Rincon context.

Pestles

The field catalogue lists nine pestles, apparently of different sizes (Fig. 6.4*c*, *d*) and materials. They are of gabbro, scoria, and gneiss, and range in length from 8 to 35 cm. Of those examined, all but two were unplaced as to phase, so that little can be stated about typological change. Phase associations determined from catalogue listings are as follows:

Phase	Number
Tanque Verde	1
Rincon	3
Rillito	0
Cañada del Oro	0
Snaketown	0
Unplaced	5
Total	9

Shaped Stones

These objects are uncommon at the Hodges site. Of the three specimens shown in Figure 6.13*a–c*, one of doubtful use has an irregular basin-like cavity on either surface (Fig. 6.13*a*). The specimen illustrated in Figure 6.13*b* is plano-convex. An unplaced specimen (Fig. 6.13*c*), similar to *b*, has both upper and lower surfaces convex. All three specimens probably served as handstones and are generally similar to the stones figured in Gladwin and others (1937: Plate XLV).

Fig. 6.13 Stone artifacts: Shaped stones, rings, and discoidals. *Shaped stones: a*, Rillito; *b*, Tanque Verde, *c*, unplaced. *Rings: d*, Rillito; *e*, Tanque Verde; *f*, unplaced. *Discoidals: g*, Snaketown; *h*, Rillito; *i*, Snaketown. Greatest diameter of *g*, 10.8 cm.

Stone Rings

Stone rings intergrade on the one hand with shaped stones, on the other, with stone bowls. The standard, doughnutlike type occurs from the Rillito to the Tanque Verde phase; generally it is lava or tufa, with the bore characteristically ridged in the center, by virtue of having been perforated from either surface (Fig. 6.13*d–f*). Included in this category are two unplaced fragments that appear to be rings in the process of manufacture, with the perforation incomplete. A variant of the doughnutlike ring is girdled (Fig. 6.13*f*); its side contour suggests a relationship to shaped stones.

Attributable to the Rincon phase are two aberrant stone rings. One, of lava, is far above average in size and has four carefully worked oval cavities on its upper surface (Fig. 6.14 *Rincon left*). The other odd form is of tufa and in its incised ornament intergrades with stone bowls (Fig. 6.14

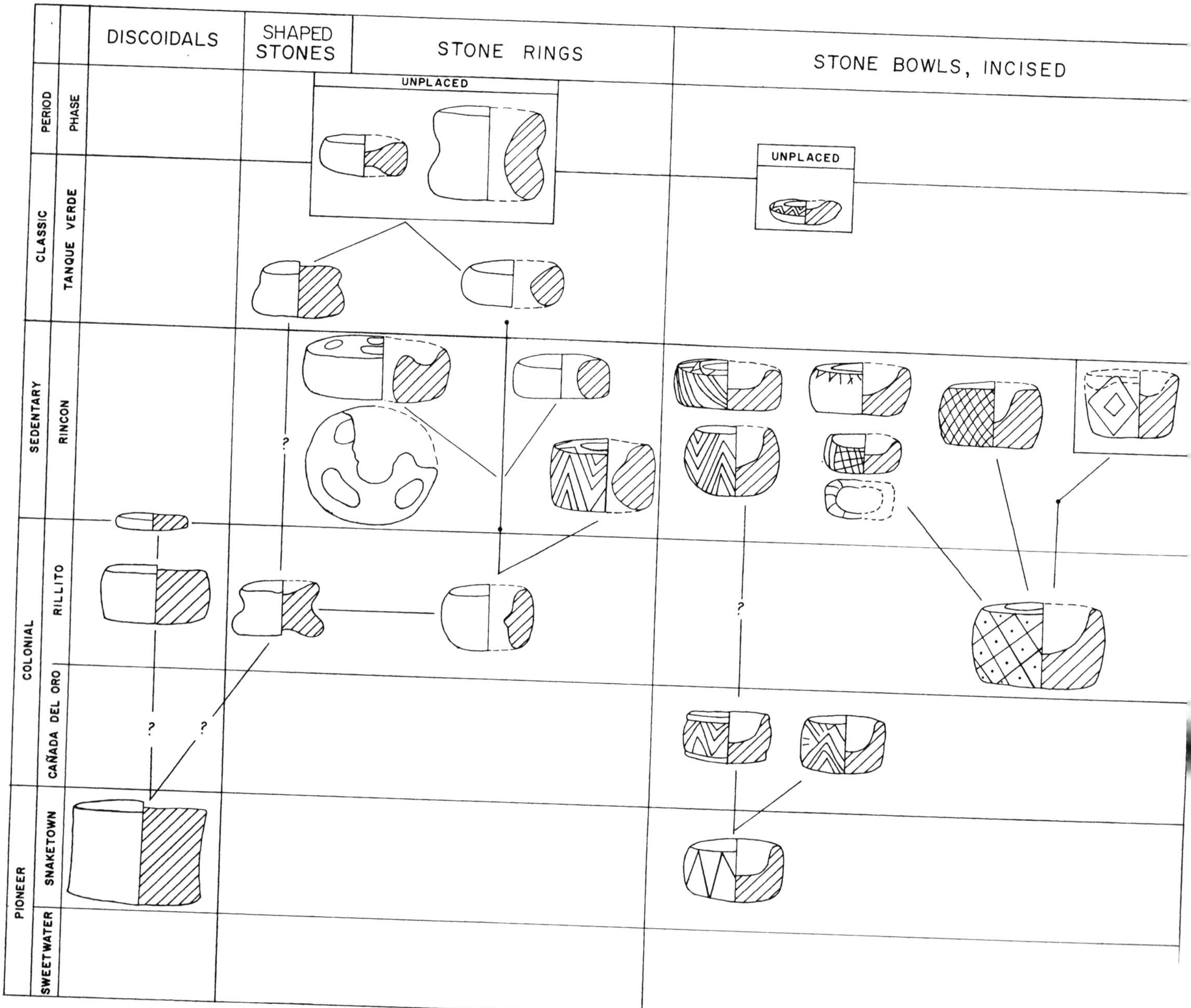

Fig. 6.14 Developmental chart of incised stone bowls, discoidals, shaped stones, and stone rings

Rincon lower right). Of the incised rings, there are three instances, one Rincon, the others unplaced.

Discoidals

Several discoidal stones (Fig. 6.13*g–i*) are of indeterminate utility. All are well worked and polished, except one Snaketown phase specimen of sandstone (*g*), which is not susceptible to polish. Side contours vary from concave through straight to convex. The few specimens range from the Snaketown phase to late Rillito or early Rincon and suggest a progressive decrease in both height and diameter. This trend appears to hold as well for the Gila Basin (Gladwin and others 1937: Plate LXXXIV).

BOWLS

Undecorated

A synoptic series of undecorated stone bowls is given in Figure 6.15. From the Snaketown phase are three well-worked bowls, two of which are oval or quadrilateral (Fig.

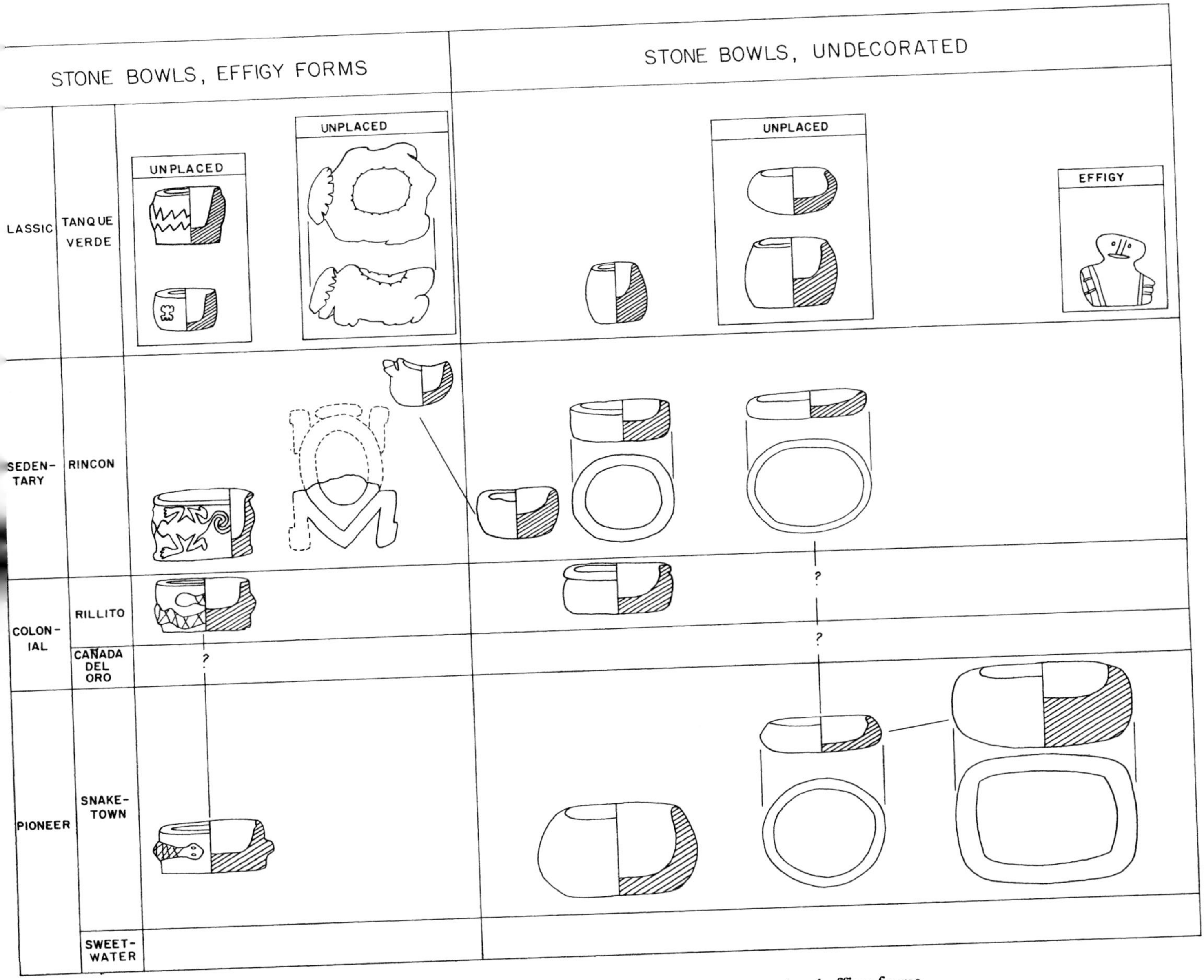

Fig. 6.15 Developmental chart of stone bowls: Undecorated and effigy forms

6.16*d*, *e*). All are convex-sided and—in contrast to decorated stone vessels—have rounded bottoms. Examples shown in Figure 6.16 from the Rillito (*c*) and Rincon (*f*, *g*) phases, respectively, are closer to the carved bowls in material and shape; they are of tufa and have flat bottoms. The same holds for the unplaced specimen shown in Figure 6.17*f*.

Classified as stone bowls are a number of large pebbles and semi-shaped stones with a shallow cavity on one surface. Two are definitely of the Tanque Verde phase (Fig. 6.16*a*, *b*); the rest are unplaced. When found, the larger of the Tanque Verde specimens (Fig. 6.16*a*) was filled with hematite, which suggests use for paint mixing. However, none of the other stone vessels, either ornamented or plain, shows obvious traces of paint. The shallow-cavity, pebble-like bowls suggest prototypes of the better-shaped ones; because of their occurrence in Tanque Verde, however, they cannot be regarded as ancestral forms.

Fig. 6.16 Stone bowls: Undecorated. *a*, *b*, Tanque Verde; *c*, Rillito; *d*, *e*, Snaketown; *f*, *g*, Rincon. Maximum diameter of *a*, 12.5 cm.

Fig. 6.17 Stone bowls: Incised. *a*, Snaketown; *b*, Cañada del Oro; *c*, *d*, Rincon; *e*, Rillito; *f*, unplaced. Maximum diameter of *e*, 9.5 cm.

Incised

Stone vessels with incised ornament evidently range from the Pioneer through the Sedentary period (Fig. 6.17). About half occur in cremations; the remainder, in trash. They may be genuinely absent from the Classic period.

As far as shape is concerned, there are minor variations. On the whole, the bowls are slightly barrel-shaped, with a definitely flat bottom. In profile, the walls vary slightly, chiefly in the rim, which may be squared or rounded to tapered. Because shape is more or less uniform, the distinctions in Figure 6.17 lie primarily in ornament.

The Rincon series is larger than others, and doubtless for this reason appears more varied in all regards. Shape variations include a rounded bottom (Fig. 6.17*c*), ovoid form (Fig. 6.14 *specimen shown in plan and cross section*), and a straight-sided, slightly flared contour (Fig. 6.17*d*). The last-mentioned specimen is unique in having its incised areas further decorated with red paint—a trait not as yet reported from elsewhere.

Unique in size, form, and field of ornament is the small, unplaced vessel shown in Figure 6.14.

Many of these little bowls are well worked. On the whole, the few early specimens (attributed to Snaketown and Cañada del Oro) are characterized by sharper and clearer cut work, both in shaping and incising. Very likely this is a corollary of material. The later bowls are of tufa which is easily worked, but not a satisfactory medium for precise craftsmanship.

Effigy

Effigy bowls (Fig. 6.18) are divisible into two categories: one with the figure in relief carving on the walls of the vessel; the other, which is three-dimensional, with the bowl cavity contained in the body of the effigy. The synoptic series in Figure 6.15 shows the former to have the same time range as the geometrically incised vessels (Fig. 6.14), namely, from the Snaketown to the Rincon phase. The three-dimensional effigies are rare and appear to be Rincon in time.

The first category of stone effigy vessels consists chiefly of a serpent entwined about the vessel (Fig. 6.18*a–f*). Of the three-dimensional effigies, there are but two specimens, with a third fragment. Figure 6.18*g* represents a horned toad, with a cavity on the back and belly. Other animals are not identifiable, but one specimen (not illustrated) suggests a lizard.

Local stone vessels evidently relate to those of the Gila Basin. Compared with the Snaketown site, they are less

Fig. 6.18 Stone bowls and effigy. *a*, Snaketown; *b*, Rillito; *c*, *h*, Rincon; *d–g*, unplaced; *i*, Tanque Verde. Maximum diameter of *c*, 8 cm.

frequent and less varied. At the same time there are some significant differences in the frequencies of the various types of stone bowls:

	Hodges site (%)	Snaketown[1] (%)
Undecorated	47	42
Incised: Geometric ornament	32	6
Effigies: Life forms in relief	17	28
Effigies: Three-dimensional	5	23
Total	101 (N = 66)	99 (N = 151)

[1]Data from Gladwin and others 1937: 113, Fig. 42.

In proportion to the total, plain, undecorated stone vessels are about equally common in both areas. It is immediately obvious, however, that Hodges has a preference for incised geometric ornament, the Gila Basin, for relief treatment and three-dimensional carving. Doubtless correlated with this fact is the complete absence at Hodges of effigies, similar to the bowls, but lacking the body cavity.

EFFIGIES

The one human effigy from the Tanque Verde phase (Fig. 6.18*i*) is without Gila Basin parallel. It is a crudely worked piece of sandstone, grooved, rather than sculptured. A certain amount of shaping has been done, yet it cannot be considered carving in-the-round. The mouth is a single horizontal groove; the nose, two parallel vertical grooves; the eyes, two dots. A line at either side of the head may represent ears. There is also some simple line ornament on the body.

The remaining effigy (Fig. 6.18*h*) is an animal head, perhaps broken from a stone vessel; it is from the Rincon phase.

SNAKETOWN COMPARISON

Following a format used by Gladwin and others (1937), Figure 6.19 shows the time distribution of placed stone implements and bowls at Hodges (solid line) compared to similar data from Snaketown (dashed line). Some 88 placed items from Hodges and 2391 from Snaketown (Gladwin and others 1937: 113, Fig. 42) were used in this graph. Approximately 269 unplaced items from Hodges and 306 from Snaketown were not included in the tabulation. Figure 6.19 shows a similar time profile for both sites, with activity peaking in the Rincon-Sacaton phases at both sites.

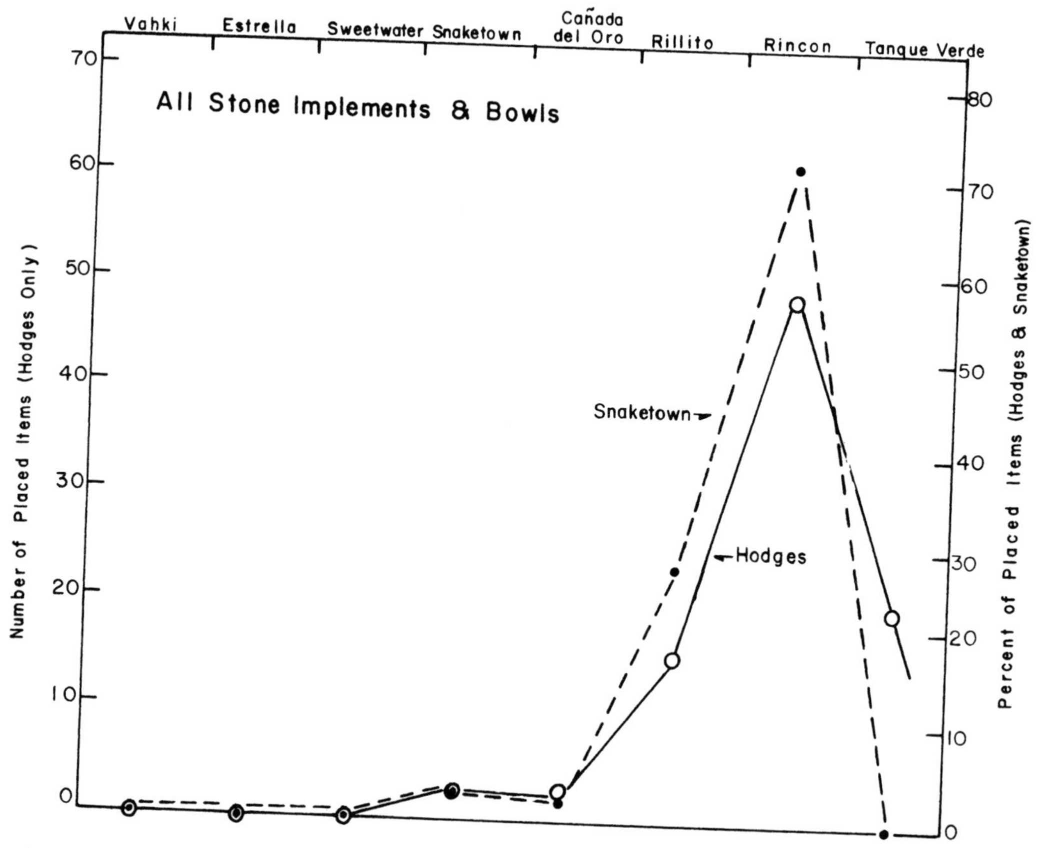

Fig. 6.19 Incidence of placed stone implements and bowls through time at Hodges and Snaketown

7. PALETTES AND STONE ORNAMENTS

PALETTES

Stone palettes similar to those from Snaketown (Gladwin and others 1937:121–126) come from the Hodges site, and, as in the Gila Basin, they occur chiefly as cremation furniture. Although less plentiful than in the Gila Basin, they are found in sufficient quantity to indicate that manufacture was local, even though obviously dependent upon Gila Basin stimulus.

With few exceptions, palettes are of schist, which is soft, easily worked, but not overly durable. Occasionally, other material is used (Fig. 7.1), but almost exclusively for

Fig. 7.1 Palettes: Various phases. *Decorated: a*, Rillito; *b*, Cañada del Oro; *d*, unplaced; *f*, Rincon. *Undecorated; c, e, i*, unplaced; *g–h, j*, Rincon; *k*, Sweetwater; *l*, Cañada del Oro. *Materials: d, e*, arkose; *j*, graywacke; *l*, schist (talc chlorite); all others, slate. Length of *h*, 15.5 cm.

undecorated specimens. Two large, worked sherds from Rillito cremations appear to have functioned as palettes; at least, their concave surfaces have the characteristic incrustation which almost invariably coats the mixing face of palettes. It has been discussed at length by Haury (Gladwin and others 1937: 122, 163–167), and, although no analyses have been made of the incrustation on our specimens, presumably the composition is the same as that determined for the Gila Basin.

Palette evolution is shown in Figure 7.2, and incidence at both Hodges and Snaketown is given in Figure 7.3. Half of the 64 specimens from the Hodges site can be identified

Fig. 7.2 Developmental chart of palettes

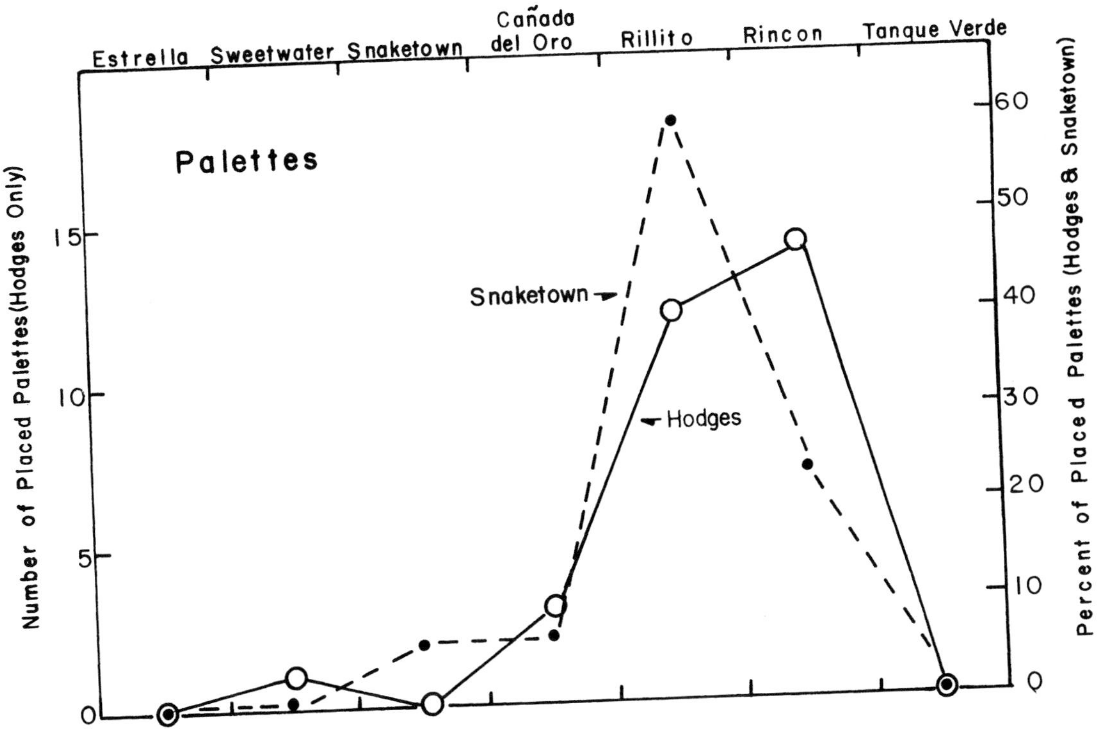

Fig. 7.3 Incidence of placed palettes through time at Hodges and Snaketown

by phase; most of the others can be placed typologically; but several more or less distinct and unallocated forms are shown in the inset of the figure just cited.

Correlated with the scarcity of early cremations at the Hodges site is the almost complete lack of palettes attributable to the Pioneer period. There is, in fact, but one fragment (Fig. 7.1*k*), and this is from the Sweetwater phase. It is the end of a schist slab, shaped but unornamented. Palettes generally similar—worked, but undecorated—are found also in the Cañada del Oro and Rincon phases. Because of their occurrence in the Sedentary period, they cannot be regarded as proto-palettes, although typologically they qualify. Haury (Gladwin and others 1937: 122–123) has noted a relationship to the abrading stone and perhaps to the metate, but we have no local evidence that is pertinent. Most of our palettes have a depression worn on the mixing surface, certainly the result of abrasion; one from the Rincon phase (Fig. 7.5*a*) is worn completely through.

For the Snaketown phase, we have no palettes. Doubtless this results from the paucity of Pioneer cremations and does not imply that palettes were not manufactured at this time. The three specimens from the Cañada del Oro phase (Figs. 7.1*b*, *l*; 7.4*d*) indicate a certain degree of specialization by early Colonial times, although the numbers are too few for safe generalization. The decorated palette illustrated in Figure 7.1*b* is tapering and more or less convex-sided, while the specimen in Figure 7.4*d* has the slightly concave sides and ends which are especially characteristic of the Rillito phase. One specimen has the border raised slightly above the mixing surface; the other has an incised line as its only border differentiation. The medial groove and notched edges evidently have become established by Cañada del Oro times.

With the Rillito phase, the selection of palettes is larger and considerable variation is evident in form, shape, size, and decoration. Shapes range from concave, through straight, to convex-sided, although of the latter there is but one example (Fig. 7.4*b*). Size varies from 5 to 13 cm in width and from 10.5 to 23.5 cm in length. A generally elongate form is favored. Characteristic Rillito treatment involves a border generally grooved and notched and raised somewhat above the mixing surface. The medial groove is consistent save for several specimens that evidently are late in the series and show predominant Rincon qualities (Fig. 7.5*b–e*, for example). One sculptured palette is identifiable as Rillito. Inasmuch as only two sculptured specimens (Figs. 7.4*e*; 7.6*c*) were found, they may be Gila Basin trade pieces. The rim of each is noticeably higher than those of the general run of the local series.

With the Rincon phase, palettes generally are straight-sided, rarely concave, occasionally slightly convex. The size range is somewhat greater than in the Rillito phase, although the maxima are almost the same (width, 3.5 to 13.5 cm; length, 6.5 to 23.5 cm). There is a slight tendency, less marked than in the Gila Basin, toward proportionately greater width than in the preceding phase. The border may be flush with the mixing surface, but this tendency is less marked than in the Sacaton phase of the Gila

Fig. 7.4 Palettes: Colonial period. *d,* Cañada del Oro; all others, Rillito. *Materials:* all are slate. Length of *f,* 23 cm

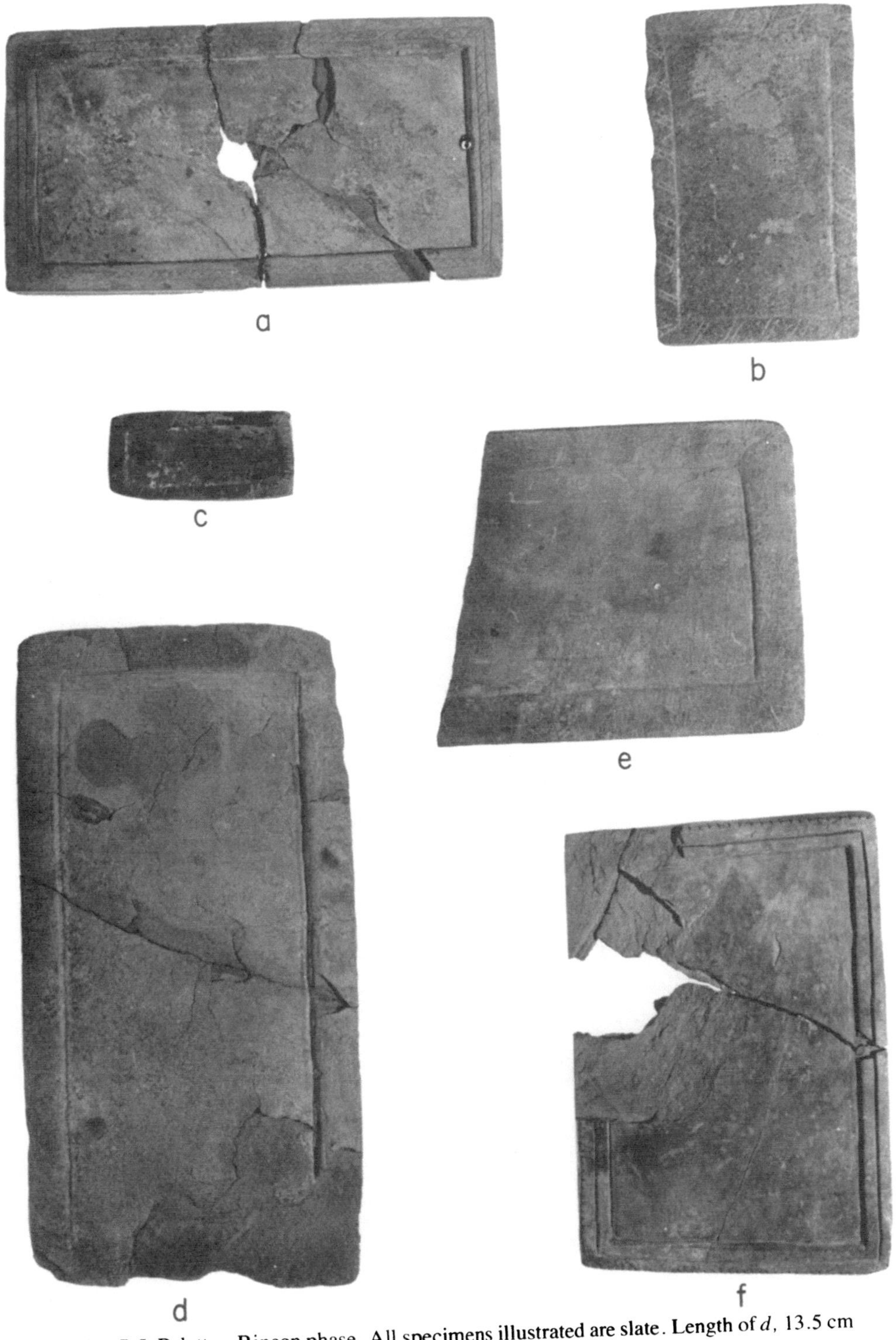

Fig. 7.5 Palettes: Rincon phase. All specimens illustrated are slate. Length of *d*, 13.5 cm

Basin. In the Rincon phase, the grooved and notched rim and the medial groove have been virtually abandoned, and borders characteristically are ornamented with running incised designs (Fig. 7.5*a–c*). The general decadence which in the Gila Basin characterizes the change from the Colonial to Sedentary periods is clearly evident. Workmanship is less precise than in the Rillito phase; shaping often is careless, and the back side of palettes is frequently unworked or, if worked, poorly finished. As in the Gila Basin, palettes appear to have died out during the Sedentary period; we have none attributable to the Tanque Verde phase despite a goodly number of cremations of that phase.

Several of the unplaced palettes (Fig. 7.6) are of interest as local variants. Moreover, the slightly convex sides occurring persistently at the Hodges site (Fig. 7.6*a*, *d*, *j*) have no counterparts in the Gila Basin unless in occasional undecorated palettes. Another trait which may be local is the heavy notching of the edge, which results in a scalloped effect (Fig. 7.6*b*). Neither of these details can be assigned to any one phase.

In palettes, as in many other aspects of culture, an essential dependence on the Gila Basin Hohokam is evident. The development, phase by phase, is in general agreement, so far as can be determined from our limited

Fig. 7.6 Palettes: Unplaced as to phase. Typologically *a–c* are Rillito; *d–f* and *h–j* are Rincon. Length of *j*, 9.4 cm

data. At the same time, the full palette complex seems not to have reached Tucson; sculptured borders are lacking, as are effigy, handled, and circular forms. In workmanship, the palettes from the Hodges site compare favorably with their Gila Basin equivalents, but in richness and variety of form, the local series is distinctly limited. Only in the occasional convex contour and the heavily notched edges, both of which are mentioned above, do the Hodges specimens show features not definitely established for the Gila Basin.

MOSAIC AND PAINTED PLAQUES

Of these plaques, there are five examples, plus a dubious sixth. Unfortunately, four of the specimens are from cremations without decorated pottery in association. These four are illustrated and described in Figure 7.7. The fifth and sixth are from the floor of an unplaced house (House 43, overlain by a Rillito cremation) and from mixed trash.

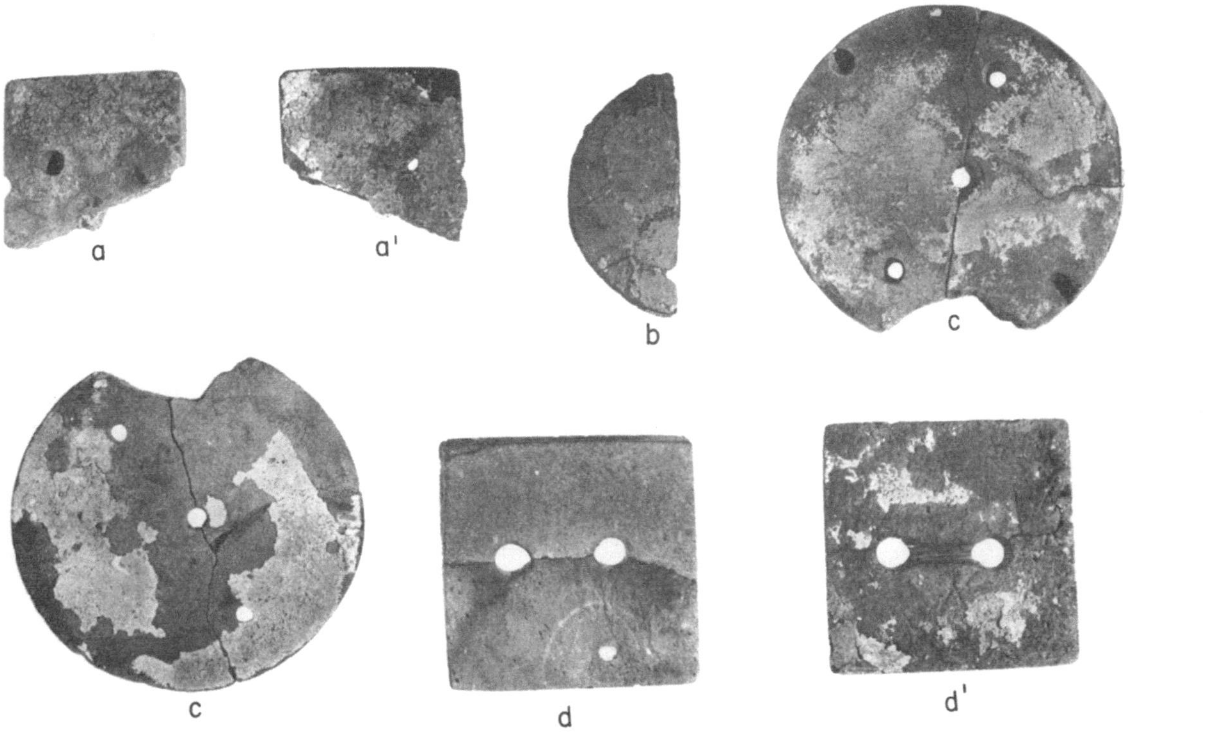

Fig. 7.7 Mosaic and painted plaques.

a, a' Lower and upper faces of rectangular plaque fragment. Perforation at left center of *a* is diagonal and is covered on upper face (*a'*) by inlay cement. The lower face may have been ornamented; there is no evidence of inlay, but it appears to have been surfaced. This, however, may be natural incrustation. Both this and the inlay cement react to hydrochloric acid. The upper face is nearly covered with 0.1 cm cement; there is clear evidence of inlay impressions. A suspension cord evidently ran from left-hand perforation at broken edge of *a*, diagonally to perforation at lower right corner. These two perforations are connected by a channel, covered with cement; the impression of a suspension strand (no suggestion of twisted cord) is clearly visible in the cement. Evidently the plaque hung horizontally, with paired diagonal suspension strands, for the channel is at a noticeable angle to the axes.

b Circular plaque fragment, upper face, showing impressions of inlay in cement. Diameter is approximately 8.5 cm; thickness, 0.7 cm. The side has a deep medial groove similar to some palettes. Perforation at lower right is bored from lower face; inlay on upper face originally covered perforation.

c, c' Lower and upper face views of circular plaque. Face diameters are 11.2 and 11.5 cm respectively; thickness is 0.7 cm. Sides are nearly vertical. Perforations are bored from lower face; perforation at upper left of *c* is diagonal, its opening on the side instead of the upper face. Opposite marginal perforation of *c* was evidently intended to be the same, but the bridge is now broken. The lower face may have been sized and painted; there is no indication, however, of pseudo-cloisonné, as in the Snaketown specimens. Upper surface was probably inlaid; some cement remains, although there are no definite inlay impressions.

d, d' Lower and upper face views of square plaque. It is 8 cm square, 0.9 cm thick; the sides are vertical. Lower face (*d*) is evidently undecorated. Upper face (*d'*) has perforations joined by channel. Ornament presumably covered perforations and channel concealing suspension cord. Some cement (0.1 cm thick) is left on upper face. At upper right of *d'* there is faint indication of red striping; the decoration may have been painted rather than mosaic.

None, therefore, can be allocated to a specific phase. Typologically, however, they are closer to the Gila Basin plaques of the Santa Cruz phase than they are to the later style found at Snaketown (Gladwin and others 1937: 132).

Briefly, it may be said that the plaques are well-worked sandstone slabs, either circular or rectangular, and are so perforated that the suspension cord was concealed from the upper or decorated face. This was accomplished by paired perforations connected by a channel and the whole covered on the upper face by inlay, or by marginal perforations bored diagonally so as to penetrate the edge from the lower face.

Two fragments (Fig. 7.7*a'*, *b*) show inlay impressions clearly. The others may have had painted ornament on a sized ground instead of inlay. There is, moreover, a suggestion of size, or of size and pigment, on the lower surfaces of two plaques (Fig. 7.7*a*, *c*). What we suspect to be sizing, however, may be natural incrustation. Both the size and the inlay cement, as well as the natural incrustation, react strongly to hydrochloric acid. In spite of the suggestion of painted surface, there is no hint of the pseudo-cloisonné ornament described by Haury for Snaketown (Gladwin and others 1937: 131), nor of the beveled face, with the inlay confined to the central section. In every case, decoration appears to have covered the entire surface.

The small number of plaque fragments suggests that this art was not well established at the Hodges site. The few pieces may, of course, have been traded from the Gila Basin; but, even if local, the craft doubtless was dependent upon Gila Basin inspiration. The general cultural implications of mosaic plaques, including a discussion of their relationship to Mexican specimens, have been given by Haury in the Snaketown report (Gladwin and others 1937: 132–134).

OTHER MOSAIC WORK

In addition to mosaic plaques, which presumably were set with iron pyrites, we have evidence of turquoise mosaic. This consists of three cut and beveled flakes, as well as a small cache of tiny rectangular bits of turquoise (2 mm and less in length), all evidently from mosaic work. Associated with the smaller pieces were a number of mica chips that might also have been incorporated in the mosaic.

Turquoise presumably was worked locally. Not only is it relatively frequent in occurrence, but a cache of almost fifty small, unworked chips and what may be part of a half-finished pendant indicate local manufacture. Unfortunately, it is impossible to date the occurrence of turquoise at the Hodges site. One bead (see below) comes from a Snaketown phase cremation; another from a Tanque Verde phase cremation; and a third fragment, worked, but with the original form indeterminate, is attributable to the Rincon phase. All other instances are from mixed trash or from plainware cremations. Although not precisely allocated, the associated pottery types in trash seem to run rather consistently from Snaketown to Rillito phases, suggesting a concentration of turquoise in the late Pioneer period and in the Colonial period, although the three placed specimens attest its presence in the Pioneer, Sedentary, and Classic periods.

ORNAMENTS

Beads

Major bead shapes are shown in Figure 7.8*a–d*. Disc-shaped stone beads with vertical sides are the most common; barrel-shaped, cuboid, and wedge-shaped (Gladwin and others 1937: 127) are rare. On the whole the series is somewhat less varied than that of the Gila Basin, although there, too, simple disc beads predominate. Most beads are perforated from either surface, with a slight ridge in the center of the bore; occasionally they are perforated by continuous boring from one face.

Strangely enough, stone beads are rare in cremations; almost all come from trash. The one bead attributable to the Snaketown phase is turquoise, the relatively early appearance of which is consonant with its presence in the Gila Basin Pioneer period. The frequency given in Table 7.1 represents the independent occurrence of each type, not of the number of individual beads. Actually, in this case, it would make little difference, for stone beads generally occurred singly, but such caution is necessary in dealing with shell beads, for necklaces of considerable size were found occasionally.

Pendants

The simple circular, oval, or wedge-shaped pendants of schist shown in Figure 7.8*m* are similar to those of the Gila Basin (Gladwin and others 1937: Plate CVII*a*). Curiously enough, the carved schist pendants of the latter area are almost lacking, and only one effigy pendant is known from the Hodges site (Fig. 7.8*l*). Although of different material, this specimen is remarkably close in design to that shown in Gladwin and others 1937: Plate CVII*i*.

Turquoise and slate were made into pendants (Fig. 7.8*e*), and, as mentioned above, there is evidence to indicate that the work was done locally. [*Ed. note*: The ornaments shown in Figure 7.8*f–j* were apparently pendants, but they are not discussed in the text and cannot now be located. Their temporal placement is shown in Table 7.1.]

Miscellaneous Ornaments

Two star-shaped ornaments, one whole (Fig. 7.8*k*) and one fragmentary, were found (cf. Kelly 1945: Fig. 74*a*). Both are of quartzite. The whole specimen is from a cremation and the fragment from the surface fill of House 69 (an undated house).

No stone finger rings, ear plugs, or nose buttons were found.

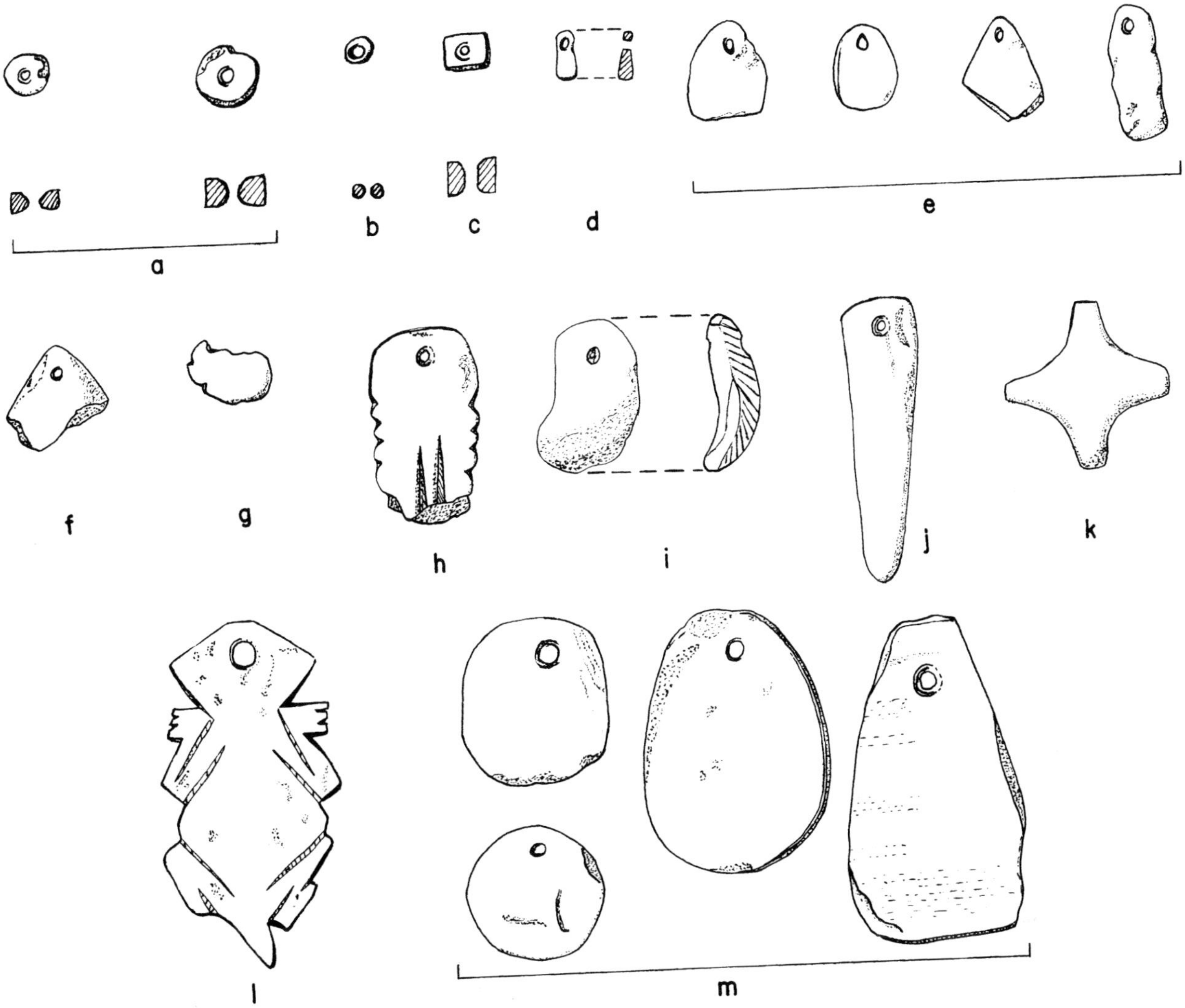

Fig. 7.8 Stone beads and ornaments. Beads: *a*, disc; *b*, barrel-shaped; *c*, cuboid; *d*, wedge-shaped. Pendants: *e*, turquoise and slate pendants; *f–j*, these pendants cannot be located and are not discussed in the text. Ornament: *k*, star-shaped ornament of quartzite. Pendants: *l*, effigy pendant of slate; *m*, schist pendants. Length of *m*, 2.5–5.8 cm.

TABLE 7.1
Phase Distribution of Stone Beads and Ornaments

	Beads (Fig. 7.8)				Other Stone Ornaments (Fig. 7.8)								
	a	*b*	*c*	*d*	*e*	*f*(?)	*g*	*h*	*i*	*j*	*k*	*l*	*m*
Tanque Verde	1												
Rincon	1							1					
Rillito									1			1	2
Cañada del Oro					1								
Snaketown	1												
Sweetwater													
Unplaced	14	1	2	2	10	1	1			1	2		3
Total	17	1	2	2	11	1	1	1	1	1	2	1	5

8. SHELL

Southwestern archaeologists have come to expect from Hohokam sites an abundance of items manufactured from marine shells. Many authorities, including Haury (Gladwin and others 1937:136), Brand (1938:9), Colton (1941:314), and McGregor (1941:226), have postulated that the Hohokam not only made use of shell but also traded both raw and worked shell to other Southwestern peoples. [*Ed. note:* Stanislawski (1961) specifically discusses this hypothesis in connection with *Glycymeris* sp. shells found within a few miles of the Hodges site.]

Excavations at the Hodges site do nothing to discourage such a hypothesis. In all, 22 species of marine shells were recovered, a total exceeded only by the number recorded from Snaketown. McGregor's (1941:215) work at the Winona and Ridge ruins produced 21 species; Pecos yielded 17 (Kidder 1932:183).

Although considerable material was recovered, the analysis of the Hodges shell collection was not easily accomplished. Most objects were found either in cremations or in trash. In the former instance fire had so altered some specimens that determination of the type of ornament and of the shell species was impossible. Whole objects were exceedingly rare and the phase correlation of many specimens was out of the question.

George P. Kanakoff and Howard Hill of the Los Angeles County Museum are acknowledged here for the following register of shell species identified from material in the Hodges collection:

Marine Species

From the Southern California Coast (5)

Cerithidea california Haldeman
Haliotis corrugata Gray
Haliotis fulgens Philippi
Olivella biplicata Sowerby
Olivella boetica Carpenter

From the Sonoran Coast of the Gulf of California (17)

Cardium procerum Sowerby
Cerithidea albonodosa Carpenter
Chama sp. Linné
Codakia distinguenda Tryon
Conus regularis Sowerby
Dosinia ponderosa Gray
Glycymeris maculata Broderip
Levicardium elatum Sowerby
Oliva angulata Lamarck
Olivella volutella Lamarck
Pecten purpuratus Lamarck
Pecten vogdesi Arnold (*P. excavatus* Turton)
Strombus galeatus Sowerby
Trivia radians Lamarck
Turritella goniostoma Valenciennes
Turritella leucostoma Valenciennes
Vermitus sp. Daudin

Fresh-water Species (2)

Anodonta californiensis Lea
Helisoma cf. *trivolvis* Say

SHELL TRADE

I consulted all the Southwestern site reports at my disposal, beginning with Brand (1938) and Tower (1945), and compiled a list of 93 marine shell species identified from ruins in this area. In addition to these 93 *identified* species, there were seven types identified only as to genera, making a total of at least 100 species in Southwestern ruins. Fifty-three of these species are native to the waters of the Gulf of California, 15 to the southern coastal waters of the state of California, and 10 to the Gulf of Mexico. An additional 15 are found in both the Gulf of California and along the Southern California coast.

With the questionable exception of three types (*Alectrion vibex* from Snaketown, *Pecten irradians* from the Starkweather Ruin, and *Pecten exasperatus* from Los Muertos), no specimens from Atlantic waters have been found in sites west of the Continental Divide. According to Tower (1945: 18–19), identification of the three Gulf of Mexico specimens listed above is open to question, since these species are nearly indistinguishable from types found in Pacific waters.

Seventeen of the shell species from the Hodges site could have been obtained only from the Gulf of California; five represent types that derive exclusively from the California coast. At Snaketown, where Pacific Coast specimens might have been brought up the Gila River, the

Ed. note: This entire chapter was prepared by James Officer in 1956. When the first person is used in this chapter, the writer is Officer himself.

positive count of far western species was only three. However, nine of the Snaketown types could have come from either Pacific or Gulf waters, as was the case with four Hodges specimens.

Brand (1938:9) postulated two principal routes by which marine shells entered the Southwest, both passing through Hohokam territory. The more important of these, in Brand's opinion, led from the Gulf of California (Río de la Concepción, on the Sonora coast, south to about the present location of Puerto Libertad), up the Concepción and Altar rivers, then overland to a point near Nogales, Sonora, where the routes split—one segment going east to Chihuahua and southern New Mexico, the other going down the Santa Cruz River to the Gila. This last route would have passed by the Hodges Ruin. Brand's other route went overland from the San Diego region to Yuma, where it divided—its principal artery continuing up the Gila, and a lesser branch going up the Colorado.

Considering that Snaketown is located at the approximate intersection of Brand's principal paths of shell commerce, the preponderance of Gulf of California species at that site argues for closer contact with the Gulf region. Whatever the reason, only *Olivella biplicata*, *Olivella boetica*, *Conus californicus*, the *Haliotis* species, and, conceivably, *Levicardium elatum* appear to have been traded in any quantity from the California coast.

Certainly, the inhabitants of the Hodges site obtained the principal part of their shell from Sonora. *Olivella biplicata*—so common at Snaketown—is scarcely represented. *Haliotis*, too, is uncommon; only two examples are included in the collection. In contrast, the quantity of Gulf shell suggests that the Indians of the Tucson area carried on a lively and flourishing trade with peoples to their southwest.

The presence of comparatively large amounts of shell at the Hodges Ruin strengthens Brand's conclusion that a major trading route passed down the Santa Cruz River. It may also point to the Santa Cruz as the major commercial highway between the Indians of Sonora and those of the Gila River. Sites excavated in the valley of the San Pedro River (DiPeso 1953: 178–179; 1958: 138–141) have produced less shell than the Hodges and Paloparado sites (Di Peso 1956: 81–114) in the Santa Cruz Valley.

It is difficult to estimate the extent to which the Tucson Hohokam may have engaged in the business of trading shell with Mogollon, Anasazi, or other Hohokam groups. Certainly, the inhabitants of the Gila River were in a more advantageous position for this kind of commerce. From Snaketown, for example, shell could be traded up the Verde, the Salt, the Gila, and even the San Pedro. From the Santa Cruz villages trade probably moved west into the Papago country and east toward the San Pedro. The presence of certain Mogollon influences (polished plainware, for example) in the pottery of the Hodges site suggests considerable contact with the east.

Shell ornaments from the Hodges Ruin show about the same degree of craftsmanship as Snaketown specimens. Assuming that the Hohokam of both sites manufactured their own ornaments—and the presence of much waste shell at both locations suggests they did—we may conclude a cross-fertilization in the area of design which produced a common standard. No specimen recovered from the Hodges site differed significantly in design from similar pieces described by Haury for Snaketown (Gladwin and others 1937:138–147).

Etched shell—reported from Snaketown, but absent from most southwestern sites—was found at the Hodges Ruin. This aspect of shell workmanship will be discussed at greater length below, since the Hodges collection includes one of the most important etched pieces known to date.

The classification of shell objects follows that used by Haury in the Snaketown report (Gladwin and others 1937: 137).

UNWORKED SHELL

By far the greater part of the shell recovered from the Hodges Ruin had been worked in some manner. Many of the pieces were unfinished, but for the majority, a start, at least, had been made toward converting the raw shell into useful or ornamental objects.

Glycymeris, *Levicardium*, and *Pecten* specimens make up the bulk of the unworked shell (Fig. 8.1). Eighteen

Fig. 8.1 Whole shell: Unworked. *Phase: c*, Cañada del Oro; remainder unplaced. *Genus: a, b, Glycymeris; c. Pecten; d. Levicardium; e, Vermitus; f, Conus*. Greatest width of *c*, 6.4 cm.

whole *Levicardium elatum* shells of varying sizes were found, including three on the floor of House 80 (Cañada del Oro) and four on the floor of House 22 (Tanque Verde phase). Five of the 18 were associated with cremations.

In addition to the 18 whole *Levicardium* specimens, literally dozens of unworked fragments of the same species were found in cremations. Piecing together these bits was seldom possible, and we provide no numerical listing to indicate their frequency. It should suffice to state that *Levicardium* ranks with *Glycymeris* as the site's most common types. All whole *Levicardium* shells that could be placed as to phase were found in houses or with cremations of the Rincon and Tanque Verde phases.

A cache of 45 juvenile, whole *Glycymeris* shells was found on the floor of House 22 (Tanque Verde phase). From this same floor (as indicated above) came four *Levicardium* specimens, as well as several *Oliva* beads. No collections of similar size were found elsewhere. Some of the whole shells had been partially worked, suggesting that the house may have belonged to someone who either elaborated or traded shell ornaments.

Isolated specimens of unworked *Glycymeris* were scattered through other parts of the site. Their usual association was Tanque Verde, with earliest examples from the Rillito phase.

Cremations produced a few examples of unworked *Pecten*. A Rillito phase association was established for one specimen (Cremation 185).

Vermitus and *Conus* specimens constituted the remainder of the unworked shell.

WORKED SHELL

Careful examination of the Hodges shell material showed no departure from working processes listed by Haury. These include grinding, breaking, chipping, drilling, cutting, and etching, in addition to the application of paint. Only one painted shell was recovered; and, despite the presence of small, turquoise fragments of inlay size, no shell was found that definitely can be said to have served as a base for either inlay or overlay.

Utilitarian

Two perforated items similar to those classified by Haury (Gladwin and others 1937: 139) as shell needles were found at the Hodges Ruin. These might actually have been pendants, as McGregor (1941:221) has suggested with respect to like objects reported from the Winona and Ridge ruins. Both Hodges specimens are *Glycymeris* and were found on the floor of House 1 (Tanque Verde phase).

Two other shell objects in the Hodges collection may have served as awls. Both are pointed but lack the holes for thread passage (or suspension?) that characterize the so-called needles. Their general appearance suggests they may be fragments of bracelets or pendants which, after being broken, were sharpened at one end to provide an instrument capable of perforating fabric or, perhaps, skin. One is from the Rillito phase; the other, unplaced.

Also found were two worked pieces of *Levicardium elatum* which, judging from their shape, may have been used as scrapers, fleshers, or scoops. Only one of the two shows the sort of wear along one edge that such use would have occasioned. Neither could be attributed to a particular level or occupation.

Apart from these objects (none of which is positively identified as utilitarian), all worked shell at the Hodges Ruin suggested ornamental or ceremonial use.

Ornamental

BEADS

Whole shell. One of the distinguishing features of the shell material at the Hodges Ruin is the lack of whole shells used as beads (see Table 8.1). Found in quantity in nearly all other Hohokam sites, such beads apparently were of negligible importance in the Tucson area.

TABLE 8.1

Kinds and Frequencies of Whole Shell Beads

Phase	Oliva	Olivella	Vermitus	Glycymeris	Total
Tanque Verde	4	0	2	1	7
Rincon	0	1	0	0	1
Rillito	0	0	0	0	0
Cañada del Oro	0	1	0	0	1
Unplaced	3	10	1	0	14
Total	7	12	3	1	23

Specimens of *Olivella biplicata* were rare, in contrast with Snaketown where, according to Haury (Gladwin and others 1937: 139): "Shells of *Olivella biplicata* were used as beads over a longer period than any other species, and their increase was marked during the Sedentary period." *Olivella* was treated as at Snaketown; that is, the spires were ground or broken off, so the shells might be strung (Fig. 8.2*c*, *d*, *e*). However, no large groups were uncovered; *Olivella* was principally represented by individual shells scattered throughout the site. Only two specimens could be assigned to phase. A specimen on the floor of House 80 is from the Cañada del Oro phase, and one found below the level of the third floor in House 65 is from the Rillito-Rincon transition. [*Ed. note*: The caption in Figure 8.2 is inconsistent with the text. We are unable to verify in which phase the specimens belong.]

Oliva beads were represented by seven examples (Fig. 8.2*h*, *i*, *j*). Four, from the floor of House 22, were attributable to the Tanque Verde phase; the others are unplaced.

Fig. 8.2 Whole shell beads and tinklers. *Phase: c, d, g, h,* Tanque Verde?; *e,* Rillito-Rincon?; remainder, unplaced. *Genus: a, Vermitus; b, Glycymeris; c, d, e, Olivella; f, Trivia; g, Conus; h, i, j, Oliva.* Length of *j,* 3.3 cm.

Two sections of marine worm casing (*Vermitus* sp.) (Fig. 8.2*a*), probably used as beads, were discovered inside a pottery duck effigy near the floor of House 19, a structure assigned to the Tanque Verde phase.

Cremation 5 was contained in a vessel of Tanque Verde Red-on-brown. It produced a complete necklace of juvenile *Glycymeris* shells embellished by a carved frog pendant, also of *Glycymeris*, and two, stylized, carved lizards, probably of *Levicardium*. This is the one instance of a group of whole shells sufficiently numerous to form a complete necklace (Fig. 8.3).

Disc. By far the greatest percentage of shell beads at the Hodges Ruin can be classified in this category. They range in size from specimens no more than 1 mm in diameter to some measuring more than 3 cm. In many cases it proved impossible to identify the shell species represented, partly because cremation fires had ravaged the specimens and partly because such identifying features as color were lacking.

Fig. 8.3 Whole shell necklace. Length of frog, 3.5 cm.

After careful comparison with other shells in his collection, Dr. Kanakoff identified the large and some of the medium-sized beads as *Spondylus crassiquama* Lamarck, a species not listed in any of the Southwestern site reports that I examined. [*Ed. note*: These large beads, with diameters ranging from 1.5 to 3.5 cm, have been re-identified by Walter B. Miller and Carl Christensen of the University of Arizona as a rock scallop of the genus *Chama* and native to the Gulf of California. The beads had been too greatly modified to permit species identification. Three complete necklaces were made from these beads (Fig. 8.4), and numerous loose beads of this type were found at the Hodges site. All of these beads had been exposed to fire and were probably parts of cremations. More precise provenience information is not available. Shell ornaments made from *Chama* are not at all common in Southwestern sites. The only published examples are those reported by Judd (1954: 93, Fig. 16) for Pueblo Bonito in Chaco Canyon. A few fragmentary specimens from the St. Mary's site are in the collection of Edward Ronstadt of Tucson. However, *Chama* is very similar to the spiny oyster (*Spondylus*), which is relatively common in archaeological sites. It is easy to confuse them in their modified states; the hinge teeth, used by conchologists to differentiate the species, have nearly always been ground off, making identification virtually impossible. Therefore, it seems that some *Chama* specimens may come from other sites but have been confused with *Spondylus*.]

Fig. 8.4 *Chama* necklaces. Diameters of beads range from 1.5 to 3.5 cm.

Disc beads were classified according to diameters (see Table 8.2). Those measuring less than 2 mm across the outside diameter were referred to as "tiny." Beads with diameters greater than 2 but less than 5 mm were dubbed "small." "Medium" beads were those measuring from 5 mm to 1 cm. Any with diameters greater than a centimeter were considered "large." Only in a few cases did individual caches yield specimens belonging to more than one of these groupings.

TABLE 8.2
Kinds and Frequencies of Disc Beads

Phase	Tiny	Small	Medium	Large	Total
Tanque Verde	1	0	0	0	1
Rincon	0	3	0	1	4
Rillito-Rincon	0	0	2	0	2
Rillito	1	7	8	2	18
Cañada del Oro	0	0	0	0	0
Snaketown	0	1	0	0	1
Unplaced	2	3	4	3	12
Total	4	14	14	6	38

One of the earliest indications of shell was a single, disc bead found in the plainware bowl containing Cremation 18 (Snaketown phase). This "small" specimen is the only example of a disc bead produced prior to the Rillito phase when such ornaments were common. It was, in fact, during the Rillito, phase that small- and medium-disc beads attained their maximum popularity. The tiny and large types seem never to have been especially common.

One might question whether we are justified, on the basis of the single Snaketown bead, to state that disc beads were being manufactured during the Snaketown phase, especially since no such ornaments were associated with Cañada del Oro.

Bi-lobed. Fairly common during the Santa Cruz phase at Snaketown and one of the most common types in the Mimbres and Chihuahua areas, the bi-lobed bead was represented by only two specimens at the Hodges Ruin. One of these could be assigned to the Rincon phase. The other was associated with material intermediate between Rillito and Rincon.

Triangular prism. The Hodges excavation (Cremation 10, Rillito phase) produced one necklace whose beads were shaped like small triangular prisms with square sides. Suspension holes passed through two of the sides in such a manner that the heavier portion of the prism swung below the string.

PENDANTS

Except for bracelets of *Glycymeris* shell, pendants proved to be the most common shell ornament from the Hodges site.

Whole shell. Species employed as whole shell pendants were *Turritella*, *Cerithidea*, and *Pecten*, especially the latter. Holes for suspension were either broken or drilled (Fig. 8.5).

Fig. 8.5 Whole shell pendants: Various phases. *Phase: a*, Tanque Verde; *c*, Rillito; remainder, unplaced. *Genus: a, Glycymeris; b, Turritella; c, Pecten; d, e, Cerithidea.* Length of *b*, 6.9 cm.

At Snaketown pendants made from whole shells were scarce, occurring principally during the Santa Cruz and Sacaton phases. The earliest Snaketown specimen was of *Cerithidea* and was attributed to the Sweetwater horizon. Of four *Cerithidea* pendants recovered from the Hodges Ruin, three were unplaced; one was associated with Tanque Verde phase materials.

Pecten pendants at the Hodges site occurred first during Cañada del Oro times and continued during the rest of the site's occupancy. *Turritella* was found first in conjunction with Rillito materials. Table 8.3 shows the types of whole shell pendants and the periods with which they are associated.

TABLE 8.3

Kinds and Frequencies of Whole Shell Pendants

Phase	Pecten	Turritella	Cerethidea	Total
Tanque Verde	2	2	1	5
Rincon	9	0	0	9
Rillito	8	1	0	9
Cañada del Oro	2	0	0	2
Unplaced	17	7	3	27
Total	38	10	4	52

Many burned fragments of *Pecten* pendants were found in cremations and are not enumerated here. *Pecten* pendants were also common on the surface and in deposits of trash. Their frequency was far greater than Table 8.3 indicates.

Cut shell. Pendants of cut shell—especially of *Glycymeris*—were extremely common at the Hodges Ruin (Figs. 8.6 and 8.7). Genera included *Cardium*, *Glycymeris*,

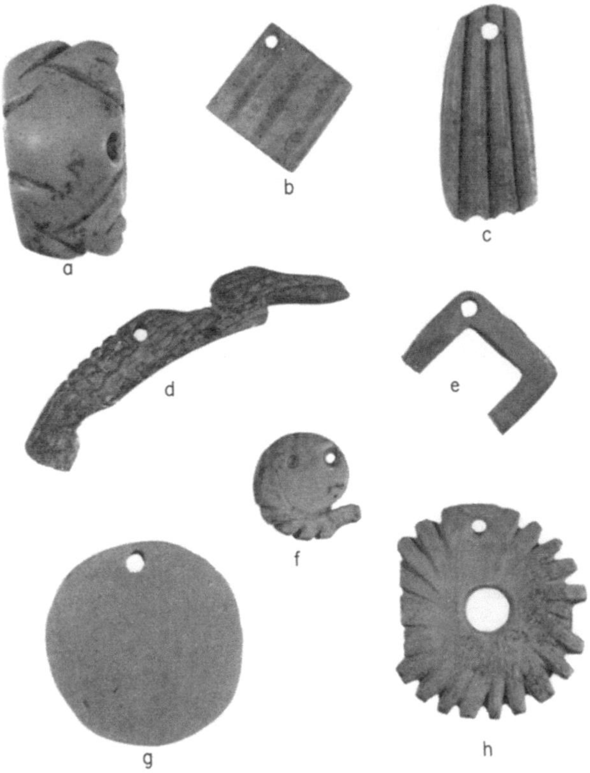

Fig. 8.6 Cut shell pendants: Various phases. *Phase: e, g,* Rincon; remainder, unplaced. *Genus: a, d, Glycymeris; b, e–h, Levicardium; c, Cardium.* Maximum width of *g*, 3.1 cm.

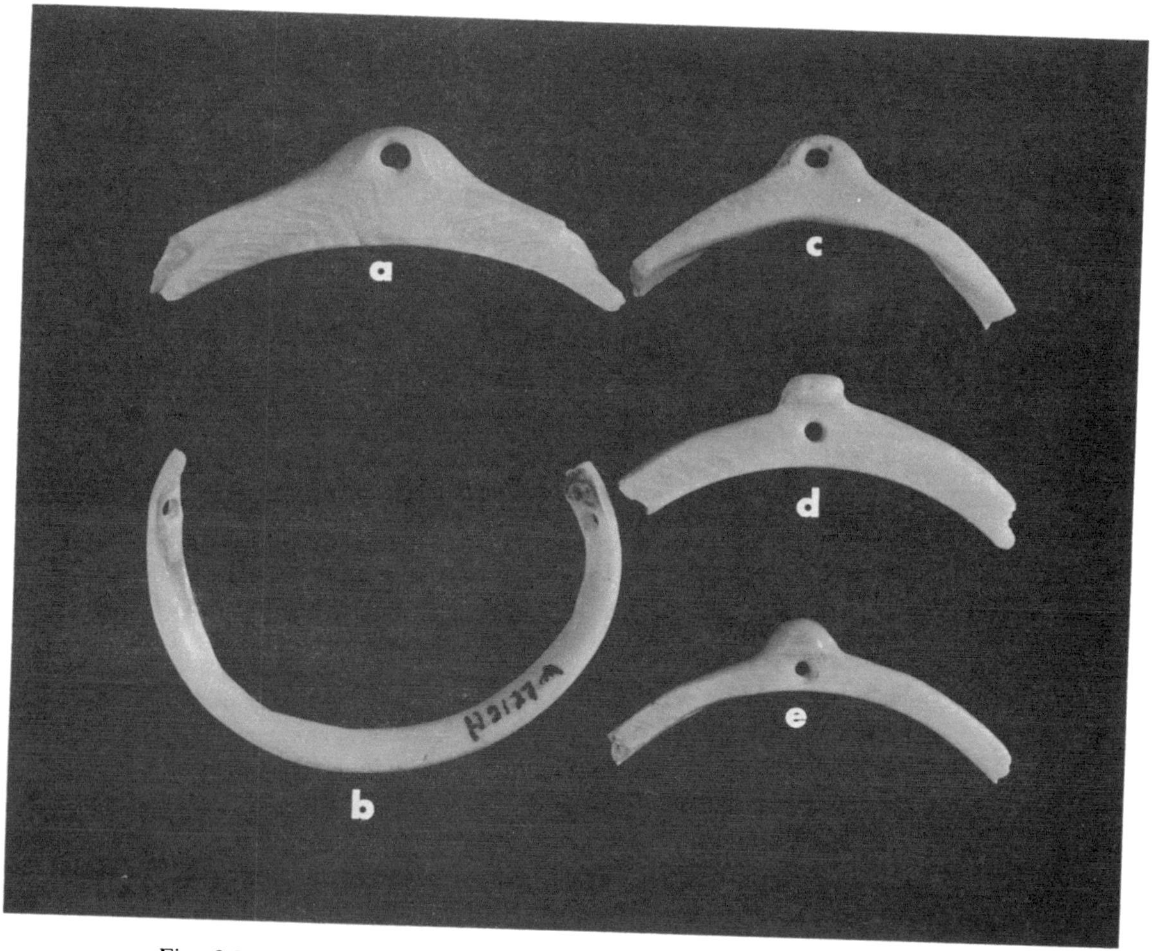

Fig. 8.7 *Glycymeris* pendants: Various phases. *Phase: a,* Rincon; *b,* Snaketown-Rillito; *d,* Cañada del Oro; *c, e,* unplaced. Greatest dimension of *a,* 5.6 cm.

Pecten, and, rarely, *Haliotis*. One cut shell pendant of *Glycymeris* (Fig. 8.7*b*) is listed in the field catalogue as dating anywhere from the Snaketown to the Rillito phase. The other datable specimens are from the Cañada del Oro phase (Fig. 8.7*d*) and from the Rincon phase (Figs. 8.6*e*, *g* and 8.7*a*).

Excluding the *Glycymeris* pendants, which will be discussed separately, Table 8.4 lists the types of cut shell pendants found at the Hodges site, with their frequency by phase. *Glycymeris* pendants are omitted from the list in order to give them separate treatment.

Many of the bracelet-shaped pieces of *Glycymeris* were of such small diameter that any idea of classifying them as bracelets or armlets seemed absurd. Yet, few of these pieces were pierced at the umbos as one might expect pendants to be. Because they might have been strung

TABLE 8.4

Kinds and Frequencies of Cut Shell Pendants

Phase	Round Disc	Serrated Round Disc	Square	Perforated Square Disc	Bird	Frog	Other Animals	Pecten	Total
Tanque Verde	0	1	0	0	0	0	0	1	2
Rincon	3	0	0	1	0	0	0	0	4
Rillito	0	0	0	0	3	0	0	1	4
Cañada del Oro	0	1	0	0	0	0	0	0	1
Unplaced	5	0	1	0	1	2	3	0	12
Total	8	2	1	1	4	2	3	2	23

through the large center hole, I have listed any such objects with diameters less than 5 cm as pendants (Fig. 8.7); those with greater diameters are listed as bracelets (Fig. 8.8). Settling on 5 cm as the dividing line was admittedly an arbitrary choice. It is conceded that some of the smaller pieces may have been children's bracelets and that some of the larger objects may have been strung as pendants.

The *Glycymeris* specimen illustrated in Figure 8.7*b* is, unquestionably, a pendant. Two holes have been drilled opposite each other on either side of the umbonal region, slightly less than half way down the body of the pendant. Suspension from a thong around the neck would have allowed the pendant to lie flat against the chest. Only one ornament of this type was found.

A number of the Hodges pendants had holes drilled below the beak. It should be made clear, however, that not all *Glycymeris* circlets with beak or band perforations were placed in the pendant category. Some—especially the larger ones—had irregular perforations that may have occurred accidentally. Circlets were classified as pendants because of umbonal perforation only if that perforation showed indications of having served as a suspension hole.

Table 8.5 shows kinds of *Glycymeris* pendants recovered from the Hodges Ruin, together with their phase frequency.

BRACELETS

The shell bracelet collection from the Hodges Ruin might easily be lost among the Snaketown material. All the carved motifs illustrated by Haury (Gladwin and others 1937: 143) are common, and the types of plain bracelets described in the Snaketown report provide generally adequate categories for classifying pieces from the Hodges site.

If the two collections differ in any significant aspect, it is in over-all bracelet size. Measurements of the inner diameters of Snaketown bracelets are not given in the report, but the specimens that Haury illustrates are, in general, larger than similar pieces from the Hodges Ruin. It is quite possible, as stated earlier, that some of the ornaments listed as bracelets may actually have been pendants.

Slightly less than two-thirds of the Hodges *Glycymeris* bracelets have diameters of 5–6 cm (Fig. 8.8). The hand

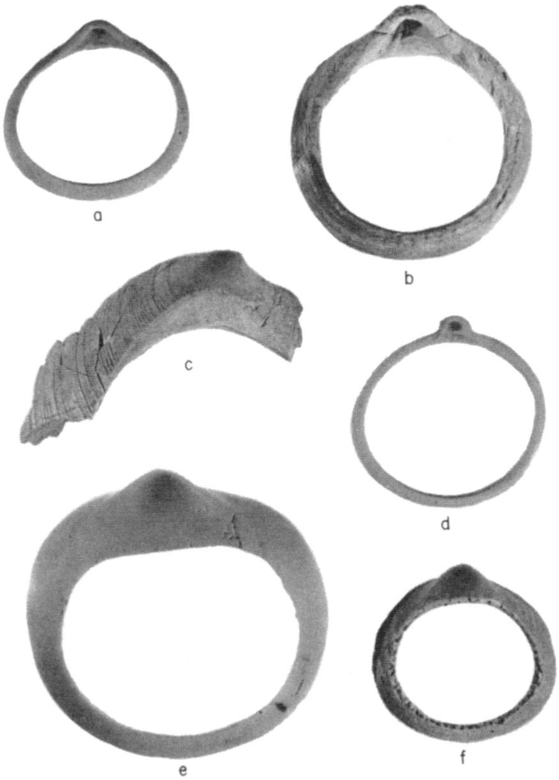

Fig. 8.8 Shell bracelets. *Phase: f,* Tanque Verde; remainder, unplaced. *Genus:* c, *Dosinia;* remainder, *Glycymeris*. Maximum dimension of *e*, 9.4 cm.

TABLE 8.5

Kinds and Frequencies of *Glycymeris* Shell Pendants

Phase	Two Suspension Holes	Suspension Hole Below Umbo	Suspension Hole in Umbo	Lacking Suspension Hole	Total
Tanque Verde	0	0	0	11	11
Rincon	0	0	2	0	2
Rincon-Rillito	0	0	4	3	7
Rillito	0	0	4	2	6
Rillito–Cañada del Oro	0	0	0	3	3
Rillito–Snaketown	1	0	0	0	1
Cañada del Oro	0	1	0	0	1
Cañada del Oro–Snaketown	0	0	0	1	1
Unplaced	0	3	3	42	48
Total	1	4	13	62	80

over which such ornaments might have passed would have had to be quite small. Only about 5 percent had inner diameters of more than 7 cm, the minimum breadth necessary to pass over the hand of a white, adult male. Few of the bracelets in the Hodges collection are of sufficient diameter to merit the classification of armlet.

The surviving group of bracelets from the Hodges collection includes fragments or whole pieces representing 136 specimens. This is undoubtedly a figure much lower than was actually represented by the excavated bits of *Glycymeris*. However, because of their size and indefinite character, many small fragments were discarded. Others have been lost.

Of the total collection only eight bracelets are complete or restorable specimens. Most of these ornaments were found either in trash or cremations. Trash finds were not datable and many of the cremation pieces have been so badly altered that it is impossible to determine their original character.

Since only 49 out of a total of 117 plain bracelets could be assigned to phase, it is not possible to make definite statements about typological progression. The thin, fragile type that Haury found to be earliest at Snaketown made up over half of the Hodges collection. This variety apparently came into vogue during late Cañada del Oro times and was absent by Tanque Verde times. What Haury called the intermediate type had about the same life span as the fragile bracelets at the Hodges Ruin. Thick types occurred only in association with Rincon-Rillito materials.

It is of interest to note that no ornament definitely identifiable as a bracelet was assigned to the Tanque Verde phase. Pendants of *Glycymeris* identified as Tanque Verde phase were, in general, of the thick type with unaltered umbo.

One worked shell object, conceivably a bracelet, represents a type not reported from Snaketown. It is of *Dosinia ponderosa*, a large and extremely heavy species (Fig. 8.8*c*). Only a small fragment was excavated. The central section of one valve has been removed and the edge has been ground smooth. The inside edge of the valve was not smoothed, indicating that the ornament was not completed. Because of the fragmentary nature and indefinite character of this object, we have not included it in our bracelet tally.

With the exception of the above questionable specimen, all bracelets from the Hodges Ruin are of *Glycymeris*. For classification purposes they are divided into four categories based on measurement of the greatest transverse diameter of the bracelet ring opposite the umbonal projection:

Thin (2 to 5 mm thick)
Intermediate (5 mm to 1 cm thick)
Thick (1.0 to 3.0 cm) with perforated umbo
Thick (1.0 to 3.0 cm) with umbo unaltered

For the thin bracelets the modal diameter was 5–6 cm; for the intermediate type, 5–6 cm; for the thick variety with perforated umbo, 7–8 cm; and for the thick variety with the umbo unaltered, 7–8 cm. This breakdown suggests that thickness was, at least in part, related to the overall size of the raw shell.

Plain shell bracelets and their phase correlations are shown in Table 8.6.

Nineteen of the bracelets from the Hodges site were carved. This is about one-seventh of the total. In the majority of cases decoration covered both the band and the umbo. As at Snaketown, the bird-serpent and geometric motifs predominated (Fig. 8.9).

Bracelet carving began early at Snaketown. Haury noted an occurrence in late Pioneer times. Only three specimens from the Hodges Ruin could be assigned to phases. One was Rillito; the others, Rincon. [*Ed. note*: None of the specimens in Figure 8.9 can be dated.]

RINGS

The surviving Hodges collection includes ten shell rings, all of *Glycymeris*; of these, two were carved with incised pendant triangles. Neither of the carved rings could be allocated to phase; of the plain rings, one each was associated with the Cañada del Oro, Rillito, and Rincon

TABLE 8.6
Kinds and Frequencies of Plain Shell Bracelets

Phase	Thin	Medium	Thick Umbo Unaltered	Thick Perforated Umbo	Total
Tanque Verde	0	0	0	0	0
Rincon	3	1	1	1	6
Rincon–Rillito	13	4	1	0	18
Rillito	5	2	0	6	13
Rillito–Cañada del Oro	10	2	0	0	12
Unplaced	30	26	3	9	68
Total	61	35	5	16	117

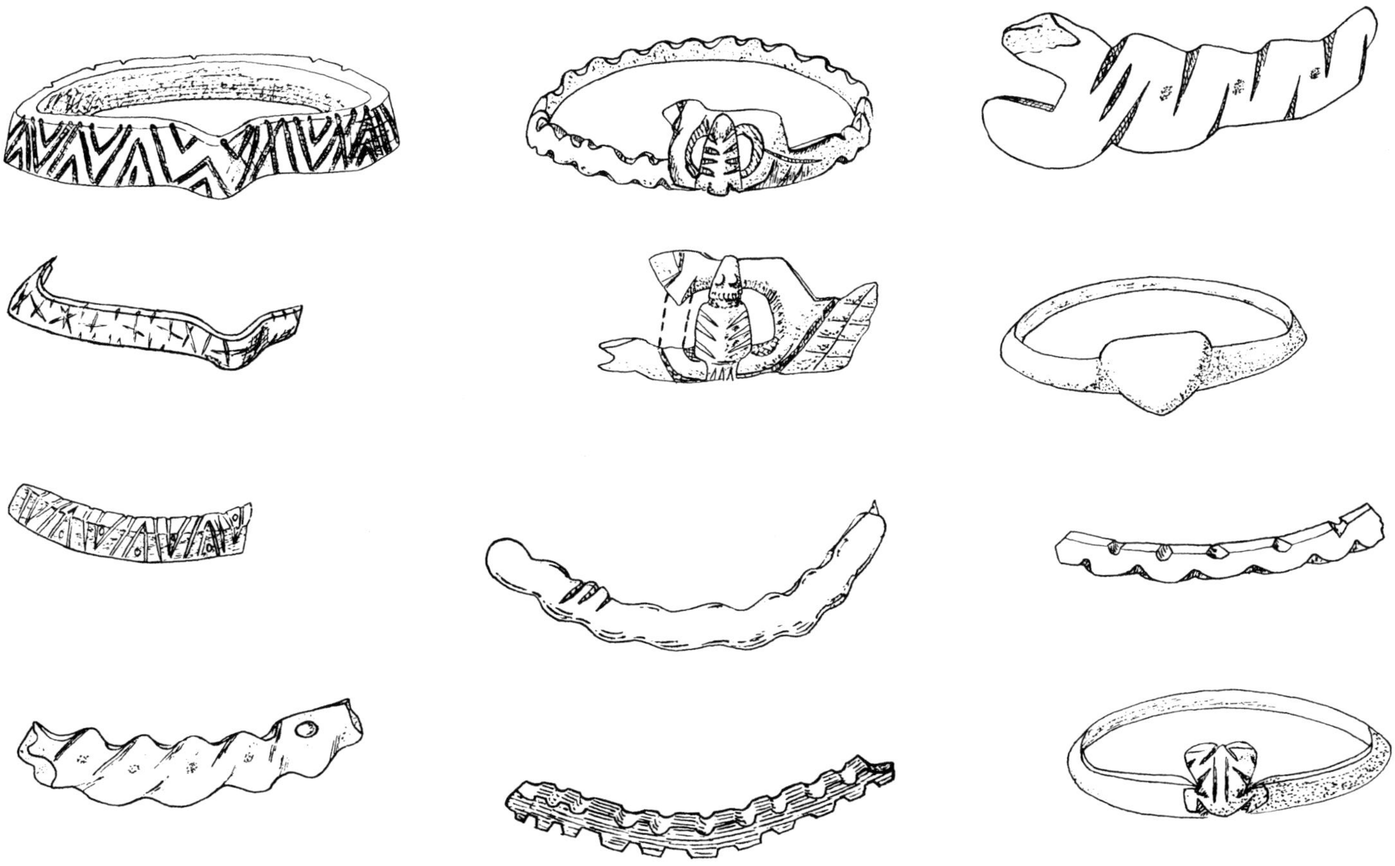

Fig. 8.9 Carved shell bracelets. All specimens are of *Glycymeris*. Maximum diameter of specimen at lower left, 5.2 cm.

phases. *Conus* rings, known from the later periods at Los Muertos (Haury 1945: 156) and the Paloparado site (Di-Peso 1956: 95), were absent.

TINKLERS

A single tinkler was found. It was of *Conus* and was associated with Tanque Verde phase materials.

Tinklers, apparently, were a late development in all the Southwest. Haury recorded none at Snaketown, a site whose occupation ended around A.D. 1100. They are usually associated with the Pueblo III period among the Anasazi and with Mimbres in the Mogollon area. I have found no reference to their appearance in the Hohokam region prior to Tanque Verde (Soho) times. They do occur throughout the Southwest from about A.D. 1100 and seemingly made their first appearance in all three major archaeological zones at about the same time.

Tinklers might be listed as ornaments with a probable ceremonial use. During dances and other ceremonial activity they could be employed to produce sound, either as part of a dancer's costume or affixed on staffs. Since apparently they were used most extensively in the Anasazi and Mimbres areas, their presence in Hohokam sites may indicate influences from either or both of these other regions.

PERFORATED SHELL

The Hodges collection includes numerous examples of perforated shells similar to those illustrated by Haury (Gladwin and others 1937: Plate CXVIII). These are principally of three genera: *Pecten*, *Glycymeris*, and *Levicardium*. It seems likely that the perforated *Pecten* and *Glycymeris* specimens may have been pendants, whereas those of *Levicardium* represent cores from which pieces were cut for the making of other ornaments.

MISCELLANEOUS

Included in this category are small, carved bits of *Levicardium* which lack suspension holes. Some, conceivably, could have been used in mosaics. Of importance in this category, also, is a carved frog, fashioned from *Glycymeris*. No phase association is possible for the frog.

Ceremonial

Except for the tinkler referred to earlier, just one example of a shell probably used for ceremonial purposes is included in the Hodges collection. This is a fragment of *Strombus galeatus*, the species commonly used as a trumpet. Like tinklers, these are generally considered to have come into the Southwest in the later periods and represent either Classic Hohokam or the Pueblo III period. At Snaketown, Haury had one *Strombus* trumpet assigned to the Sacaton phase, the earliest previously reported incidence of the use of shell trumpets in the Southwest.

The fragment of *Strombus* from the Hodges site could not be positively dated, but its association strongly suggested the Cañada del Oro phase. This constitutes a hint, at least, that shell trumpets have a longer history in the Southwest than had been previously assumed.

PAINTED SHELL

One whole *Levicardium elatum* shell from the Hodges Ruin apparently had been painted with red pigment, probably hematite. No design was discernible, the paint having been applied to the entire surface. The specimen could not be placed as to phase and, unfortunately, most of the paint was washed off in cleaning the shell.

ETCHED SHELL

Haury (Gladwin and others 1937: 150–151) describes experiments at the Gila Pueblo Archaeological Foundation to determine whether the design on certain Snaketown shell specimens was produced by an etching process or by incision. First, examination of some of the Snaketown pieces under a microscope showed the designs to be undercut slightly along the edges. Next, by way of experiment, both surfaces of a piece of *Cardium* were coated with paraffin, leaving a design area uncovered, and the prepared shell was soaked a few moments in a weak solution of hydrochloric acid. Upon removal from the acid, the piece was examined under the microscope, and it was seen that the exposed portions, now somewhat etched by the acid, were undercut as was the case with the Snaketown artifacts.

With the likelihood of shell etching thus established, Haury set out to determine what etching liquid might have been available to the Indians. He experimented with the fermented juice of saguaro fruit and found that shell left in it three days was etched to about the same degree as many of the archaeological specimens. Accordingly etching of shell may be considered a technique practiced by the ancient Hohokam. Subsequently, Paul Ezell confirmed these findings in experiments at the Arizona State Museum.

One specimen from the Hodges site further corroborates shell etching as an ancient skill. An unfinished ornament (of *Levicardium elatum*) had been prepared for etching; its surface was covered with a resist, scratched through in places to produce a geometric pattern (Fig. 8.10).

Fig. 8.10 Etched shell. The shell is *Levicardium elatum*. It probably dates to the Rillito phase or later. Length is 6.6 cm.

Members of the Department of Chemistry at the University of Arizona examined the Hodges specimen and reported that a determination of the exact substance used for the resist would be costly and time-consuming. They stated, however, that numerous plant materials available in the Tucson area could have served the purpose. The resin of the mesquite tree (*Prosopis*) was suggested as the most likely possibility. Mesquite is common throughout the area and often grows near the saguaro cactus, the juice of which might have provided the etching acid.

The specimen from the Hodges site demonstrates that the Hohokam, in addition to possessing etched shell, practiced the etching technique. Although the evidence is meager, it may be suggested that etching entered the Hohokam area during the Rincon phase (A.D. 900–1100). Of the five Hodges pieces, three were closely associated with materials identified as Rincon phase, and two of the Snaketown pieces were assigned to the corresponding Sacaton phase.

Geometric designs were the most popular for etched items at the Hodges Ruin. Two of the specimens recovered were decorated with small squares. Another, the only shell found etched on the inside, had small, round, unetched islands for the design. One fragmentary specimen evidently was part of a zoomorphic design, probably a horned toad similar to the one found at Snaketown. The fragment covered with resist had been prepared for a squared scroll decoration much like those commonly found on Tanque Verde Red-on-brown pottery.

9. BONE, TEXTILES, AND VEGETAL REMAINS

BONE

Parallels with Snaketown are strongly evident in the inventory of bone from the Hodges site. Although some kinds of bone tools were fairly common, stone and shell seem to have been more popular for tools and ornaments.

Of the bone artifacts, awls were overwhelmingly in evidence. Fifty-six such items were excavated, a number considerably greater than for Snaketown. The earliest of these were splinter awls and awls made with unmodified joints associated with the Cañada del Oro phase. Those with modified joints occurred in the Rincon, Rillito, and Tanque Verde phases, with splinter awls also present in the latter.

No notched awls of the Mogollon type illustrated by Haury (Gladwin and others 1937: Plate CXXV*b*) were found at the Hodges Ruin. Over the head of one modified joint awl (unplaced as to phase) a resinous substance had been molded. There is no impression of any kind in this material to suggest that the awl had been hafted.

Incidence of placed bone awls through time at Hodges and Snaketown is shown in Figure 9.1.

Ed. note: This section of Chapter 9 was prepared by James Officer in 1956.

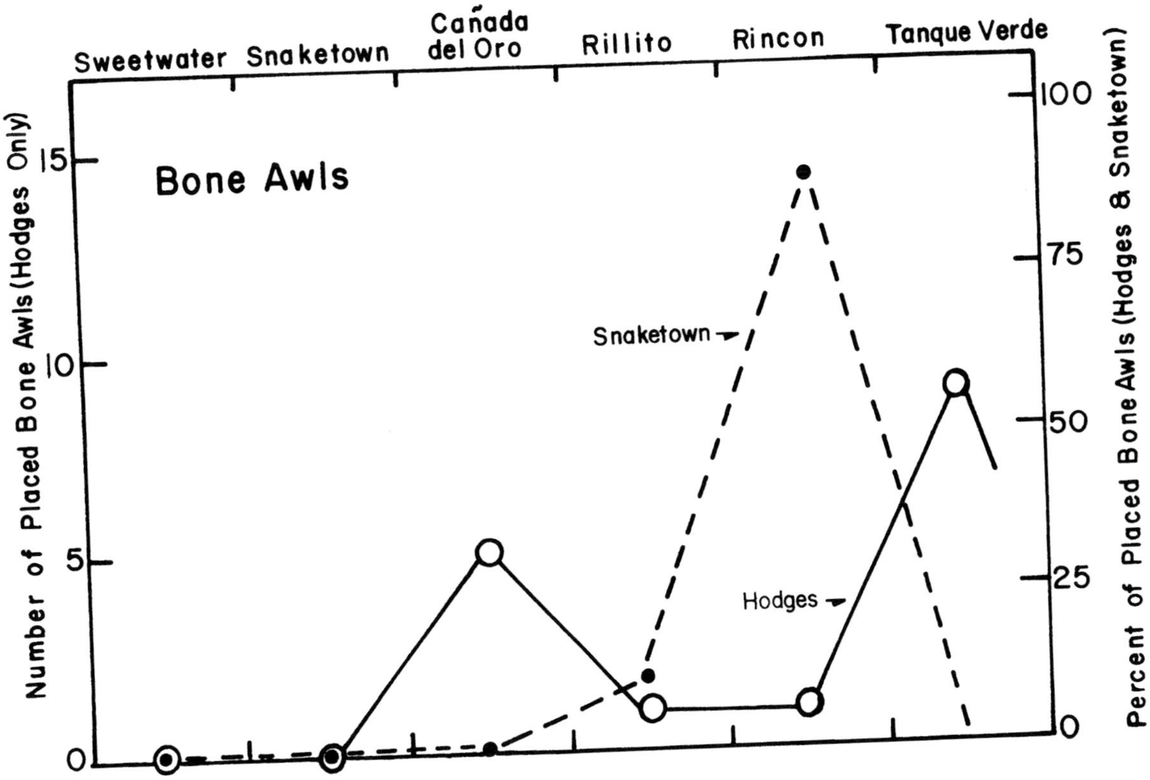

Fig. 9.1 Incidence of placed bone awls through time at Hodges and Snaketown

Ranking next to awls numerically were bone tubes. Haury (Gladwin and others 1937: 155) has pointed out that these items are fairly common in Hohokam sites. The Hodges Ruin contributed 28 plain and incised examples. Unfortunately, only one of these, a plain specimen, could be given a phase assignment. It was associated with Rincon materials. Four of the tubes were incised as compared with 11 at Snaketown. Incised designs were exclusively rectilinear, consisting principally of straight lines, triangles, and some hatching.

Likewise of indeterminate use were two other carved pieces. Designs on these did not differ significantly from those described above, although one (which may have been part of a hair ornament) was decorated with lines diagonal to the long axis of the piece and separated from each other by dots. This specimen was also notched.

The dagger-like implements, which Haury has postulated (Gladwin and others 1937: 154) may have been hair ornaments, were not especially common at the Hodges site, although 10 were excavated. Two of these are Rincon in phase; the others are not placed. One of the unplaced specimens was deeply grooved on the convex surface perpendicular to the long axis.

Seven flattened, spatula-like tools are included in the Hodges collection. Four were found in Tanque Verde phase association; the others are without phase correlation. These were generally similar in form, except for one unplaced specimen shaped much like a modern butter knife.

Four unplaced antler flakers were found, as well as a quantity of worked bone most of which seemed to represent partially completed artifacts of the types just described. The firepit of House 71 (unplaced) produced four small, tubular pieces probably used as beads. Except for these and the possible hair ornaments just mentioned, no other purely decorative items were discovered.

Animal bones representing domesticated dog, mountain sheep (*Ovis americana*), and mule deer (*Odocoileus hemionus*) have been identified from the Hodges site, although species identification of bone artifacts was not attempted. However, the striking similarities between the Hodges and Snaketown bone artifacts make it fairly safe to conclude that the animal bones represented at the two sites are the same. Haury lists dog, mule deer, and pronghorn antelope as having provided the material for many of the bone artifacts at Snaketown.

In contrast with Snaketown, few of the bone implements and ornaments at the Hodges site came from cremations. Many more—especially awls and bone daggers—were found on house floors and in trash. Like clay figurines, bone does not seem to have been especially popular as an item of grave furniture in the Tucson area.

TEXTILES

Of textile processes, we have only indirect evidence. One is a clay imprint of a simple twilled mat of Cañada del Oro age. A somewhat similar fragment evidently was either twill or checker, with each unit composed of several elements. The latter appear to have been rods rather than flat splints. This specimen is from the Colonial period, associated with Cañada del Oro and Rillito phase sherds. A third imprint, unplaced, is of a simple checkerwork mat.

A coiled basket imprint comes from a Tanque Verde phase cremation. The basket evidently had been filled with fine seeds (probably saguaro) which, upon contact with the cremation fire, became solidified and retained the basket impression.

In short, for the Colonial period, there is one clear instance of twilling, plus a specimen which may be either twilled or checkered; an additional case of checkerwork is unplaced. From the Tanque Verde phase alone is there indication of coiled basketry.

VEGETAL REMAINS

From the apparent density of population at the Hodges site, an agricultural economy can be assumed. Substantiating evidence occurs in the form of charred corn and beans, as well as corncob impressions in clay.

Our earliest evidence of maize is from the Snaketown phase, for which there is an unmistakable cob imprint. Charred corn is mostly unplaced, but one instance is definitely from the Rincon phase and another from the Tanque Verde phase. In addition, 10 specimens are unplaced. The span from Snaketown to Tanque Verde is expectable and doubtless correct. Professor A. T. Erwin, of Iowa State College, to whom corn and other plant remains were submitted for identification, reports the corn all to be a form of the flint type of *Zea mays*.

Charred beans were less plentiful: one occurrence is from the Rincon phase, one is Rillito to Rincon, and seven are unplaced. Of the bean identifications, Professor Erwin is less certain. He believes, however, the following to be represented: kidney bean (*Phaseolus vulgaris*), five instances; Lima bean (*Phaseolus lunatus*), two instances; and possibly the tepary bean (*Phaseolus acutifolius* var. *latifolius*), one doubtful case. [*Ed. note*: Years later, the bean specimens were examined and all were identified as *Canavalia ensiformis* (jackbean). This point is discussed in Chapter 11.] Other plant material includes a charred mesquite bean and two occurrences, in cake form, of some unidentified seed, perhaps saguaro (not identified by Erwin.) None of these is placed as to phase.

10. DISPOSAL OF THE DEAD

INHUMATIONS

Portions of only six unburned skeletons were excavated. As had been anticipated, cremation proved to be the preferred method for disposal of the dead. Two of the skeletons might have been parts of cremations buried nearby. Of the unburned skeletons, two associations with the Rincon phase and one each with the Rillito and Tanque Verde phases could be surmised.

Only one skeleton, that from Burial 5 (Fig. 10.1), was sufficiently intact to be examined. Norman Gabel studied the material and his report is summarized here. (The complete report is in the Hodges documents in the Museum library, archive number A-117, vol. 14: 16–28.) The burial was of an adult female between the ages of 56 and 70. Most of the skeleton was present including the cranium, pelves, humeri, femurs, sacrum, tibiae, scapulae, and radii. The teeth were of very poor quality and showed pronounced wear; 17 were lost before death and two after death. Gabel (n.d. A-117, Vol. 14:28) concluded his report with a comment on pathology as follows: "In addition to the severe abscessed condition of the alveolar border of the right maxillary, there are a number of parts indicating what likely was arthritis—best seen at the sacro-iliac joint, the lower vertebrae and to a lesser extent at other joints."

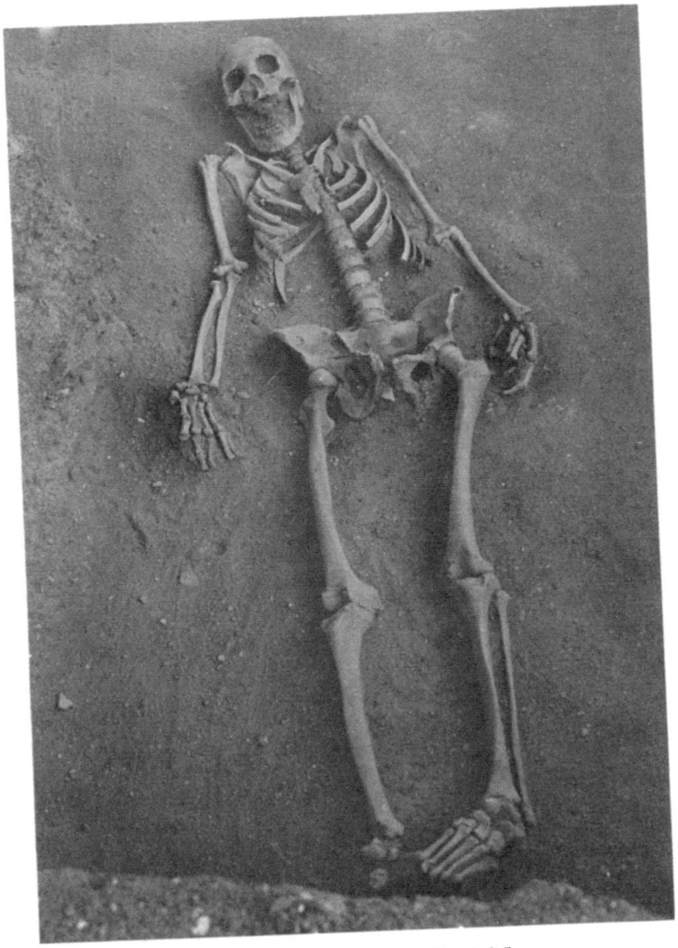

Fig. 10.1 Skeleton from Burial 5

CREMATIONS

Clear-cut phase patterns of cremation are not apparent from the evidence at hand, but some general statements concerning cremation practices during the various phases can be made.

Sweetwater Phase

Two cremations (Nos. 155 and 218) were identified with the Sweetwater phase. The arrangement of one could not be determined since the ashes and accompanying furniture were widely scattered. The other consisted of small bits of calcined bone in association with the sherds of a small bowl which evidently had been placed upright in the burial pit. It was not apparent whether the bone had once been situated in the bowl. A few plainware sherds that could not be pieced together were also present.

Snaketown Phase

There were six cremations from the Snaketown phase; the most spectacular of these was No. 186. Along with human bone it contained a stone ax, a stone bowl, fragments of two more stone bowls, a stone cylinder and a clay cylinder, plain jar and bowl sherds, and sherds attributed to

Ed. note: As mentioned in the preface, this chapter is based on a draft by Officer. However, the original source material appears to be somewhat confused, and there are some discrepancies between it and Officer's descriptions. Some of the artifact descriptions have been modified to agree with the original field notes. Also, the description of Burial 5 has been added.

both the Snaketown and the Tanque Verde phases. These materials were contained in an oval pit (75 x 60 x 20 cm). Incineration evidently took place on the spot for the walls of the pit were burned and the offerings had clearly been through the crematory fire.

A second cremation (No. 27) contained burned bone in a small plainware jar and included a hobnail sherd and a gourd-shaped vessel.

Three other Snaketown phase cremations consisted of crushed pottery mixed with ashes. One of these, No. 18, contained a single disc bead. A sixth cremation was badly scattered. All of these last four contained painted sherds; sherds from three of the cremations were identified as from the Snaketown phase; the sherds from the fourth were identified as Cañada del Oro phase or earlier.

Cañada del Oro Phase

Seven cremations can be dated to the Cañada del Oro phase, two of which were in pits. One of these, No. 179, was in an oval pit dug into sterile soil; it contained assorted stone tools including a stone ax, a stone bowl, stone bowl fragments, and stone blade fragments. It also contained Snaketown phase sherds. Cremation No. 165 was in an irregular pit with a small Cañada del Oro bowl turned on its side, plainware sherds, and a decorated scoop from the Snaketown phase.

Of the other five cremations, two were with inverted vessels, two were in an undetermined arrangement, and one was with sherds evidently from a bottle-shaped vessel (Fig. 4.7*m*).

Rillito Phase

Thirty-three cremations are Rillito in phase; for 27 of them, something of the original interment could be inferred.

The important innovation of the phase consisted of the inversion of vessels or of large sherds over or about the cremated bone, in a specially prepared pit, which seems not to have been the original crematory basin. Four such interments were found. Offerings were fairly elaborate. Ceramics included painted, red, and plainware vessels, with scoops, jars, flare-rim bowls, and plates popular. From one pit came miniature vessels, which may have accompanied the remains of a child. Other grave furniture included shell beads, shell pendants, and palettes.

In contrast, eight Rillito cremations were in pits in which the incineration of the corpse evidently took place. The prepared cavities ranged in size from 45 x 45 x 15 cm (No. 101) to 120 x 100 x 20 cm (No. 203). In one instance (No. 117), the pit has been lined with sherds. The flare-rim bowl was the most common ceramic offering; other furniture included a carved slate effigy pendant (Fig. 7.8*l*), projectile points, shell bracelets, large shell beads, and stone pendants.

Fourteen Rillito phase cremations were in pits either too small to have been crematoria or whose walls show no sign of burning. Accompanying ceramics were plentiful, including plainware, Rillito Red-on-brown, and Santa Cruz Red-on-buff. In eight of these cremations, the pottery consisted of unrelated sherds; in each of the remaining six, at least one entire or restorable vessel was present. Likewise included were palettes, rubbing stones, shell ornaments, and points (two of these are shown in Fig. 6.7*b*, *f*). Bones from one of the pits (No. 116) had been filed at one end.

Urn interment was uncommon, with only one example (No. 192). The burned bone had been placed within a flare-rim bowl identified as either Rillito Red-on-brown or Santa Cruz Red-on-buff; a worked sherd was also associated.

Rincon Phase

Forty-one out of 56 Rincon cremations were in more or less their original burial arrangement. The custom of burying the burned bone in the crematory pit—which apparently reached its maximum importance during the Rillito phase—declined in favor during Rincon times. Just four examples were noted. One of these (No. 216) might properly be termed a trench burial since the excavation in which it was located was 280 x 130 x 70 cm. The other three were within the over-all size range quoted for Rillito cremations of the same type. Grave furniture with these pit and trench cremations consisted of pottery (both sherds and whole vessels), shell ornaments, palettes, rubbing stones, stone bowls, and, in one case, a bone awl. Shouldered jars and bowls with outcurved rims were the most popular vessel forms.

Especially favored during the Rincon phase were burials in pits with inverted vessels and sherds either over the burned bone or nearby. Fifteen examples of this type were uncovered. Grave furniture was similar to that described in the preceding paragraph.

Six Rincon phase cremations had been placed in urns. The most popular vessel form was the shouldered jar. In four cases a small bowl had been inverted over the top. Shell, palettes, and rubbing stones, as well as pottery, comprised the grave offerings.

Sixteen Rincon cremations were in small pits with sherds, whole pots, and other furniture. Three of these, Nos. 161, 169, and 182, were especially large and provided much of the ceramic information for the Rincon phase. In the other thirteen, the sherds were badly crushed and no vessels could be reconstructed from them. The abundance of such fragments suggests either that they themselves were considered satisfactory offerings or that only portions of the entire vessels which disintegrated in the crematory fire were collected and interred with the ashes. Sayles (Gladwin and others 1937: 95–96) has discussed both alternatives.

Tanque Verde Phase

The number of Tanque Verde cremations at the Hodges site represents a considerable decline from the preceding period. Only fifteen were found. Of these, all but two provided information concerning their burial arrangement.

Burial in the crematory pit had apparently passed out of vogue by Tanque Verde times and the most popular form was that of the urn burial. Six cremations had been placed in large decorated jars. In none of these was there evidence of a covering bowl or sherd. Accompanying furniture included stone bowls (both plain and effigy), palettes, and occasionally, shell. Cremation No. 5 included the *Glycymeris* necklace described in Chapter 8. Plainware potsherds were frequently a part of the cache, sometimes being placed in the burial urn itself.

Inverted vessel burials also occurred in Tanque Verde times. However, neither of the two examples was accompanied by other grave offerings.

Five cremations had been placed in small pits with offerings of pottery. Crushed sherds constituted the bulk of material in four of these. In the other (No. 13), several Tanque Verde bowls and a plainware scoop were found, plus shell pendant fragments, and the impression on the pit wall of at least one coiled basket.

Unplaced

The styles of cremations described above hold likewise for those lacking phase assignment and for the 11 of "mixed" context (Cañada del Oro-Rillito, Rillito-Rincon, and Rincon-Tanque Verde). Furniture also is similar, but the presence of figurines with one unplaced and one Rillito-Rincon cremation may be noted. By and large, figurines were not popular as funeral offerings at the Hodges site.

SUMMARY

Because of the scarcity of data, little can be said of the earliest cremation customs at the Hodges Ruin. Our first evidence of interment in the crematory pit or trench comes from the Snaketown phase. This was the most popular pattern in Rillito times and continued into the Rincon phase. There is no indication of this disposition of the dead during the Tanque Verde phase.

The custom of placing inverted vessels or large sherds over or around the cremated bones—depositing all in a special pit—was first evident during the Rillito phase and was the most popular form during Rincon times.

The use of urns for the cremated bones occurred in all phases, with the possible exception of Sweetwater, and reached maximum popularity in the Tanque Verde phase.

During all periods cremated bones were deposited in a small pit with pottery offerings. These burials are of two types: those with crushed sherd offerings and those with pottery vessels as furniture. The latter were never particularly popular, and the former reached their height of favor during Rillito and Rincon times.

In conclusion, it should be noted that cremations for the most part were recovered from portions of the site that seem to have been reserved for that purpose. An overwhelming number were in trash deposits. A few were in areas occupied by houses, and four of these seem actually to have been dug into the house floors during the time of occupancy.

As indicated by Sayles (Gladwin and others 1937:95–96) for the Snaketown site, Hodges cremations that were buried in jars or outside the area of the crematory pit frequently were incomplete. In some cases they consisted of a few pieces of bone or a handful of sherds. This tends to substantiate Sayles' (1937:96) statement that "there were no fixed rules as to what should be gathered up and buried."

Not all the offerings found with cremated bone showed signs of having passed through crematory fires. This was the case especially with pottery. No crematory mounds such as those Sayles described (Gladwin and others, 1937:95) were found at the Hodges site.

11. CONCLUDING THOUGHTS

Emil W. Haury

The long span of years between the excavations and the reporting of Isabel Kelly's work in the Hodges village may be viewed in two ways: First, had the report appeared soon after her studies were completed, the Snaketown findings, published in 1937, would have been immediately reinforced and complemented. Snaketown's "uniqueness," so labeled because no other site approached its chronological and cultural record, was occasionally cited as a reason to suspect its story as being representative of the Hohokam. Some of the confusion of the 1940s and 1950s might have been spared. The similarity in the chronicle of the occupation of the two villages and the geographic separation by nearly 75 miles (120 km) served notice that the history of the Hohokam followed similar paths over a wide area, phenomena which ought to inspire confidence in the record.

Second, the delay has permitted us to compare the original interpretations of the 1930s against the independent (and often bizarre) ideas that have been proposed in the meantime. Among the original interpretive work in the Hodges report were the dating of various horizons, judgments on the ebb and flow of living patterns as caused by immigrants or other forces, and the conclusions on apparent loss of cultural vitality at the end of the 14th century. Seen in the light of the 1964–65 studies in Snaketown, many of the early interpretations of the Hodges material have stood up well. The only tragedy is that we cannot go back to restudy the Hodges village, employing new techniques as was done at Snaketown, to verify and expand what was learned before. The old settlement is capped by a new occupational layer of 20th century fixed and mobile homes.

Physically, Snaketown and the Hodges site shared certain characteristics and differed notably in a few others. They were both extensive villages. The 30 acres (0.12 sq. km) noted for the Hodges village should be at least doubled, taking into account the part removed by gravel exploitation and those extensions of the site to the north and southeast lying beyond the property acquired by the Hodges. Sixty acres (0.24 sq. km) represent a village of respectable size and larger than most, but it is still far below the minimal 250 acres (1.0 sq. km) of Snaketown.

Both villages were situated at the edge of the second terrace of the Santa Cruz and Gila rivers, overlooking the fields on the lower terrace close to the life-giving streams. Both exhibited ball courts as prominent surface features, and both had stratified architectural remains in the subsurface matrix resulting from long occupancy.

The principal differences were a lack of prominent refuse mounds and of platform mounds at the Hodges site. Trash was scattered as sheet deposits in contrast to the scores of mounds, some with heights of 4 m, at Snaketown. Though puzzling, the absence of platform mounds may be a reflection of the Hodges village marginal location with respect to the Hohokam hearth in the Gila Basin. Another lack at Hodges is the clear evidence of a canal system, on either the first or second terrace. It is doubtful whether canals ever existed on the second terrace—and the traces of those that must have been on the first terrace have been eliminated by late 19th and early 20th century farming and other activities. In spite of the lack of direct evidence of canals, we must accept the assumption that the residents were farmers and that they irrigated. The similar geographical setting of both villages in essentially the same environment predicates parallel economic pursuits.

On the basis of these features alone, an investigator would suspect a kinship between the residents of the two villages. Comparing the cultural remains fully confirms the suspicion.

Using the old information (Gladwin and others 1937) as well as the fresh data from Snaketown (Haury 1976) as the baseline, let us look at a few other aspects of the two sites. Both occupational records are long, but they are not equal. Snaketown's beginning date of about 300 B.C. (Vahki phase) precedes the founding of the Hodges village (Sweetwater phase, A.D. 200–350) by about 500 years. Snaketown's life as a village ended about A.D. 1100 (Sacaton phase), whereas the Hodges village lasted on to about A.D. 1300 (Tanque Verde phase). These differences call for speculations.

My postulation is that the immigrant Hohokam first entered the arid Southwest in the Gila and Salt river valleys, having found there the ideal land and water resources on which to apply their skills in irrigation technology. From the Gila Basin hearth, in time, they moved up tributary systems of the Gila-Salt river systems, and the Santa Cruz was one of them. The record suggests this took place during the Sweetwater phase, after the people were well established to the north. We may recognize this as a kind of colonizing effort, an expansion of territory, which was to continue through the Colonial period.

Snaketown's terminal years came near A.D. 1100. Why the village was vacated is not clear, but we do know that life continued for several centuries in a number of newly established settlements in the immediate environs. In other words, there was a geographic rearrangement of people, but not a total displacement or evacuation of the region by them.

The Hodges village lasted to about A.D. 1300, when it was also vacated, although here, too, the region was not abandoned. Certainly, the descendants of the Hodges site residents lived on in other villages of the Tucson Basin.

The beginning of the 14th century is close to the arrival time in the area of a foreign cultural complex, the Saladoans, introducing a new architectural form of puebloid derivation and differing cultural attributes, such as polychrome pottery. Whether this intrusion of a new element had anything to do with the death of the Hodges village remains to be determined. But at the moment, because no traces of the Saladoans were seen, one infers the abandonment was due to other causes.

Turning to an examination of attribute details in both sites, we note a phenomenon that must have been operative generally through the Southwest, namely, parallelism at first in the early centuries of coexistence of the two villages, as a prelude to regional diversity later. A group of people moving from a settled nucleus to establish themselves elsewhere should most closely match the home group at the start. With diminishing contacts and the passage of time, a certain independence of development set in and a regional imprint, so important to archaeologists, emerged.

In the Hodges site, for example, we note that Sweetwater Red-on-gray and Snaketown Red-on-buff are indistinguishable from countertypes at Snaketown. However, thereafter the ceramic tradition was no longer exactly parallel, though a common denominator clearly held the diverging branches together. The differences are enough to warrant separate type status in the eyes of the archaeologist. Hence,we have Cañada del Oro Red-on-brown at Hodges, the equivalent of Gila Butte Red-on-buff in the Gila Basin; Rillito Red-on-brown matching Santa Cruz Red-on-buff; Rincon Red-on-brown matching Sacaton Red-on-buff; and Tanque Verde Red-on-brown equating with Casa Grande Red-on-buff.

A review of the total sample of above-named types from the Hodges village shows that other kinds of differences existed too. Tucson Basin ceramics manifest a smaller range of vessel forms and less variety and flamboyance in depicting scrolls, small repeated elements, and life forms. These may be the consequence of distances from the "mainstream" of cultural vitality.

While this kind of branching is enormously helpful in understanding regional developmental trends, it also emphasizes, seen in reverse, the nuclear nature of the initial group of Hohokam who reached the Southwest.

Regional imprints in other cultural features (for example, palettes, figurines, shell products, bone artifacts, and common utilitarian stone tools) are not so readily discerned. The comparability in all of these with Snaketown is high, doubtless reflecting the existence of a close contact between Hodges and the villages to the northwest. The greater divergences noted in ceramics may be attributed to the fact that the fragile nature of pottery demanded a high production rate and a greater energy expenditure relative to other attributes. The frequency with which pottery was made may well have stimulated local form and design modes to account for the differences we see. Also, there were variations in the locally available raw materials.

Death practices follow the pattern set by Snaketown with respect to the disposal of cremated bones. Pit deposits in early phases were superseded by enshrining bones in pots in later times. How the fragmentary inhumations of several phases are to be interpreted is not clear.

An unresolved taxonomic problem in the Gila Basin concerns the transition from the Sacaton phase of the Sedentary period to the Soho phase of the Classic period. The ceramic changes are inexplicably abrupt and changes in architecture are noted as well. Gladwin inserted the Santan phase to smooth out the transition (Gladwin and others 1937: 264), but the attributes of a solid cultural nature characterizing the time were not acceptably defined. Hammack's (1969) Las Colinas excavations in Phoenix so far have produced the most likely material in the right time position to make the Santan phase a reality.

The record in the Tucson Basin, luckily, is somewhat clearer. Ceramically, the changes from orthodox Rincon Red-on-brown to Tanque Verde Red-on-brown seem to be less abrupt. The apparent abruptness of the Gila Basin is not there, and it would appear that a phase in the Tucson sequences comparable to the Santan is not needed. This will require, however, a lengthening of the Rincon phase toward the present, perhaps to A.D. 1150, as well as an early extension of the Tanque Verde phase from A.D. 1200 to about 1150.

Kelly's work in the Hodges site sheds light on a vexing and neglected botanical problem which may be labeled "The Case of the Cliff Dweller Bean." For many years there have been persistent reports of the discovery of large white beans, particularly in the cliff dwellings of Central Arizona. The astonishing aspect of the report is that the beans germinated when planted. These finds, consistently, appear to be made by amateurs. This fact, plus the improbable viability of a bean that dated back at least to the 14th century, raised doubts as to the credibility of the discoveries.

Botanists identified the legume as the jackbean (*Canavalia ensiformis*), and some expressed doubt as to the antiquity of the plant in the Southwest. However, in recent years archaeologists have also found *C. ensiformis* in indisputable archaeological contexts (Bohrer 1962: 106–107; Greenleaf 1975: 106). It is reasonably certain that the plant is native to America and that it has been in the Southwestern United States for a long time.

Of special interest now are the large charred beans found by Kelly in several contexts in the Hodges village. Initially, these were identified as lima beans (Carter 1945). However, a review of the specimens by Kaplan (1956: 246) shows that, instead, they were *Canavalia ensiformis*, an identification verified by Frank S. Crosswhite in July 1975. Sauer and Kaplan refer specifically to the Hodges material as having a pre-A.D. 1300 date (1969: 418). Had the identification of the bean been correctly made long ago, and had these discoveries become generally known soon after the excavation in the late 1930s, we would at least not have been skeptical so long of the presence of this cultigen in the Southwest in pre-Spanish times. As far as we know, Kelly was the first archaeologist to find the species in an ancient context.

Three of these occurrences were in different features of House 71 (H-899, H-1111, H-1115), dated by Kelly as Rillito-Tanque Verde phase. [*Ed. note:* This house does not appear in Table 3.3 because it covers too broad a time range.] Two samples came from the fill and near the floor of House 65 (H-943, H-959), attributed to the Rillito-Rincon phases. One sample from Trench 2 (H-793) could not be assigned. The various dates, all post-A.D. 700, suggest then, that *C. ensiformis* was one of a number of plants cultivated by the Hohokam since that time. Rillito and Rincon phase assignments have been made for several occurrences of the same bean in Punta de Agua, a Hohokam village, south of San Xavier Mission (Greenleaf 1975:24–25,106).

I believe we may confidently accept the idea that jackbeans were an important crop to the Hohokam at least since A.D. 700, and that the plant survived as a cultivated crop as late as 1938 in Pima agriculture (Bohrer 1962: 106–107).

The viability problem does not directly concern us here because we are dealing with charred remains, but the verification of *C. ensiformis*' antiquity makes the alleged viability of the cliff dwelling–derived specimens all the more intriguing.

REFERENCES

Amsden, Charles A.
1936 An Analysis of Hohokam Pottery Designs. *Medallion Papers* No. 22. Gila Pueblo, Globe, Arizona.

Bohrer, Vorsila L.
1962 Nature and Interpretations of Ethnobotanical Materials from Tonto National Monument, 1957. In "Archaeological Studies at Tonto National Monument," by Charlie R. Steen and others, pp. 76–114, *Southwestern Monuments Association, Technical Series* Vol. 2, Globe, Arizona.

Brand, Donald D.
1938 Aboriginal Trade Routes for Sea Shells in the Southwest. *Yearbook of the Association of Pacific Coast Geographers* Vol. 4. Cheney, Washington.

Carter, George F.
1945 Plant Geography and Culture History in the American Southwest. *Viking Fund Publications in Anthropology* No. 5. New York.

Colton, Harold S.
1941 Prehistoric Trade in the Southwest. *The Scientific Monthly* Vol. 52: 308–19. Washington.

Cosgrove, Harriet S. and Cornelius B.
1932 The Swarts Ruin: A Typical Mimbres Site in Southwestern New Mexico. *Papers of the Peabody Museum of American Archaeology and Ethnology* Vol. 15, No. 1. Harvard University, Cambridge.

DiPeso, Charles C.
1953 The Sobaipuri Indians of the Upper San Pedro River Valley, Southeastern Arizona. *The Amerind Foundation* No. 6. Dragoon, Arizona.

1956 The Upper Pima of San Cayetano del Tumacacori: An Archaeological Reconstruction of the Ootam of Pimería Alta. *The Amerind Foundation* No. 7. Dragoon, Arizona.

1958 The Reeve Ruin of Southeastern Arizona. *The Amerind Foundation* No. 8. Dragoon, Arizona.

Doyel, David E.
1974 Excavations in the Escalante Ruin Group, Southern Arizona. *Archaeological Series* No. 37. Arizona State Museum. University of Arizona, Tucson.

Gladwin, Harold S., Emil W. Haury, E. B. Sayles, and Nora Gladwin
1937 Excavations at Snaketown, Material Culture. *Medallion Papers* No. 25, Gila Pueblo, Globe, Arizona. [Reprint edition 1965 University of Arizona Press, Tucson.]

Gladwin, Winifred and Harold S.
1930 Some Southwestern Pottery Types, Series I. *Medallion Papers* No. 8. Gila Pueblo, Globe, Arizona.

1933 Some Southwestern Pottery Types, Series III. *Medallion Papers* No. 13. Gila Pueblo, Globe, Arizona.

Greenleaf, J. Cameron
1975 Excavations at Punta de Agua in the Santa Cruz River Basin, Southeastern Arizona. *Anthropological Papers of the University of Arizona* No. 26. University of Arizona Press, Tucson.

Hammack, Laurens C.
1969 A Preliminary Report of the Excavations at Las Colinas. *The Kiva* Vol. 35, No. 1: 11–28. Tucson.

Haury, Emil W.
1936 Some Southwestern Pottery Types, Series IV. *Medallion Papers* No. 19. Gila Pueblo, Globe, Arizona.

1945 The Excavation of Los Muertos and Neighboring Ruins in the Salt River Valley, Southern Arizona. *Papers of the Peabody Museum of American Archaeology and Ethnology* Vol. 24, No. 1. Harvard University, Cambridge.

1976 *The Hohokam: Desert Farmers and Craftsmen, Excavations at Snaketown, 1964–65.* University of Arizona Press, Tucson.

Hayden, Julian D.
1957 Excavations, 1940, at University Indian Ruin. *Southwestern Monuments Association, Technical Series* Vol. 5. Globe, Arizona.

Huntington, Ellsworth
1914 The Climatic Factor as Illustrated in Arid America. *Carnegie Institution of Washington,* Publication 192. Washington.

Judd, Neil M.
1954 The Material Culture of Pueblo Bonito. *Smithsonian Miscellaneous Collections* Vol. 124. Smithsonian Institution, Washington.

Kaplan, Laurence
1956 Cultivated Beans of the Prehistoric Southwest. *Annals of the Missouri Botanical Garden* Vol. 43: 189–251. St. Louis.

Kelly, Isabel T.
1945 Excavations at Culiacán, Sinaloa. *Ibero-Americana* No. 25. University of California Press, Berkeley.

Kidder, Alfred Vincent
1932 The Artifacts of Pecos. *Papers of the Phillips Academy, Southwestern Expedition* No. 6. New Haven.

Kinkade, Gay M. and Gordon L. Fritz
1975 The Tucson Sewage Project: Studies at Two Archaeological Sites in the Tucson Basin. *Archaeological Series* No. 64. Arizona State Museum, University of Arizona, Tucson.

McGregor, John C.
1941 Winona and Ridge Ruin, Part I. Architecture and Material Culture. *Museum of Northern Arizona Bulletin* 18. Flagstaff.

Russell, Frank
1908 The Pima Indians, *Twenty-sixth Annual Report of the Bureau of American Ethnology.* Washington. [Reprint edition 1975, University of Arizona Press, Tucson.]

Sauer, Carl and Donald Brand
1931 Prehistoric Settlements of Sonora with Special Reference to Cerros de Trincheras. *University of California Publications in Geography* Vol. 5, No. 3: 67–148. Berkeley.

Sauer, Jonathan and Laurence Kaplan
1969 Canavalia Beans in American Prehistory. *American Antiquity* Vol. 34, No. 4: 417–24. Salt Lake City.

Stanislawski, Michael B.
1961 Two Prehistoric Shell Caches from Southern Arizona. *The Kiva* Vol. 27, No. 2: 22–27. Tucson.

Steen, Charlie R., Lloyd M. Pierson, Vorsila L. Bohrer, and Kate Peck Kent
1962 Archaeological Studies at Tonto National Monument. *Southwestern Monuments Association, Technical Series* Vol. 2. Globe, Arizona.

Tower, Donald B.
1945 The Use of Marine Mollusca and their Value in Reconstructing Trade Routes in the American Southwest. *Papers of the Excavators' Club* Vol. 2, No. 3. Cambridge.

Wasley, William W. and Alfred E. Johnson
1965 Salvage Archaeology in Painted Rocks Reservoir, Western Arizona. *Anthropological Papers of the University of Arizona* No. 9. University of Arizona Press, Tucson.

INDEX